LEADING IN A SOCIAL WORLD

Stop social media marketing and build social capital instead

R. AARON TEMPLER

ISBN: 978-1-7376397-0-1 (Hardback)
ISBN: 978-1-7376397-1-8 (Paperback)
ISBN: 978-1-7376397-2-5 (eBook)

Front cover art and illustrations by Sonja Calhoun
Author photography: Flor Blake Photography

First printed edition 2021

Templer Tantrums, LLC
Denver, Colorado
www.templertantrums.com
info@templertantrums.com

Contents

How to Read This Book

The pandemic of 2020 forced us to confront many important questions. Not least, *how do we as individuals and organizations maintain social connections while maintaining social distances?*

That's what this book is about. It was conceived and started a long time ago but gained momentum during the stay-at-home orders of Spring 2020. It's a book about social capital and how it can be built and used in online social groups like social media. It lays bare the pitfalls of an all-too-prevalent preoccupation in business and organizations to think of social media through the lens of marketing tactics that, widely used though they may be, ultimately yield little value and in some cases may diminish it. Marketers have had their hands on the levers of social media for too long, and I'll make the case for companies, brands, and their marketing departments and agencies to redirect their energies toward building and using social capital within these online social constructs, to view our actions and interactions online as means of leading people rather than converting them. I'm convinced that it's the only way to create genuine value for most organizations in online social circles.

Part One explores our socially-wired brains, the meaning of social capital, and how those dynamics are in play and stand in contrast to social media marketing. This necessitates a bit of marketing (and especially social media marketing) deconstruction, and I intentionally want us marketers to question some of our practices and feel uncomfortable about our biases in order to find a better way for our brands and clients. I think you'll find the tone and approach a little fun if you're willing to embrace the discomfort (#notallmarketers, if that makes you feel better).

Part Two, I think, is a decent playbook for any leader looking to identify specific ways to build and use social capital as a leadership skill, and to do so in any setting. It's my intention to also challenge marketers to elevate our thinking about our work, our role in business and organizations, and ultimately to view our day-to-day skills as transcendent into other areas of our professional lives.

This was always the focus of *Leading in a Social World*, primarily for marketers, organizational leaders, and others involved in influencing people and groups. But watching huge swaths of human populations feel real pain as we disconnected from one another through physical distancing (a much more accurate term for social distancing, in my opinion) and tried substituting our need for connection with digital tools, convinced me that this book treats a much broader theme than I originally thought.

Then, almost overnight, the pandemic essentially (and remarkably) became a backdrop as we faced a different disease: yet another reminder of our country's ugly roots in racism and white supremacy. The demonstrations following the killing of George Floyd were stunning to behold, certainly the most important social justice and civil rights movement of our time and probably the most significant since the civil rights movement of the 1960s. With no sports highlights to consume us or movie theaters or concerts to escape to, activists finally had the attention of those of us in positions made comfortable by privilege and power. All it took was a global pandemic to prioritize the issue.

The antidotes to racism and white supremacy share many of the characteristics of what it takes to build social capital, and those of us interested in pursuing solutions to injustice do so because our brains are wired to feel social exclusion very deeply (we explore this in detail in Chapter 2). We innately want to rid ourselves of a palpable pain. And so the civil and human rights issues we addressed during the spring and summer of 2020 added even more timeliness to the concepts in this book.

Then, amidst all of it, with the book finally gaining momentum, I stumbled into a discovery.

I've been dealing with and studying social capital in one form or another for over 20 years. It wasn't until July 7, 2020, when, like so many of us, I was in the midst of processing the flood of extraordinary events that I discovered the term was first coined by Glenn Loury, a Northwestern welfare, income distribution, and labor economist and professor. My belief, one I think I shared with many who study social capital, was that sociologist James Coleman coined the term.[1] But this wasn't the case. Dr. Loury invented it, as he confirmed. "I did coin the term," he told me. "I did not do very much with it beyond the use of words. It was left to the late sociologist James Coleman and the political scientist Robert Putnam to apply the concept in a systematic way."[2]

The origin of the term was not terribly important to me as I worked my way through the manuscript, since it seemed to have little bearing on the meaning of social capital (which we spend the entirety of Chapter 4 defining). But things changed when I discovered Loury is Black, and that he invented the term in his 1976 paper *A Dynamic Theory of Racial Income Differences*.[3]

Loury was exploring "the moral and political developments of the late fifties and early sixties [that] created a climate [of] legitimacy for a system which denied the full opportunity for achievement to its minority citizens."[4] Loury coined the term to describe the measurable capital and advantages white people have gained through decades of systemic government-mandated programs that have accumulated and been handed down through social systems. Outwardly a far cry from the focus of this book, which examines the value built and exchanged in social groups (like knowledge sharing, idea generation, and access to other networks). Still, here we are, social capital students, scholars, and practitioners, tackling social capital concepts like trust; the importance of taking the third perspective first; how our brains feel social separation the same way we feel physical pain; and equal and sustained reciprocity all under the umbrella of a term that has its origin story in social justice and systemic racism. The irony was striking. Social capital scholars, writers, and practitioners are operating in that space while erasing origins and appropriating the work of a Black leader, as those of us in positions of privilege and influence so often do when the architect doesn't fit our conventions and when the topic is too uncomfortable for white people to face.

So, this is a book for our times. The very concept is a reflection of them, energized by many of the same emotions that are driving change on a larger scale today. It doesn't have a big, silver-bullet answer for our larger challenges. But I think it addresses more than a few smaller ones. It's also a reflection of our times in that we'll move forward in these pages with the commonly held, yet appropriated, definition of social capital. As I mentioned, we spend Chapter 4 exploring the meaning of social capital, but it might be helpful to offer a definition at this point just to get it on the table. For now, and for our purposes, let's think of social capital in business and similar organizational settings as a resource of value for individuals and groups, created by investing and managing the configuration and operation of social networks and their durable social relationships.

You don't have to be in marketing or business or nonprofit management to find value in this book. You can read the marketing and leadership principles as placeholders for influence, and the social capital principles, focused on business though they are, as concepts that can easily transfer into your particular community, family, or circle of friends. Or maybe to a group you are seeking to enfranchise or bring justice to in some way. My intent is to draw easy lines of sight from the companies treated in the book to almost any working situation and take care that the examples should be relatable to a wide variety of contexts. Apple and Starbucks are lodestars for many best practices, but they operate in an orbit so very different from most of the rest of our worlds that it's often hard to tease out which practices can be adopted and which are aided by other activities funded by and integrated with their vast pools of resources. I spoke to several recognizable brands—Zappos and Xbox, to name two—but I think you'll find them and their approach to building social capital accessible and real for a variety of organizations.

I've tried to keep things accessible and real because it's my belief that we all have an obligation to consider how our social world operates and what our responsibility within it is. As you'll discover, building social capital, particularly when we bridge different groups of social clusters, is the thread that connects communities and the infrastructure for ideas. When we practice social capital-building activities, we clearly receive value for ourselves. But we're engaged in a pursuit much larger and more important than that.

Connecting in meaningful ways while physically separated is the challenge of our times. COVID-19 was more stubborn than some first anticipated, and its future is murky even now as new strains mutate and some groups refuse to vaccinate. Variants of another virus may send us back into our homes at some point (at least those of us privileged enough to be able to do so). Or maybe there's a sea change afoot as we realize the efficiencies inherent in remote, flexible work. Whatever the case, regardless of whether we're leading teams (marketing or otherwise), organizing political issue campaigns, engaging religious committees, or keeping a dance studio's rehearsal schedule on track, we all need skills to build and use social capital in digital spaces. It will help us as individuals achieve what we need to achieve, but these skills will also be necessary for rebuilding our teams and the social relationships within them as physical distances start to close.

Virtual spaces make connecting with one another more challenging but even more critical. The need to double down on social capital during times like these was identified in 2001 by social capital scholars Laurence Prusak and Don Cohen in a *Harvard Business Review* article titled "How to Invest in Social Capital." As they made clear, "social capital is under assault because building relationships in turbulent times is tough—and tougher still with many people working off-site or on their own."[5] It's hard but important work for all of us. I hope this book will help.

You might learn a little something about marketing and social media along the way, too. The pandemic was a reminder of the rather precarious nature of employment, generating a second surge of the self-employed, side-hustle economy we saw in the early 2000s. It's important for any working professional to keep their marketing chops honed, but especially those who find themselves surfing the free agent wave. If you're a leader of a unit or organization, I think this book will help you manage and lead your marketing and customer care functions, be they internal or by way of agencies, with a new lens, as well.

The broader lens is this: as a community we need to take these issues seriously. If we don't find ways to stay connected while physically distanced, it can damage us deeply.

Because we're wired to be social. We can't help it. As you're about to find out.

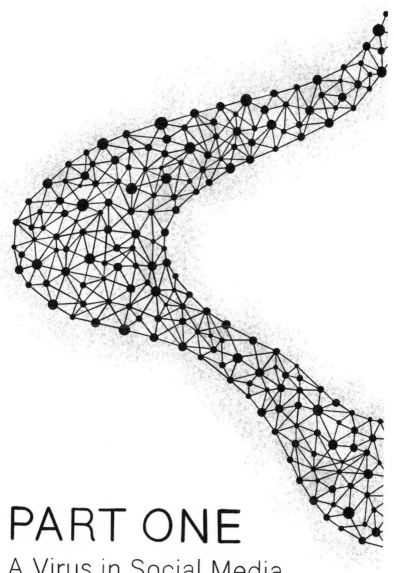

PART ONE
A Virus in Social Media

Chapter 1
ROOTS OF BIAS: THE GREAT PROMISE OF SOCIAL MEDIA

It was in the middle of the great recession of 2008 that Erik Proulx became one of 130,000 ad agency professionals to lose his job. It sent him into the deepest period of self-reflection of his life, not so much because it was the third time it'd happened to him, although that was certainly a jarring part of it. It was the third time in a career during which he had followed all the rules and that should have provided him a lifetime of security. The third layoff for an award-winning ad agency senior copywriter with brands under his belt that would make any ad man proud (and employable). Volvo. Nokia. Fidelity. MTV2.

We can learn a lot from our current pandemic situation by looking back at the Great Recession of 2007–9, and particularly how it impacted those in the marketing world like Erik and his ad agency reality. It was a time when we marketers were developing a new perspective for online social connections, when necessity was driving invention, and joblessness was the pressure under almost everything we experienced. It was the closest we had come to the kind of economic shifting we seem to be facing today.

For Erik, this particular layoff was different. Felt more…permanent. Not just because advertising as an industry was facing perhaps the greatest challenge to its relevance it had ever experienced, though that was a big part of it, as anyone working in business and especially marketing around 2008 could tell you. For Erik it was more a case of something inside him that was pleading for him to get off the merry-go-round.

We'll get back to Erik's story in a moment, but it's interesting to think back about this time and how it affected marketing, and really all, professionals. Social media was on the rise and we were on our way to using it in remarkable and unprecedented ways. We were bringing people together across the globe, uniting every overlooked data point on the long tail. Turns out, people like Erik were laying the groundwork for us to live and thrive through periods of social distancing such as we've experienced during the COVID-19 pandemic. A groundwork that manages to keep team members connected when they're no longer together in offices. One that embraces opportunity amidst challenges while flexing toward new directions, that turns to creativity and invention when things are upside down. And, most importantly, one that allows us to connect with one another and exchange value over distances.

If only we had listened. Somewhere along the line we lost our way. Marketing certainly had something to do with it. In a way, we marketers killed what was sustaining us. Today the shifts in usage of major social media platforms away from social purposes—down as much as 16 percent—and toward activities like following celebrities and celebrity news—up 27 percent—are very telling.[1]

The Great Recession wasn't just the last time we were envisioning social media as something larger and more world-changing than marketing. It was the last time our way of working was as disrupted as it is today. Like today, albeit voluntarily, many people—over 15 percent of the workforce[2]—retreated to home-based and remote working conditions. Many of us marketers, laid off from agencies and in-house corporate marketing communications departments and concerned (convinced) that the traditional way of doing things was dying, flipped on our innovator switches and started to thrive. We pushed our socially-driven technologies into a new area of growth and possibilities. We saw ourselves as the creative juice in an entrepreneurial renaissance.

Our investments and biases in what social media could do for marketing efforts quickly followed. Before we knew it, it was uncontroversial to proclaim social media's potential and staying power for moving groups of people to take action. And we started to see the commercial potential for it. Instead of just passive consumption, interceding in social groups could yield financial returns.

At first, social media didn't simply represent new marketing channels. It represented a way out. A way out of spin, trickery, and manipulation. A democratized place for us to practice our powers of influence. A place where the promise of the long tail meant we could find smaller groups to motivate and we could finally afford to reach them. Digital makers. Activists. We could connect, and connect in meaningful places. The old, expensive models were dying and we could be a part of a new frontier. Someone coined the term *disruption,* and we pushed our cards all in.[3]

So layoffs, typical for the ad agency industry, started to look a little different for the likes of Erik Proulx during this time:

> It became clear to me after three layoffs that there is no sure thing. You can turn your life over to your employer, give them your nights and weekends and holidays, win them clients and awards, do your timesheets on time and abide by the employee manual, and even then your job is not safe.[4]

That feeling of safety is what sometimes causes us to embrace the status quo. When you're invested in a process, it's hard to lift your head above the noise and make an honest assessment of what's going on. Neuroscientists call it 'the endowment effect,' a cognitive bias that makes us think the investments we've put into things in our lives are worth more than they actually are when we're presented with the prospect of changing them. Many of us were simply shocked out of this bias during the stay-at-home orders of 2020. Forced to rethink how we connect when not together, we had to grapple with how to lead teams when the closest we could physically get to them looked something like a *Brady Bunch* opening sequence. What can this mean for the status quo? Who'll be the innovators that emerge from this time?

Who'll seize the opportunity to turn crisis into opportunity and find new ways to lead during times of physical separation?

Fueled by similar questions in his unique time, Erik Proulx found the courage to question the payouts from his career endowment. They clearly weren't what they used to be. How sustainable and meaningful can a career really be when the employment peaks and valleys follow the ethereal ability to please a client, and the capricious reality of boring them?

So he did what any self-respecting, unemployed ad agency creative would do in 2008. Just as the forced-to-stay-at-home professionals of today start podcasts and publish recorded Zoom interviews, Erik started a blog.

As he told me, at first Erik simply "wanted to give ad agency people who were experiencing their first layoff some help."[5] There was never a business model, never a focus on revenue. Just a place where Erik could keep his writing chops sharp in "a space where I could speak openly and honestly about what I was going through. A space where new unemployed people could read some words of comfort and know that it was going to be okay."

Please Feed the Animals was born. The blog's name reflected the sense of empowerment Erik was interested in exploring: "We're hungry, capable, and aggressive," and getting laid off wasn't about to change that. Motivated by a laid-off ad guy who wanted to use his transition as a chance to reinvent himself and maybe help others do the same. "To connect to something bigger, and to people outside of myself."

It was a focused blog, specifically for unemployed ad agency professionals. Erik kept it that way because that was his world, his people. He could be himself and write with honesty and directness, an authenticity that trying to appeal to a broader audience would most certainly water down. Everyone knew the acronyms, the job titles, the sacrifices demanded by the industry, and the creative-mind-meets-capitalism-hustle vibe so unique to ad agencies. It was a community familiar to so many like Erik, only virtual and without the pressure of pesky client work.

The tight community made it a little easier to find, follow, and engage people across the social web. With some hashtags and a narrative specific to the advertising industry, Erik built a community on Facebook and Twitter in addition to the blog. And there turned out to be plenty of hungry, laid-off ad pros out there eager to connect.

He asked a few others to write for the blog, welcomed and facilitated dialog through comments, and shared posts across the social web. People started coming in droves to *Please Feed the Animals*, the blog and the social web community. A post about *Please Feed the Animals* on a popular ad agency blog threw some more fuel on the fire, and before long there were Animals across the country and the world joining Erik's community to commiserate, share leads, and find project partners.

The community was a safe place, a democratized space where no one person held a rank or title. There was also no commercialization. No subscription list, no ads. For many today who work day in and day out trying to commercialize constructs like this, this may be hard to imagine but there was a certain purity to *Please Feed the Animals*. People felt they could be vulnerable there, and they started to share their own stories of reinvention. These stories began to grow into a mini-movement within the community. "These were stories that were much bigger than advice for the unemployed. Here are some people who're facing their fears and making something new."

It became obvious to Erik that everyone should experience these stories, that there were probably many people out there who could use the validation and encouragement. So he put an idea across his social network to film a few people telling their stories for "a simple video of people sharing what happened to them and how they dealt with losing their jobs. Something with production qualities similar to what you see on YouTube."[6]

Something remarkable followed. First, in an amazing outpouring of mass vulnerability, 75 people came forward in a matter of days to share some of the more intimate details a person can face with the world.

And then professional filmmakers came out of the woodwork to volunteer their time to document it.

Picture Park, a Boston-based film company, heard the buzz online and offered their production services, gratis. Sony was listening, and connected Erik with a few companies—Rule and Abel Cine Tech—who donated the equipment.

Then came Bug Editorial Inc., Finish Editorial, Soundtrack Group, and Mir Internet Marketing for the sound mixing, interactive work, and postproduction. Friends from across the *Please Feed the Animals* community pitched in time. And a few professional directors helped Erik make it all into a movie (Picture Park's Mark Carlucci directed and Peter Nelson, director of photography on Michael Moore's *Sicko* donated weekends).

During the production Erik even mobilized a few Twitter friends to urge Virgin America Airlines to become "the Official Airline of the Unemployed Ad Agency Professional." Within two hours Virgin America's CMO offered up free flights for the crew to shoot a story in California.

A few PR professionals, friends of friends connected through the online community, placed Erik and his story in *FastCompany*, *AdAge*, *The Christian Science Monitor* and on ABC News, NPR, and others. The momentum was so great that before he knew it, Erik had a professionally produced documentary and the kind of buzz surrounding it that would feel like an accomplishment within any professional movie studio.

It was called *Lemonade*, a half-hour documentary profiling a few laid-off ad agency pros who decided to take their moment of transition and treat it like a catalyst instead of a roadblock. "Hope porn," as Erik once put it to me. At one point it was the most viewed documentary on Hulu. And the community achieved it all by exchanging capital of a different kind. Most film people will tell you that films of this caliber cost seven figures to complete. *Lemonade* was made entirely with donated equipment—from cameras to lights to flights—$400 on a credit card, a bunch of time, and a whole lot of love from people connected across the social web and with a shared vision.

The movement also launched Erik into the trajectory he was looking for that day in 2008 when he first launched *Please Feed the Animals*. He's now an accomplished film director, "finally doing," as he says in *Lemonade*, his "life's work." Through his company Fighting Monk, he has directed industrials for Yahoo! and Dell, and completed a documentary, *365 Days*, about life at Penn State after the Sandusky scandal. He's also still a free-agent creative in the truest sense: writing, taking the occasional project gig, and in general using his storytelling powers for good.

A community using social web tools that created a film and a movement and changed the career for "an unemployed ad guy who wrote a blog for unemployed ad people."

What's going on here?

It's important to stop and think about Erik's story in a context other than that of a marketer. Now, I understand this is hard for most marketing people because marketing people (like me) are paid to find audiences, engage them, and motivate them to do something. When we hear about someone who has motivated so many to do something so significant with so small a price tag, well, let's just say us marketing wonks are rather motivated to want to understand how that's done.

It's what motivated a bevvy of authors and thought leaders at the time to create blogs and books from *Trust Agents* to *Tribes* that tried to take old marketing concepts and twist them a bit to fit social constructs. Learn the technical capital of the web, apply a few easy-to-remember rules, and watch the value fuel new-found success. The pressure under Erik's story is 'The Great Marketing Promise' of the social web. It's what makes marketers drool. Millions and millions of eyeballs to be reached and audiences to engage at a cost accessible to all of us.

Even more opportunely, these networks seemingly give marketers an unprecedented opportunity to find people who are friends of friends, or friends of friends of friends, who'll do the promoting for us. And if they're the ones doing the selling? Well then, hey, that's not marketing at all. That's crossing the uncrossable line in marketing. Because if there's one irrefutable truth in business, it's this: we do business with people we know and trust. And fundamentally marketers know, deep down behind our marketing mettle, in those places we don't like to go, there's a truth we don't like to talk much about: in the end people can't trust a brand because *shhhh: a brand isn't a person.*

To marketing people, the social web looks like a loophole in the system. The thing that we've been waiting for. Finally.

So I understand the temptation to be drawn into this story looking like some emoji with dollar signs for eyes. But as hard as it may be, as strong as our own endowment effects may be, take off your marketing hat and try to open yourself to the lesson of Erik Proulx through a different lens. Because when you stop to honestly think about it, do you really believe Erik made a movie and launched a new career without any capital because of his savviness with social media marketing? Because he knows the secret to the most compelling Tweets and which day of the week is best to post on Facebook? Because he has all the social media secrets you and I don't have, secrets everyone around us is memorizing and throwing out with their LinkedIn updates like opinions at a bar, secrets like Facebook posts have a 63-percent higher engagement rate when there's a video or 46-percent more when there's a link (or whatever)? Does Erik have a better grasp of the technology than you do? A better technical sense of the digital tools he used and what makes these so-called marketing tools tick?

To paraphrase Clay Shirky, a seminal thought leader on groups and the effect of the social web on our society, for Erik Proulx it wasn't the technical capital that mattered. It was the social capital.[7]

Whether he knew it then or could even articulate it now, Erik was leading people and doing it by attracting them with a shared set of ideals and values. He wasn't marketing to them. The context in which he was operating—a world of constructs that are socially organized—required him to use the only skill that could possibly engage people to get behind a vision with no promise of return: building and using social capital.

And that's a leadership skill. Not a marketing one. It's long overdue that we as marketers expand our thinking, step up, and acknowledge that we need to lead people in social constructs, not market to them. And that requires a much more sophisticated set of skills and aptitude than we've been willing to accept.

Erik, and others like him then and today who are successfully generating real value on the social web are exhibiting the classic characteristics of leaders who deliberately build and exchange social capital in organizations, learnable skills of the sort explored in this book.

Like seeing his *ad hoc* reputation for expertise in the world of advertising not as a certain rank or position in a hierarchical system, but as a person in service to a diverse set of stakeholders in a democratized system. In my interviews with Erik I couldn't compel him to describe his role as anything other than a guy in service to those in the community he built. It's truly what drove him. He reminds me of Darwin Smith, the CEO exemplar Jim Collins uses to illustrate a Level Five leader in *Good to Great*. When asked what he attributed his success to, Smith said "I never stopped trying to become qualified for the job."[8] When you talk with Erik about his days making lemonade out of lemons, you get the sense that he simply kept trying to deserve the role.

Another leadership skill is that of balancing achievement with collaboration. Erik and his team stayed true to their values by keeping *Lemonade* free to their community because it just wouldn't seem right to ask someone who's been laid off to pay to watch a movie about being laid off. This came with a compromise: it created the right reputation for *Lemonade* and attracted more of the right people to engage and volunteer their time. On the other hand, it would be ineligible for certain awards without a commercial run, not to mention the revenue streams he passed up.

Then there's this: Erik contributed value to a system with the tacit understanding that social systems operate under laws of persistent and recurring reciprocity. These laws don't tolerate any individuals in the system aiming primarily to gain from it. When pressed, Erik will tell you there were thoughts about pulling together some of the talent across the *Please Feed the Animals* community to create a new, reinvented version of the ad agency model. But it never gained momentum because it was never about that. It was about helping unemployed ad professionals feel like they weren't alone. And that's what stuck.

Erik also at some intuitive level, probably not intentionally or even very consciously, galvanized a community with three social capital principles that keep groups together and generate value—*bonds* as I've come to call them. Social capital-savvy leaders who build and exchange social capital understand the importance of these bonds and intentionally curate them. You'll learn about them later and what the role of curator (or leader) entails. For now, consider how Erik's story exemplifies them.

One example is *structural bonds,* a new frontier of sorts for social capital marketers but very much at the core of social capital development and curation from a leadership perspective. Erik's dedication to keeping his audience specific, it turns out, uncovered the power of *appropriability.* The trust and norms of the advertising agency office moved fairly seamlessly into the online advertising agency world. Identifying appropriable social organizations is one powerful way to consider how to build social capital in online spaces, and Erik exchanged a powerful element practiced by social capital-savvy leaders when he stayed true to his original audience.

This approach to remaining focused on a specific audience also lent itself to the second bond used to build and leverage social capital: *cognitive bonds.* Anyone who's worked in or even around advertising knows that there's a very specific language among ad agency pros. The industry-specific terms for things like job titles, processes, and common client roadblocks were peppered throughout *Please Feed the Animals,* giving it its unique appeal. This helped to create a cognitive system of meaning, a 'conceptual apparatus' for someone to evaluate a community's potential value and thereby whether someone should join in and add value to it.[9]

The third bond for leaders interested in building social capital is *relational bonds.* Erik was (and is) vulnerable in blog posts, to the point of being self-effacing at times, and is one of the most humble people you'll ever deal with. He says what he'll do and apologizes freely if he misses a mark. And when he said he wouldn't look to make money from *Please Feed the Animals,* he meant it. He never has. He epitomizes that Level Five Leader: a seemingly paradoxical mix of humility and tenacity that draws people to him because he's someone you want to listen to, while at the same time getting shit done. This is where social media marketing runs into such friction in social systems and where Erik can help us understand why: relational bonds are all about trust.

And in systems where trust is high, people are more willing to participate in social exchange.[10] When we sense a salesman's agenda in social
systems, we retreat. Fast.

Without a marketing lens clouding things it's easy to see how, in
the end, Erik wasn't marketing. He wasn't branding. Erik hard-earned
and cashed in the only currency that can be spent in systems created
by freewill and are organized cooperatively instead of by coordination:
social capital.[11]

He built and cashed in a resource of value for individuals and
groups, created by investing and managing the configuration and
operation of his social network and their durable social relationships.
He built social capital and it returned value specific to his context, just
as it returns value to organizations that build it in a myriad of other
ways specific to theirs. Social capital can increase knowledge transfer,
enhance knowledge creation and sharing, collaboration, and cooperative behavior. It can reduce transaction costs and accelerate and focus
innovation and intra/entrepreneurship. It can focus the coherence of
teams. It helps with talent flow and can result in stronger human
capital development efforts. And, yes, it can provide access to privileged information, networks, and opportunities, the myopic focus of
social media marketers.[12]

It's a lot more fun (and useful) to explore the meaning of social
capital than to define it. Again, that awaits in Chapter 4. But back to
the concept of *organized cooperatively instead of by coordination*. This is
generally what I mean in this book when I say 'the social web' or refer
to online social groups. It's important to conceptualize the social web
as more than a specific tool, or website, or category of channels to
reach an audience. It's also important to differentiate my focus on the
social web and how we use it to our benefit as compared to what's
called 'the commoditized self': the use of a social platform by an individual to create a reputation strong enough to charge others for
promotions. Nor am I referring to so-called social or cryptocurrency
online, like a blue checkmark on Twitter or Non-Fungible Tokens. The
social capital we're dealing with is also very different from the
exploitation engaged in by companies developing platforms that
derive value from the people participating in them, 'conspicuous

prosumption' as Kane X. Faucher termed it in *Social Capital Online: Alienation and Accumulation*.[13] Or as the Netflix documentary *The Social Dilemma* puts it, "holy shit, what kind of manipulative poison-monster is this?"

This book is decidedly not dealing with online activity that garners empirical praise for an individual's shared content aimed at building capital by way of eyeballs for an advertising platform, either for the individual or the company. The social web we're interested in is a dynamic. The reality is that the web has evolved and continues to evolve into a way for us to connect, share, and cooperate. Facebook can continue its monopolistic climb toward worldwide dominance, and you may be among those who believe that it's a myth that Facebook and its main competitors and cohorts are actually democratizing anything. But the web itself is social, always will be, and we will continue to evolve it to find new and meaningful ways to allow us to connect. This book is not about predicting the future, and I've never been one to try. But forecasting the idea that the web is social and always will be is easy enough because the web is evolving into exactly what the humans who invented it need it to be: a way to connect with one another. We're simply wired to do this.

Wired, in fact, in a primal way.

What would you say if I told you social connection is actually responsible for meeting primal needs after birth? What if I told you Maslow didn't have the base of his model right? That's right: the base of our *Hierarchy of Needs* isn't physiological. It's social. Because without the ability to form a social connection we couldn't connect to a caregiver to provide for us the basic needs of survival during our comparatively long development period outside the womb.

That's not me taking down Maslow. That's social neuroscientist and author Dr. Matthew D. Lieberman. He's a leader in the field of biobehavioral science and his experiments have produced powerful evidence that we're wired, in a primal way, to be social. The activity during our brain's down time, when our brains aren't concerned with specific tasks like balancing a checkbook or practicing guitar scales, defaults to exercising a region of the brain used for social interaction.

It's our "default network," what we work on when we don't have a specific task in front of us.[14]

That's because acquiring the skills necessary for navigating the intricacies and sophistication of social networks is so important to our survival that we work on it literally, as Dr. Lieberman would say, whenever we have a free moment. Navigating social networks to identify a friend or a foe (or a marketer) was necessary for our survival. Until we evolve this out of ourselves we're stuck with it, and we'll continue the pursuit of finding new and creative ways to connect with one another.

And while connecting with one another is a fairly straightforward proposition, generating value in our networks is especially difficult. We tend to think of networks as a line of dominoes, or a bucket brigade where information or value is passed from one person to the next. We believe that the stronger these ties are the better, and that our best friends are our most valuable contacts because of the trust we have with them. Turns out our networks are far more complex than this.

Social networks are sophisticated systems with histories, memories, even agency, and with very different roles among their various members. The friend who introduces you to your next date plays a very different role than the mentor who shows you a new approach to a professional problem. Nicholas Christakis and James H. Fowler in their book *Connected* emphasize that social network "ties do not extend outward in straight lines like spokes on a wheel. Instead, these paths double back on themselves and spiral around like a tangled pile of spaghetti, weaving in and out of other paths that rarely ever leave the plate." Not exactly a bucket brigade. Nor a market segment.

And contrary to most people's intuition (and the arguments of Putnam and his colleagues in *Bowling Alone*[15]), weak ties are often the most valuable. More people find jobs through their networks from near strangers than friends,[16] and ideas that benefit organizations are generated better from those sitting near structural holes in networks, as opposed to so-called transitive ties (tightly-knit connections of three or more) which tend to simply circulate value among themselves.[17]

Not only that, but consider the exponential problem your brain faces when evaluating agendas among your social network. You have a friend named Shefali. Shefali needs something from you, and you from her. This tacit reciprocity is the stuff of social relationships and is handled subtly, without a formal contractual relationship. It's a nuanced cognitive skill to stay on top of, but fairly straightforward for all that. Now imagine that Shefali introduces you to her friend Conrad. You have a triad of agendas to consider. What does Conrad owe you? You him? What is your loyalty to Shefali if Conrad provides value to you? How does this change things with Shefali? And what happens when you find out Conrad is friends with Shefali's ex-boyfriend? Look out. As people come into a social network the prospect of untangling and understanding the nuances becomes exponential. Fast.

Like driving a car, we navigate and negotiate these social relationships without thinking. You don't think about turning on the turn signal, applying the brake, positioning your hands on the steering wheel, and turning after a pedestrian is out of the crosswalk while talking on your phone. Social networks build exponentially, and our minds must be finely tuned to spot the friends and the foes (and the marketers). Otherwise we get into trouble pretty quickly.

No wonder we work on the social region of the brain whenever we can. We need the exercise.

We'll dive much more into Dr. Lieberman's work and the complexities of social systems—systems that sacrifice a certain degree of coordination in favor of cooperation—later on. For now it's important to agree that the web will continue its evolution toward an increasingly social system because our brains can't stop it. Our technology is in service to a primal social urge, the urge we work on when we don't have anything else to do.

Social media platforms understand certainly this. Dr. Anna Lembke, Medical Director of Addiction and Medicine at Stanford University School of Medicine goes so far as to call social media "a drug" in the documentary The Social Dilemma.[18] Reinforcing Dr. Lieberman's work, Dr. Lembke understands why so many of us can't help ourselves from scrolling and liking and sharing and emoji'ing and selfie'ing, and why by extension we'll continue to find new and inventive ways to connect online. "We have a basic, biological imperative to connect with other people" says Dr. Lembke "that directly affects the release of dopamine in the reward pathways. Millions of years of evolution are behind that system to get us to come together."

Certainly one of the more important lessons from the stay-at-home orders of 2020 is that our understanding of social systems and leading people in different contexts is, now more than ever, a leader's most critical task. The pandemic has also exposed how little we actually know about it, not least the urgency around finding ways to connect remotely during periods of social distancing put front and center. Combine this with the exponential nature of change across the internet and its wildly unpredictable nature, and you begin to see why it's so critical for leaders to start thinking more broadly about social: what drives it, the forces that underpin it, and what moves people within it. Far from a tactical marketing issue, the relationship between social distancing and the social web demands that we come to terms with the fact that the ability to motivate and influence people within social systems—in person or online—will be a fundamental skill for leadership success in the coming years.

My argument is that leadership is a social exercise. That effective leaders hone their emotional intelligence, self-awareness, and relationship-building skills to meet the needs of others. So maybe it's more accurate to say that to lead effectively in the coming years is to acknowledge this basic leadership tenet and that it now intersects with the need to do it across a range of social systems.

In her book *Daring to Lead*, Dr. Brené Brown quotes the director at the London School of Economics in putting a finer (if oversimplified) point on this: "Once work was about muscle. Now it's about brains. Tomorrow it will be about the heart."[19]

How far we have still to go in understanding and leading social groups online is illustrated starkly in our use of video conferencing. We saw a spike in the demand for a more social approach to coming together over video as millions of us were forced to learn, work, and socialize at home during the pandemic. A report from App Annie, which tracks app downloads and other industry data, shows an unprecedented 62 million video conferencing app downloads during an early week of the social isolation period. It was a 90-percent increase for the category, never before seen for any category in any time.[20]

The Zoom video conferencing platform grew from 10 million users in December 2020 to 200 million by March 2020, a mind-boggling explosion that blindsided its CEO Eric Yan completely. "We did not design the product with the foresight that, in a matter of weeks, every person in the world would suddenly be working, studying, and socializing from home," he wrote. "We now have a much broader set of users who are utilizing our product in a myriad of unexpected ways, presenting us with challenges we did not anticipate when the platform was conceived."[21]

During the period of physical distancing, we unexpectedly used these tools, which were designed as conferencing tools for business and organizations, for decidedly social purposes. Happy hours, dinner parties, streaming concerts, weddings, family brunches. I have an image seared into my mind, shared by a family physician on Twitter, that starkly brings this abrupt need for technology-driven social connection: a storage room in a hospital, filled with dozens of iPads on stands, at the ready for the surge of end-of-life visits brought on by COVID-19.[22] Unexpected uses of technology indeed.

New security and privacy shortcomings arose quickly, and with it a recognition that online video conferencing platforms aren't very social-friendly. Harassment through so-called Zoom bombing became a very real problem. Political organizing meetings and religious gatherings were hijacked by a myriad of anti-social bullies, racists, and creeps.

Zoom allows for breakouts (Zoom Rooms, as they're called) where smaller groups can meet separately from the larger gathering, and there are nuances that allow some interactivity (reacting with a few emojis, for instance). But the technology is built for presenting and for simple meetings, not real-time social interaction. The bandwidth issue alone erects barriers. Imagine something like a karaoke party through the lens of your online conference experience—*Can you hear me? Sorry, go ahead. No, you go. No, I thought you were done. Oh, sorry*—constantly interfering.

Unsurprisingly, more socially-focused solutions have sprung up as our hard-wired social brains create more demand for them. Houseparty, with its ability to find friends online and suggest hangouts, its gesture-based interface, integration with Snapchat, and bundle of games users can play while video chatting, saw 50 million additional sign-ups during the first month of physical distancing. App industry experts say that's some 70 times above normal, and doesn't even take into account Houseparty's browser users.[23]

Real time, online social interaction is clearly where the evolution of the social web is headed, an unprecedented demand for social connectivity generated by forced physical distancing.

We must also face the ever-increasing reality that connecting with people on the social web is becoming a task in discovering what a real connection is in the first place. Some have estimated that as much as 40 percent of the internet is fake. Bots, acting like humans, creating content, views, clicks, and links, distorting what we're interacting with. We're moving ever closer to a concept called *The Inversion*: an age where there are more fakes and deepfakes than there are actual people online.[24] Perhaps we're already there.

A rather ironic example of this recently came to light when the Federal Communications Commission (FCC) asked for public comments on its net neutrality laws. An industry advocacy group funded by the nation's top internet providers hired three firms to generate "volume and intellectual cover" for FCC Chairman Ajit Pai to roll back the Obama-era regulations intended to maintain fair treatment of internet traffic. Operating in an "influence industry that generates made-up comments and often attaches the names of real people caught up in marketing ploys," the scheme generated the bulk of more than 18 million fake comments—80 percent of all the comments received. The majority of the comments submitted in favor of keeping the regulations—over 7.7 million of them—were contrived by one 19-year-old college student in California. This and other campaigns like it are creating all kinds of headaches for policy makers as they try to sift through what's real and what isn't, what's grassroots and what's so-called 'Astroturf lobbying.' "Americans' voices are being drowned out by masses of fake comments and messages being submitted to the government to sway decision-making," said New York State Attorney General Letitia James who led the investigation.[25]

And this isn't at all confined to social media and fake comments. Follow the work of Dr. Augustine Fou on Twitter (@acfou) for some serious emperor-has-no-clothes research on this subject. One study he conducted demonstrated that fully two thirds of digital ads purchased through programmatic exchanges (and monitored through anti-fraud services) are shown to bots, not humans.[26] Let that one sink in: How would your boss or board of directors feel about two thirds of your marketing budget simply making money for someone else?

Determining what's real online will require some technology, yes. But what will really help us navigate this new reality will be our skills in finding new ways to connect at a human level through values that can't be replicated by machines (at least not for a while). We must learn how to transfer genuine human values like trust, reciprocity, and sharing of belief systems to and in the digital world. In my opinion, the only way we'll be able to wade through what's real and what's not—to be effective red-pillers (a term taken from *The Matrix* where we take the red pill to melt away the computer simulation)—is to be savvy leaders of people, not better technologists. Certainly not better marketers.

It could very well be that these same abilities will also move us away from the beasts that Facebook and Google built. As so acutely illustrated in *The Social Dilemma*, so-called social media platforms understand all too well our hard-wired need to connect, and have built AI and machine-learning algorithms that are manipulating us for little reason other than to make a small group of shareholders a lot of money. The imperative of our time is to learn how to interact with the online world by building and exchanging social capital, something AI can't generate nor shareholders trade. It's the anti-cryptocurrency, a social vaccine in the time of quarantines, the only value-exchange that's human.

And here it comes again: building and exchanging social capital is a leadership skill. Not a marketing one.

Another takeaway from Dr. Lieberman's work: we've been exercising the brain's region responsible for social interaction for quite a while now. Millions of years, as he and Dr. Lembke will tell you. It's what set us on our evolutionary course as a species, and as an individual you've been doing it from your very first butt-spanked cry (as a matter of fact, your social wiring is responsible for that cry). The result? We're really good at it. This is not good news for marketing and sales people in social systems. We have hard-wired alarms that tell us when someone is a threat to our social connections.

Stop and think about it. You can tell, can't you? When someone is selling during a networking happy hour. When the speaker at your conference isn't as interested in spreading ideas as they are in selling their book or consulting service. You can sniff it out, and while some of us are more sensitive to it than others, we all have the alarms. Our social senses tingle when someone has an agenda in a social setting. It's no different than the person at the networking reception handing out brochures. The street team member with the energy drink sample that breaks into your family circle at the festival. The telemarketing call at dinner.

We're motivated and highly skilled at interacting in social systems. We've created and will continue to create systems through which to engage and communicate online, and they're very different from the passive media groups of the past, systems that have an implicit agreement of transaction. I could simply point to Dr. Lieberman's evidence that our brains use entirely different regions to process buying decisions than they do when interacting in social settings and leave it at that.

Change won't be easy. Prising the controlling hands away from us marketers and facing the sophisticated nature of online social systems is to swim against a very strong current. This is true in organizations with budgets and plans and staff and structures built to support the status quo, and it's true in the agency industry that's deeply entrenched in keeping billions of billable hours. As the great thought leader James O'Toole told us, we have to construct a compelling vision of a better future than could be achieved by continuing down the path we're on.[27]

Try this vision on for size: stop marketing to us. Start building our communities instead.

Chapter 2
A TELEMARKETING CALL AT DINNER: WHY MARKETING DOESN'T WORK IN SOCIAL CONSTRUCTS

If you're I-remember-phones-tethered-to-walls years old, you'll remember an analog telephone's ringer. Electric charges set loose a hammer on the inside of a steel bell that would beat the hell out of it until someone, so vulgarly interrupted from whatever they were doing, picked up the handset and accosted whoever decided now would be a good time to insert themselves into the privacy of a home. No pre-call text message to ask if it was a good time. Just an analog barging-in of the most barbaric kind.

To my memory, the only people pleased by this process were teenagers, a morning dew still on their perception of human relationships. The ring would spring them into action, ever-convinced the caller was bringing news or gossip from a friend or love interest, and screaming "I GOT IT" through their braces lest anyone else in the house get to the phone first. To a teen the telephone was a portal out of homework, three-channel television options, and smelly younger siblings.

When Clay Shirky mentioned the telephone in his 2009 TED Talk *How Social Media Can Make History*, it was with a bit more reverence.[1] As one of the five periods in human existence that created media revolutions, the telephone (and telegraph) allowed for real time, one-on-one conversations. This was a huge shift from the broadcast-based revolution of the printing press (an invention that brought changes so vast and significant we can still hardly get our arms around it). Shirky goes on to illustrate the other pre-internet moments in media revolution: recorded media other than print—photos and sound—and then "the harnessing of the electromagnetic spectrum to send sound and images through the air: radio and television."[2]

His three-part point, a decade ago at a time when the Erik Proulxs of the world were pushing and exploring new ways to connect, is still an important one as we build a foundation to consider how social groups and marketing coexist today (and why a book about social capital begins by considering the ringing of an analog telephone). First, before the internet, we had media that was effective at either creating conversations or groups. But not both. Conversations were had one-on-one, or messages were broadcast *at* groups, without conversations. The internet is the first medium for both. Second, the internet is the first medium to collect, store, and deliver all other media. Which puts it all together in one place, ready for intersectional comparisons, conversations and criticisms. A site of coordination, as Shirky so sharply put it.

The third part of his broader point is that consumers and producers are now one with the internet. Without judgment about quality or intent, this is an important shift to remember. It didn't used to be this way. Not putting "too fine a point on it," Shirky rightly says that the internet basically gave laymen a printing press and a recording studio complete with a broadcast tower. While we consume, we also create. The curtain is pulled back, the audience is ours. Have at it.

I'd like to add a fourth point to Shirky's seminal TED talk. Marketers having mass and cheap access to social groups is also a very recent reality. Something we're still getting used to, still understanding. Industries and wealth have been built atop sacred principles of reaching and targeting groups and segments within the traditional marketing landscape. I'm hardly the first to talk about this, but it's still important to remember when we think about peeling back the cognitive biases and financial interests blocking us from seeing how social groups actually work, and how we can intervene to have an influence within them for our needs.

Our needs, as in those of our organization or brand, as opposed to *their* needs, as in our customers' or stakeholders', which is why our organizations were formed in the first place. Let's put a placeholder on that one for the moment.

For those of us old enough to remember, the old media landscape also gives us a nice entry by way of an analogy for today's social media marketing: telemarketing. When that hammer beat the bell during a dinner party or a family game night, the vitriol came fast and hard. It actually generated physical pain: an annoyance which was at times unbearable. Defenses—armor, to borrow a term from Brené Brown—were immediately erected, resulting in many an abusive rant hurled across the lines at faceless salespeople. Parents broke all kinds of conduct codes with words and phrases not typically used in family settings. Red faces, embarrassed spouses, slammed-down handsets, money deposited in the curse jar.

When social constructs—gatherings of opted-in groups brought together for activities decidedly not concerned with financial transactions—are interrupted by sales and marketing, we react instinctively and strongly in defense of our social bubble. Nothing matches it, really. Maybe driving comes close, where we set aside normal empathetic responses as someone comes into conflict with our Feel Good by way of a stolen parking space or an open lane without a turn signal.

This is not a book about telemarketing, so I'll skip commenting on its virtues (which, to be fair, still exist in certain contexts). The point is this: the minute companies and brands recognized they could generate leads for their sales efforts in other ways, they largely abandoned the telemarketing ship and moved into waters where groups were gathered in such a way that a sales pitch wasn't so unwelcome. We invented marketing disciplines like permission marketing and opt-in lists in response, and even reverted to channels of traditional advertising. As consumers, we're generally aware of the arrangement in these settings, and far less likely to respond with contempt when someone makes a sales pitch in them. When we know the exchange for value is, say, commercials that pay the bills on a TV channel or pop-up forms gathering our email address to pay for a free industry white paper, we're quite literally (as we'll see later) in a better headspace to receive such messages. When we feel we're a part of the arrangement, when it's what we've signed up for, we're at least more tolerant. That is the nature of transactional relationships.

Tolerance, of course, isn't what we're aiming for with our social media communities. Tolerance isn't sustainable, and it's passive. There's no real value in tolerance, no relational depth. We'll get to all that, but it's important to acknowledge that in some arrangements we're more receptive to marketing messages than others, and when given the choice marketers will always take the option that gets their brand some sales leads while at the same time avoiding a hit to their brand's reputation. By and large this seems intuitive: not many of us need convincing that interrupting meaningful social constructs with random peddlings from sales and marketing wonks run contrary to our internal sense of what's effective and ineffective.

We know it intuitively, but we also know it professionally. Social media marketers are quick to suggest 'value-added content' as a key ingredient to effective social media marketing, conjuring ratios of non-branded, value-added-content-to-promotional-content as a path to engagement. And even if social media marketers don't have a proven, scientific formula to back up their intuition, research backs up the concept. One academic paper in the *Journal of Business Research* studying online consumer engagement empirically found what we all know: "online communities welcome marketers only if they are contributing to the community [...] businesses need to listen to and 'engage in engaging' consumers in brand communications, which consumers perceive to be 'non-commercially driven.'"[3]

As it turns out, this is because we're actually hard-wired to protect social relationships, and protect them from a variety of threats, including, I argue, sales and marketing. In fact, it's central to our wiring, intertwined and inexorable from our being. We're talking primal. Not squishy-teambuilding/Myers & Briggs/it-might-generate-better-performance-in-the-workplace theories. No, protecting ourselves from social loss is so strong that it motivated Dr. Lieberman, after years of award-winning research, to challenge Maslow over the issue. "Maslow had it wrong," he wrote. As infants, we are "absolutely useless when it comes to surviving on [our] own [...] our biology is built to thirst for [social] connection because it is linked to our most basic survival needs."[4]

In other words, creating and protecting social connections is a primal function for our survival. We can't get our hands on food, water, and sleep—the physiological needs for survival—without help. We must bond quickly, deeply, and for the long term to help us through what is an unusually long development period.

Taking on Maslow's Hierarchy of Needs[5] comes at the beginning of Lieberman's book *Social: Why Our Brains Are Wired to Connect*. The book goes on to detail the science behind our primal need to connect with others and how painstakingly we've evolved to protect these connections. He's an incredible writer—an amazing talent because he's also so clearly a brilliant scientist and those two worlds don't often intersect. He makes brain and social neuroscience with its Latin labels and endless acronyms accessible. He's the kind of communicator who makes laymen like me feel like an expert in waters they have no business wading into, let alone extrapolating from. It's on this basis that some clear lines of sight can be drawn from his world into marketing (narrow a reading of his book though it may be). The effect is to deepen our intuitive sense that marketing in social constructs creates dissonance, and is ultimately an ineffective way for a brand managers to influence customers. Let's wade in.

With the rise of fMRI technology, the field of neuroscience has never been more exciting. Dr. Lieberman uses a combination of this technology with other traditional psychological research techniques to better understand our 'central mammalian' need for social connection. Evolution, he illustrates, has given us a certain wiring that bonds us to a caretaker immediately after we're born, and allows us to create bonds with people as we grow into adulthood. This happens in two essential ways. First, we process social disconnection in the same way as we experience physical pain, which also sounds alarms to motivate us in addressing threats to such events. Second, we develop the ability to mind-read so as to understand the psychological meaning from the physical actions of others which, combined with *mentalizing*—the applied ability to understand that all people have unique thoughts that drive their choices and behaviors—allows us to create reason behind others' actions and interpret their thoughts, feelings, and yes, their agendas. These two key neural networks, along with other psychological abilities, give us a path to mitigate pain by avoiding those things that might sever social connections.

The process of understanding, recognizing, and making social connections is so important (and complex) that infants turn on the network responsible for it before they're aware of anything else. Before we see, smell, or control movement we literally cry out for connection, and provide feedback to the reward systems of the people who give it to us. From the moment it's switched on, the regions responsible for social connection go to work, and as we discussed earlier we exercise it during downtime to maintain it. As a result, these areas of our brain are bigger and much more developed than in other mammals. By a long shot.

The idea that rewards for social connections and the pain we feel when we lose them are hard-wired into our brains—that we have no choice—should give all of us clarity around why social media is such a force in our world. We're driven to connect, even online. Zombie-like we thumb through our phones in line at the grocery store, seeking that latest Like or Friend Request while our child tugs at our shirt tail. Billion-dollar companies are built upon this innate human reflex.

The kicker here, as Dr. Lieberman lays out in detail, is that the pain we feel when we lose a connection takes part in the same places of the brain as physical pain. Let that sink in: we experience social pain the same way as physical pain. It explains a broken heart after a breakup. A kick to the gut after a rebuke. Why we use physically-derived words like broken, ill, shattered, empty, and sick when describing a lost relationship.

And while it may seem a bit crude in comparison, is it any wonder that we feel drawn to fans and followers, and feel bewildered when we lose them? For our purposes the important point is this: the parts of our brain that are activated when we experience physical pain—a threat to one of our most fundamental survival needs—are the same parts of our brain that are activated when we recognize social threats.

The same part of the brain that monitors and issues alarms for social distress does so for threats against our physiological well-being, too. The network that alerts us to social conflicts and *faux pas* is the same that motivates us to take our hand away from the stove when we feel it heating up.

"Our sensitivity to social rejection," writes Dr. Lieberman "is so central to our well-being that our brains treat it like a painful event, whether the instance of *social rejection matters or not* (my emphasis)."[6] And this has been tested in the field of social neuroscience across the phenomena of human error, bereavement for a loved one, being negatively evaluated, or simply looking at disapproving faces.

Dr. Lieberman doesn't mention sales and marketing people in this array of contexts. But is it such a stretch? Doesn't it hurt a little when a hawker shoves a flyer in our face while we're walking along with a date at a music festival? When a canvasser knocks on the door during game night? And don't we sniff that stuff out? Don't we all have a radar for such intrusions, alarms going off at a biological level when peddlers disguised as regular people approach our families when we're traveling? When the sales pitch is about to hit us at church?

There are other areas in Dr. Lieberman's book that support why marketing and selling in social contexts runs contrary to our biology. Like how strongly the cognitive bias for *loss aversion* (psychologically we're more predisposed to avoid losses than we are to take advantage of gains) works to help us avoid social loss. To social media marketers this bias should sound the most ominous of alarms: in a social setting the deck is simply stacked against us. Our target is deeply biased to lose the social connections they're interacting with, much more strongly than they are to gain a new product, or a discount, or even a nugget of value by way of some branded content.

Dr. Lieberman also details how our cognitive ability for self-control actually works as social cohesion, which sheds yet more light on why the social and marketing minds are at odds. Self-control is often thought of as some self-actualized driver of separation, but the opposite is actually true. We're wired to seek ways to harmonize our beliefs and values with groups, not separate from them. Social settings, online or otherwise, are formed around mutually agreed-upon values. We gather in them to share pictures of our lives, exchange knitting tips and tricks, offer advice for hidden hiking trails, or discover a new chord progression. Market to someone in that setting and you're asking them to mentally introduce something new. To disharmonize. To dissent.

Moreover, to market to someone in a social construct is asking for a person to allow the marketer into the group without the permission of others in the community. Marketers are essentially asking community members to jeopardize not only their place in the construct, but the integrity of the entire construct itself. This isn't a concept from Dr. Lieberman but one that's aligned closely with his work, so is important enough to mention here.

Some of the best examples of online communities rich in social capital uncovered by our research aren't staffed with marketers. The managers of these communities know, even if only intuitively, that a marketing mindset is a virus inside social groups. For example, McKenzie Eakin built Xbox's record- and ground-breaking customer service team called *The Elite Tweet Fleet* and a thousand-plus-member Ambassador Chat program composed of Xbox users who provide peer-to-peer support.[7] She told me she didn't even have a Twitter account when she started the project and didn't hire social media experts. Instead she looked for people with a passion for Xbox so they'd have a deeper understanding of the problems their users were experiencing. This resulted in more authenticity online, and acting passionately in solving problems.[8] Rob Siefker, Senior Director of Customer Loyalty at Zappos, told me he doesn't look for marketers when staffing his Customer Loyalty Team, and doesn't care about their social media chops. "Everyone knows how to do social media," he said. Instead he looks for people who understand what it means to "go above and beyond. We ask about this in interviews: 'Do you remember a moment when someone went above and beyond, and how that made you feel?' We need people who recognize it, because how would you give it if you don't know it."[9] Nichole Kelly built a million-strong online community for debt consolidation nonprofit CareOne. She told me she staffed her team with customer-oriented talent so she "wouldn't have to train them to unlearn marketing." She says she's been dealing with that dynamic her entire career as her community-building professional practice has developed. "Recognizing opportuni-ties for human connection is very different from opportunities for conversion," she told me.[10]

Madison Leupp, a Social Support Manager at Adobe who oversees a team of twelve reps as part of a 40-team social media support team, looks for communicators. "The challenge [is finding people] with a social voice. Tone, and expressing that they get the internet culture. Posting marketing and writing content is irrelevant. It's easier to teach the social media aspect."

Dr. Lieberman, blissfully outside the marketing sphere, seemingly (and wonderfully) quotes science fiction authors and poets almost as often as he does scientists in his book. He points to philosopher Alain de Botton to underscore an important point about our social hard-wiring: "Living for others [is] such a relief from the impossible task of trying to satisfy oneself." When we participate in social settings we're following the comfortable mandate of our wiring to harmonize with a group. As a marketer, you're asking someone to break away from that and consider something entirely—and selfishly—different: a transac-tion that benefits oneself.

Here's another biggie: while we're interacting socially, we aren't, to take the colloquial to a literal place, in the right headspace for sales and marketing. I mean this not in a cognitive bias or emotional way. I mean it in a physical way.

The neuroscience behind social thinking has demonstrated that the network responsible for it is distinct from the abstract reasoning section of the brain associated with general intelligence. Dr. Lieberman describes their relationship with each other as at odds, as an "antago-nism between social and nonsocial intelligence [...] like two ends of a seesaw; as either side increases (goes up) in activity, the other side decreases."[11]

Dr. Lieberman frames this in the context of leadership, suggesting that some leaders are perhaps more adept at activating and deacti-vating these networks for the complicated leadership task of balancing empathy and reason. Think about what that means as a marketer (like a leader you're in the business of influence, after all). At best, when you market in social constructs you're asking someone to switch their mindset entirely, to turn off a network actively engaged in social activity. You're asking them to stop connecting with friends by way of funny selfies and to access and switch on an entirely different neural network to calculate the need for another pair of socks. At worst they simply can't do it.

This holds important meaning to marketers. As expected, some people are more adept at switching these networks on and off (Dr. Lieberman suggests that some of us are simply genetically predisposed to it). The fundamental calculus for the marketer here is that, given the near impossibility of segmenting in this way, is it even worth the risk of sending that marketing missive, given the negative consequences and the likelihood it will miss its mark?

In other words, when you market to people in social settings you're taking a shot in the dark from a market segmentation perspective. Identifying the types of people with the biological predisposition to switch to a transactional mindset in social groups seems like an incredibly daunting, if not impossible, task from a marketing analytics perspective. Segmenting and targeting customers with a biological predisposition for a certain neurological flexibility? That's some serious next-level AI stuff right there. LinkedIn can't even seem to flag spam in their direct messages right now. I continued to see ads served up in my social feeds for a specific kind of Adidas a full two months after I bought a pair of them. And again, the calculus here isn't just wasting time and money. The potential negative consequences are quite real.

In the next chapter we get into the data about social media marketing including the negative consequences of it. And to say its benefits are flimsy actually gives it too much credit. What's solid, though, is the disconnect between marketers' belief in social media marketing and what the data tells us, between the "triumph of hope over hard evidence of [its] commercial return" as one industry study on social media marketing puts it.[12] From my observations and our research, the predominant thought leaders in the social media marketing space are marketers, and as marketers we engage in social media marketing data with our work hats on. Or, more in keeping with Dr. Lieberman's work, with our non-social network activated. Our social alarms don't tingle with danger when we see someone selling on social media like non-marketers do. We see potential, creativity, and possibilities. Very different from the way a potential customer reacts.

A long time ago a boss gave me a piece of advice (maybe you've received this one, too): "Never use yourself as a data point. Because you're in marketing, you're inherently unreliable. You think about these things differently than a customer. I don't ever want to hear you say 'I think this or that' about what we're doing. You need to say 'The data shows.'"

I pass this advice along in my classes with new marketing students, or when I have the chance to give some advice to a young marketing professional. Reading Dr. Lieberman's book and putting some neuroscience behind this bit of wisdom was a validating moment for me (thank you, Dr. Lieberman). And I think it should become a critical starting place for marketers when considering and evaluating social media marketing for brands and clients.

So social and nonsocial thinking are at odds with each other in the brain; they're a seesaw. We have strong cognitive biases when we're engaged in social activities. We're wired to find harmony within our social groups. We experience pain from social separation with warnings to prevent it and rewards from social acceptance in the same way we feel physical pain and rewards. And it's all the result of millions of years of evolutionary development to ensure our very survival.

We're adept at a hard-wired level to recognize when to sell and when not to sell—except when we put on a marketer's hat. When that happens, it seems that the allure of social media as a marketer's golden utopia of peers selling for us, of low-cost access to eyeballs, of being on the front curve of The Next Thing, is stronger than biology.

That's probably why some of you need some numbers to demonstrate the ineffectiveness of social media marketing.

Chapter 3

THE STRAW MAD MAN: MARKETING'S TOXIC RELATIONSHIP WITH SOCIAL MEDIA MARKETING DATA

It used to be that a person could find some reliable data about social media marketing. That didn't mean that marketers would listen to it, of course. But for people who were interested in evaluating where and how their marketing dollars should be spent, various organizations obliged us with studies.

Due in no small part to the volume of content created by digital and social media marketing companies with vested interests in demonstrating the value of the services they provide, quality, agenda-free digital marketing studies are drowned out these days. And marketers are making ill-informed digital—and especially social media—marketing decisions. It's a problem that's spreading like a coronavirus set loose. We no doubt have the rise of content marketing to thank for this, not without a small measure of irony. Marketing agencies (yes, like mine) tout content marketing as a way for brands to earn the trust of their stakeholders. They (we) tell clients: produce (or better yet, *hire us* to produce) content that seems as if it's a purely value-add and customers will view your brand as acting in their best interest. The law of reciprocity takes things from there.

Companies that offer digital and social media marketing solutions (the HubSpots, the Sprout Socials, the MailChimps) are also churning out 'reports' and 'studies' for their own marketing purposes. Naturally this content validates their business model and the value they bring to the industry. Those of us who look for objective data to help guide our marketing decisions don't always identify the connection to this content-marketing ouroboros: the product of the thing that is driving the marketing content is marketing itself.

Studies (signals) of the more objective kind are now drowned out and subsumed by content marketing (noise). Having waded through more than my share of them and compared them to those produced by more agenda-free publishers, it's becoming increasingly hard to find meaningful, consistent, and reliable data about digital marketing, and especially about social media marketing. Marketers beware: if we're not careful we're going to kill that which sustains us.

What's worse, marketers are listening to these biased studies. The agency blogs with posts that promote the value of a certain marketing tactic, supported by a citation from such content, are legion. I've judged marketing plans in competitions that use them. And no doubt they've snuck into my plans and consulting as well.

By way of comparison, back in 2014 Augie Ray published what I consider a seminal blog post about the effectiveness of social media marketing that uses what I think are the kind of agenda-free studies we don't see as much anymore.[1] Augie is a customer experience expert these days, working and thought-leading on the subject across the social web and for the consultancy and research company Gartner. Before establishing himself as a must-know expert in the customer experience space, he worked in the social media sphere, using it for strategy and customer experience insights at American Express and Prudential.

Augie doesn't suffer fools or their data and he had his finger on the pulse of social media marketing as well as anyone. For instance, Augie was warning of a 50-percent decline in organic Facebook posts reaching audiences before most were willing to talk about it. Today Hootsuite reports that all of 8-percent of organic reaches an eyeball.[2]

His 2014 blog post takes a methodical approach to evaluating social media across the key marketing dimensions that every MBA student and marketing executive is told to care about. He used around 15 industry and academic studies to back up some solid conclusions (spoiler: everything we knew about social media marketing in 2014 was wrong). Candidly, I think of his post as timeless, and even though the studies he cites are old by internet standards, the dynamics at work in online social constructs haven't changed enough to undo most of his points. If anything, matters have gotten worse for marketers, as evidenced by the 8-percent Hootsuite stat.

Attempts to go back and find updated versions of Augie's cited sources in the course of researching this project yielded exactly zero results, so new ones were amassed: more than fifty studies no older than 2017 that directly relate to marketing-centric numbers similar to what Augie collected for his blog post. Ignored were what I call 'Promise Keeper' studies: growth of social media, how many people are on social media and which channels, and how much time people spend on social media. These aren't marketing studies. They're at best census data, at worse propaganda for social media marketing plat-forms and their pick-and-shovel (an investment term for companies that produce supplies associated with the actual output, named after the tools needed to take part in the California Gold Rush) affiliates. The studies were also evaluated by their source: the practitioner world (and if so what kind of company might have sponsored it) or academia.

Two major takeaways from this research have broad-ranging impli-cations. First, social media marketers don't know what they're measuring or how to measure it. Either that or they're ignoring what they're seeing or their biases have so calcified their thinking that they *can't* see it. Marketers have plenty of data, but it seems we're too fueled by our desire—and quite often our clients' and bosses' desires—for social media to work as a marketing tool. In other words, our confir-mation biases are pegged.

That's casting a lot of shade on social media marketers, and we'll take a look at some studies we found that will back it up. But there's a fairly obvious implication in all of this: we're recommending and acting on incorrect information. We need a new, honest relationship with the data in order to do right by our organizations and clients.

The second takeaway from our research is a bit more abstract, but as important. Marketers' lack of data acuity puts the rest of the marketing research milieu in question. Seeing as how marketing effectiveness studies rely significantly on data and measurements reported by marketers, and marketers themselves are reporting low confidence in their ability to measure their activities, how can we trust the data?

Let's dive into some specifics.

Garbage in, garbage out. 'Twas ever thus.

- You've probably heard some version of this before: According to the 2020 Duke/Deloitte/American Marketing Association CMO Survey, 67 percent of executive marketers can't quantitatively measure the impact of their social media marketing. That number balloons to as much as 77 percent in some B2B sectors.[3] Social media marketing consistently falls into this category in other studies we looked at as well. Again: how are we supposed to trust marketing reports that rely on data reported from these sources if the sources themselves don't know what they're looking at?

- Sprout Social released a content marketing-oriented 'report' titled *Turned Off: How Brands Are Annoying Customers on Social* that puts data behind an elephant in most agency and marketing department rooms. In their report, they warn that social media users will unfollow brands if they promote too much: 46 percent report unfollowing a brand because of too many promotions. (Wouldn't surprise me if the other 54 percent who don't unfollow a brand because of too many promotions are social media marketers.) Confusingly, the same respondents tell Sprout Social that they need to see a product or service 2–4 times before purchasing it and 20 percent need to see it 5–8 times.[4] Does your brand promote too much or too little on social media? Good luck.

ROI, schmaROI

- In the same study, CMOs rank their social media spending right around 3 on a scale of 1 to 7 in terms of how it contributes to business performance. This metric is almost perfectly flat over four years, while CMOs continue to increase and plan to increase their spending on social media marketing. Is a three-out-of-seven a waste of an organization's marketing budget, or is it just... *bleh*? Seems like one of those non-committal, we're-in-some-kind-of-malaise, we-don't-really-understand-our-data scores to me, especially since it hasn't changed in four years. Doesn't it also seem odd to keep spending on something that is at best so unremarkable?

- Of the 3,000 HubSpot users surveyed in its 2020 *Not Another State of Marketing Report*, only 35 percent said that understanding the ROI of their social media campaigns is "Very Important" or "Extremely Important."[5] When all the data measuring social media marketing effectiveness across all the years is piled up, this seems like the jeweled crown that rests upon it. Most of us are just doing social media because... well, just because.

- Side note: Shout out to HubSpot's content marketers who in a moment of refreshing self-awareness decided to call their 2020 state-of-marketing report *Not Another State of Marketing Report*. I see you, HubSpot.

- In the same study, 66 percent of marketers say they use (what I call) non-results-oriented metrics when measuring the effectiveness of their social media efforts (Likes, Shares, and Comments). Some 93 percent use non-results-oriented metrics to evaluate effective influencer campaigns (Reach, Clicks, Comments, Impressions, and Views ranked 1–5, respectively). And Engagement (60 percent) and Traffic (51 percent) top their measurements of effectiveness when advertising on social. All of these are ranked ahead of Leads and Sales. Studies sponsored by social media companies insist on calling these 'top-of-the-funnel' metrics, but that's just gaslighting. Leads or inquiries are the top-of-funnel measurements that matter, and when you really look into it, social media isn't producing much of either (more on that shortly).

- A study by Buffer and AppSumo, the latter with a racist character/logo that I guess we're just supposed to ignore, found that brands are increasing their Facebook page posts while reporting 50–70-percent declines in engagement with them.[6] If you're claiming engagement is an important metric —a fairly questionable position to take in the first place—*and* you see it declining *while* continuing to invest in it, then I worry that even the best marketing minds can't help you.

- A 2018 Social Media Examiner *Industry Report* found something similar: 56 percent of their (pro-social media marketing, it should be noted) audience can't be sure or are unsure if they can measure their social media marketing ROI. Still, 62 percent report intentions of increasing their organic activities.[7]

- Over half of B2B marketers in the *Chief Marketer's 2019 B2B Outlook Survey* cite "Measuring ROI" as the biggest challenge of social media lead generation.[8] When I see these stats, which have been in B2B marketing studies for years, I have this strange vision of the Netflix documentary that will chronicle the brave soul who finally said 'enough' to their B2B boss, stopped investing in social media marketing, and now sits atop a mountain to which marketers trek to gain wisdom.

- From the 2017 Altimeter/Hootsuite report, *Beyond ROI: Unlocking the Business Value of Social Media*: a mere 26 percent of marketers say they tie social media marketing metrics to business results, and the rest simply use what's available in the tools.[9] Sit with that one for a minute: we're measuring the effectiveness of a tool by using the tool's measurements. Talk about the fox running the hen house. *And it's Hootsuite who's reporting this.* What's the saying about the greatest trick the devil ever pulled? More on that question in a minute.

- This sentiment from a marketer running Arby's social media efforts captures the dynamic well: "It's difficult to tie what we're doing in social with hard metrics around sales or store visits [...] However, when we take a deeper look into the quantitative results and look at the sentiment and passion intensity of the comments [on our Instagram posts], we're driving significant positive conversations around our brand."[10] That's an awfully athletic way to arrive at a 'positive conversations' metric. I see this kind of vague thinking a lot in these studies. It's vaguely better than negative conversations, I guess, but not exactly a result that definitive-minded C-level execs care much about, or what marketers should aspire to.

- In case you're resisting my assertion that social media engagement metrics aren't top-of-the-funnel metrics that marketers should aspire to, consider a 2021 report by e-commerce app developer Bango.[11] They surveyed 200 CEOs and found that 66 percent of them think us marketers focus too much on these tactical analytics, and we aren't demonstrating enough business results. 65 percent of them aren't interested in likes, 76 percent aren't interested in retweets, and 66 percent aren't interested in impressions.

What can be measured can be managed. But only if you decide to try to understand it.

- Some 20 percent of marketers surveyed in Buffer/Social Chain's *State of Social* say they're uncertain if social media is effective in their marketing efforts.[12] A promising minority, but in the same study over half of the respondents said their organization doesn't have a documented social media strategy. So what are we to make of the people who *do* claim certainty around the effectiveness of social media marketing? How can you measure something when you don't know what it's supposed to be doing for you?

- The 2017 Altimeter/Hootsuite report, *Beyond ROI: Unlocking the Business Value of Social Media*, finds 85 percent of marketers in agreement that social data is accessible, but fully half of them say their organization lacks the skills needed to work with it.

- In what I think is becoming the most glaring example of marketers flummoxed by their own data, customer service/care using social media is showing significant promise in terms of returns for organizations (we tackle this topic in Chapter 5). Yet a surprising number of businesses are ignoring it. A Sprout Social content marketing report claims a 146-percent rise in social messages that require brand responses over three years, but the brands' response rate has actually decreased (on average they respond to only 1 in 10) in the same timeframe.[13] Marketers, we need to ask ourselves why we're not pushing harder to move social media activities to customer care. Is it because we're paying attention to the data or because we don't want to lose the billable hours, FTEs, or budget?

It's remarkable that we're still talking about the potential and hope for social media marketing at all. The Bango study mentioned earlier found that a full 60 percent of the CEOs they surveyed think that the potential for social media marketing is exaggerated.[14] Market research and digital marketing agency Good Growth spent a few months in 2017 researching social media marketing for their fourth annual digital marketing growth book. Quite a bit of our research coincided with theirs, and they concluded that "investment in social media [marketing] continues to be a triumph of hope over hard evidence of commercial return. [...] There remains a lack of clarity regarding the commercial outcome from the investment."[15]

Social media marketing companies' content marketing 'reports' and 'studies' strengthen the cognitive biases that are preventing social media marketers from seeing what they don't want to see. Our research illustrates marketing's need for less data on the one hand, but more data that is directly tied to business results on the other. I'm hardly the first to write about this, but less data and a refusal to buy into the vanity of what is (at best) the leading indicator data offered by social media tools may give us a clearer picture of the results social media marketing is actually generating.

We need a back-to-basics relationship with marketing data, especially social media marketing data. Maybe we can find inspiration from the minimalist movement, or the *Simple* magazines of this world. Whatever the case, it's clear that, as Nassim Taleb warned us, we're in the midst of a calamity in the information age: the toxicity of data has increased much faster than its benefits.[16]

The truth is that marketers don't do data very well, and it's obfuscating our ability to understand the efficacy of social media marketing. Let's now look at the facts around social media marketing, and wonder why we as marketers seem so intent on ignoring it.

The Greatest Trick the Devil Ever Pulled

As discussed, a large part of the problem with determining the effectiveness of social media is the source from which we get our information. Social media companies, with a vested interest in our enduring faith in the effectiveness of the medium, churn out content marketing materials masked as objective studies and reports like a candy factory while social media marketers, like Lucille Ball, try to gobble it all up. Some content released in 2018 by Sprout Social called *Creating Connection: what consumers want from brands in a divided society* is a good example of what you'll have to slog your way through these days.[17] They surveyed 1,013 people, defined only as "U.S. consumers," though most unlikely to be a representative sample, asking a variety of questions about how they feel about connecting with brands on social media. When you dig into the content though, it's much more accurate to say how they *want* brands to connect with them on social media. Asking people what they want in such research projects is what clapping on one and three is to rhythm and blues: you're going about it the wrong way and even someone casually familiar with the discipline will probably make fun of you for it.

The study's main takeaway proclaims that *"When* [my emphasis] customers feel connected to brands, more than half of consumers (57 percent) will increase their spending with that brand and 76 percent will buy from them over a competitor." The probability of 'when' someone will feel connected to a brand on social media is a highly questionable issue in the studies we looked at, so the conclusion is suspect from the jump. But the study asks this of respondents along with other multiple-choice questions that fill their heads with a picture of a brand-customer utopia where brands take up the social causes the respondent cares about. Do we want, they ask, a brand to bring people together for a goal, act as a leader in society, and perform other deeds of benevolence that brands are traditionally terrible at actually demonstrating, let alone doing? Under those circumstances, why, yes, of course I'll feel connected, and I'm practically guilted into admitting that I'd increase my spending. What kind of jerk wouldn't?

In response to this finding, David Kennedy, CEO of market research firm Corona Insights, told me that "respondents giving socially acceptable answers and rationalizing their behavior is definitely an issue in research." Social media and content marketing 'reports' are replete with this kind of thing.

I was able to connect with a very kind and responsive PR rep for Sprout Social about this study, but she was unable to add much clarity. I asked her how they arrived at whether or not a customer feels connected to a brand, and she replied "For that stat we prompted respondents to select statements they agreed with to complete the sentence, 'When I feel connected to a brand or business, I am...' and then gave them several options to select from—including increasing their spending and choosing that brand over competitors." So there isn't much there, there. "Respondents are trying to rationalize their behavior," as David put it in response to this. "We can't always explain why we do what we do (or what we think we'll do) so we fall back on the rational explanation." Other than an assumption (not based on any actual spending or loyalty) that social connects brands to consumers,

Sprout Social's entire exercise seems intended to promote the virtues of social media marketing for Sprout *Social*.

Self-guided, self-motivated studies of this kind might make good content marketing, but they don't serve as objective reasons to use social media for marketing purposes. Marketers, however, *do* use them as such. We cite studies like this without doing much digging into their legitimacy.

One other note from David on this: "Attitudes in general can take a long time to form or change," he said. "One post, one action from a brand probably won't change many minds. A sustained effort is almost always needed to change awareness and attitudes." This is a foundational underpinning of social capital, actually, and serves a nice bit of foreshadowing of Chapter 7.

Until then, here's another issue with these reports: their careless use of case studies (you can check out another Augie Ray 2014 perspective on this topic as well).[18] Many content marketing-oriented 'reports' use them without regard to the many shortcomings of case studies, such as their tendency to illustrate outliers (e.g. user-created content can skyrocket sales; all your business has to do is produce GoPros). Later I discuss how the vast majority of the more thriving social media communities tend to be built under three relatively narrow contexts, representing outliers rather than standards. Case studies feed off of these, leaving the rest of us wondering if we chose the right employer as opposed to an actual lesson we can bring back to our marketing departments.

The research for this book also uncovered that social media case studies almost always come up short when demonstrating actual business results. The above-mentioned Sprout Social report is peppered with little #brandsgetreal case study vignettes, inserted ostensibly as an attempt to prove the concepts they're driving at with their biased survey data. The authors wrap up these sketches with 'results,' all focused on views and impressions and vague claims of success. One #brandsgetreal measures the value a social media campaign brought to a company by bundling it into the brand's overall $1 billion market valuation while making no attempt to hide its inability to tease out the number. Another of these #brandsgetreal case studies doesn't even try to conjure up a legitimate business outcome, concluding that the brand "hopes to raise awareness—and generate solutions" from its social media marketing campaign. Actually, having written that it occurs to me that this is perhaps the best way to approach the issue of results in social media case studies. Just be transparent: you're all just hoping it works.

There are also plenty of sneaky incongruencies between the questions asked and the reported results in these pro-social media marketing content marketing pieces. Like a study by Curalate, a digital marketing platform that hired OnePoll, a brand-driven research company "used extensively for PR, media and brand exposure campaigns" that delivers exactly the kind of conclusions you'd expect from such a cabal. The study, *Social Content is the New Storefront*, makes "broad" claims about "U.S. Consumers" (which they culled from 1,000 names and 10 questions) to explain how social media marketing drives purchasing behavior.[19]

Some 52 percent of "U.S. Consumers," they conclude, report seeing a product they were interested in on Facebook, but make no mention of the likelihood that the respondents will be following the brands they're already advocates for. Over the years many studies have exposed the tendency of social media users to follow brands they're already aware of (we look at a few later), a fact simply ignored in Curalate's report and the many studies like it that amplify social media marketing as an effective sales tool. It's a detail that's easily (or willingly) overlooked by marketers, blinded as we are by confirmation bias and anxious as we are to justify our billable hours.

Later in that same study, the authors boast this finding: "65 percent of U.S. consumers say the link in a social media post led them to a product they weren't interested in." The implication, I guess, is that consumers have purchased a product, thanks to social media, they weren't previously interested in. The actual question asked of respondents was "Have you *experienced* [my emphasis] a link in a social media post that *led* [my emphasis] you to a product that you weren't interested in?" Both are clumsy, and, depending on how you interpret them, in conflict. And of course being "led to" could mean a number of things, including a bevy of options that have nothing to do with an action. Sure, it could mean purchase. But it also could mean putting it in a comparative set of other products, or even simply becoming aware. Or maybe it just means "Yeah, I've seen links of products I wasn't aware of."

If you're willing to wade through this malaise and find some studies with less bias, the news is not at all good for the effectiveness of social media marketing. Our research found that everything Augie wrote about back in 2014 essentially holds true. Since his post, organizations have poured billions of dollars into an area of marketing that isn't returning very much of it. Augie's blog post is, in my opinion, still relevant so I won't rehash it in detail. But he convincingly and systematically points out what our research confirms: social media isn't making a significant difference in any area for which marketing communications are responsible.

- It isn't a preferred channel for consumers to learn about brands
- It isn't a preferred channel to find more information about purchase decisions
- It isn't reliable in effectively building brand trust
- It isn't reliable in effectively building brand awareness
- It's a poor lead-generation tool
- The fans and followers that make up its audience do not equate to brand affinity
- It doesn't drive purchase intent; and
- Social media isn't a cost-effective reach tool

Here are a few highlights of our research that augment Augie's:

Brand Awareness and Affinity

- 'The Value of a Facebook Fan: Does "Liking" Influence Consumer Behavior?,' a 2017 study published in the *Journal of Marketing Research*, found strong evidence that consumers not only like brands they already have a fondness for on social media, but "the mere act of 'liking' a brand has no positive first-order effect on consumer attitudes or purchases."[20] In other words, social media engagement is a consequence, not a cause, of brand affinity. And get this: two meta analyses suggest that "if anything, its effect is detrimental."

- This confirms many other studies over the years drawing the same conclusions which in my opinion have all kinds of cascading effects, to the point of becoming a factor in every equation looking at purchasing behavior. If a customer buys something as a result of something they saw in their social media feed, to what extent did their existing affinity for the brand play a part? You can't count on the social media industry to tease that out for you.

- Another 2017 *Journal of Marketing Research* study, 'Effects of Traditional Advertising and Social Messages on Brand-Building Metrics and Customer Acquisition,' found traditional advertising is still more effective as a tool in building brand awareness and customer acquisition than social media posts by brands, and even by consumers on behalf of brands. That's right: Traditional advertising is driving more recommendations than social media.[21]

- A 2017 Harvard Business School study found that liking a Facebook page does not change customer behavior.[22] On its face this may seem simply disappointing, but I think it actually subverts what we know about the basic forces of influence. Robert Cialdini, essentially the founding father of modern influence theory, lays out five principles of influence based on human hardwiring in his book *Influence: The Psychology of Persuasion*. One of them is consistency: we experience a cognitive dissonance when our actions don't reflect our beliefs.[23] Liking a brand on social media, it would seem, is that rare place where we're immune to this long-held understanding.

Purchasing Behavior

- Another 2017 Harvard Business School study found, across 16 studies, "no evidence that following a brand on social media changes people's purchasing behavior." Nor does a friend's endorsement. The study found that social media had "no enhancing effect on the purchasing habits of friends."[24]
- The above-mentioned *Value of a Facebook Fan* study discovered that liking a brand on Facebook is viewed as a "token" action in terms of friend endorsements.

Reputation and Trust

- A 2017 University of Maryland study, *Bias on Your Brand Page? Measuring and Identifying Bias in Your Social Media Community*, dug into 170 million unique users of 3,000 brands and found that word-of-mouth on social media is often subject to bias, that this bias is typically negative, and when it affects brand performance it tends to damage it. The study also found that the larger the following, the more likely word-of-mouth is to be negative, while smaller followings lean more positive.[25] Think about that the next time you report social media follower growth to your boss, or demand it from your marketing department.
- This also has interesting implications for those who insist on touting the power of social media as a tool for customer insight. Social media biases can "certainly decrease the quality of insights marketers can extract," according to the study.[26]
- Avinash Kaushik, one of the most respected analytics thought and practice leaders on the Internet, makes a similar point about social media encouraging and amplifying negative sentiment in a blog post that urges all brands to stop organic social media marketing posthaste. Looking at Expedia social media posts, he finds "pretty much every single comment on pretty much every single Expedia post is

a complaint about how horrible Expedia is […] If your Facebook presence is solely to inspire people […] why are you on Social Media?" This combined with some compelling math related to his Conversation, Amplification, Applause, and Economic Value social media marketing metrics motivated Avinash to appeal to "the intelligent rational assessor of reality" in all of us to "kill all the organic social media activity by your company. All of it."[27]

Lead Generation, Funnels, and Preferred Channels

- Social Media Today, a social media blog, and Sharp Spring, a sales and marketing platform company, came together to produce a 2019 report called *The State of Social Lead Generation*. Over half the marketers surveyed were either neutral, somewhat dissatisfied, or extremely dissatisfied with social media as a lead gen tool. Some 38 percent notched Somewhat Satisfied ratings.
- Nearly 70 percent of those same marketers were either neutral, somewhat dissatisfied, or extremely dissatisfied with the quality of leads social media generates for them.[28]
- Chief Marketer's *B2B Outlook Survey* reports that social still ranks behind email, search, content marketing, and live events for generating leads. It falls behind email, content marketing, in-person meetings, calls from sales, and account-based marketing for lead nurturing. It's second to last on the list of tactics to move leads through sales funnels.[29]
- Keiler Perkins' massive annual *Internet Trends* report for 2018 shows barely marginal growth in traffic referrals from social to e-commerce sites (from 2 percent to 6 percent over three years) and Facebook e-commerce click throughs (1 percent to 3 percent over two years). These barely perceptible gains don't even keep up with the growth of the Internet: 19 percent according to the report.[30] As the Internet matures and continues to attract new minds, new technologies, and new techniques, traffic referrals from social aren't budging.

Having presented and consulted on this topic for a decade, the most common pushback I hear from marketers when presenting this data is around the sales lifts and boosts some brands are able to measure from their social media efforts. "I can offer a coupon on Twitter, and sales jump," a common declaration goes.

To those ends, it's important to consider the tendency to measure short-term gains from social media marketing, while ignoring the long-term value. Or worse. As a marketing researcher from global data-aggregator WARC put it when summarizing their company's *Seriously Social* report, a short-term social media marketing focus is "ultimately undermining long-term effectiveness."[31]

Sales lifts and follower boosts from special offers abound in the social media case study milieu, but very little of it is associated with long-term business success. WARC has released several reports on social media effectiveness based on hundreds of social media case studies, and in their top-four takeaways for the study as a whole the authors of their most recent report lament how "social campaigns [are] constrained to work over short timescales [and] unable to deliver the same benefits as long-term ones."

As marketers our job is to balance short-term lifts in sales through activation tactics like discounts and trials without damaging long-term business necessities like profitability, market share, and customer churn and retention. Deep dives into social media marketing's so-called success stories reveal the trumpeting of short-term wins while distracting us from the balanced marketing results marketers are responsible for delivering.

Whether it's Starbucks' limited-time Frappuccino offer, New Zealand Bank's 'Like Loan' campaign, or Mattessons stopping a decline in sales with their Fridge Raiders campaign, social media marketers like to confirm biases with measurements and data that demonstrate sales lifts.[32] This is not without its downside. As the WARC report puts it, "the inevitable consequence of short-term measurement is a drift to strategies that deliver better in the short term. Unfortunately, these tend to deliver poorer long-term performance and so short-termism ultimately undermines long-term effectiveness."

It's ultimately your data that matters, of course. If you can measure business success from your social media efforts, more power to you. There are outliers, usually located within three brand categories that I outline below. But if your data isn't demonstrating business success, you aren't alone. Maybe this chapter will help you find the courage to defund social media in your marketing mix, or garner the support you need to make the case to your boss.

I'm fascinated as to why marketers are so insistent in disbelieving the data as it relates to social media marketing. I resonated deeply with Nichole Kelly when, as you recall, she told me she's spent a career asking and training people to "unlearn marketing" for purposes of building online communities. I suppose this is at the core of it. Marketers, with their hands on the social media levers, have some unlearning to do. The difficulty in this, I think, is a combination of several factors that are ripe for addressing and changing.

Social media marketing is a huge industry with deep, vested pillars that are very difficult to move. We're wandering in a vast place, a megalopolis with global ad agency high rises on the east side to red light district shingle-hangers on the west side. All of them contribute to interests heavily vested in the billable hours and freemium business models social media marketing represents, all of them intent on ensuring marketing department budgets have a nice chunk allocated to them.

HubSpot's *Not Another State of Marketing Report* finds that 74 percent of marketers invest in social media marketing, and the 2020 AMA *CMO Survey* found that outside agencies deliver a quarter of it.[33] That 74 percent is feeding a seemingly insatiable appetite for social media marketing. A Lyfe Marketing agency blog post claims there are 50 million social media marketing companies, agencies, and freelancers across the globe (we've reached out to Lyfe several times to ask for their source on this and are still trying to reach them).[34] Online ad agency WordStream's *State of the Digital Marketing Agency in 2018* report found 82 percent of digital marketing firms offer social media marketing services.[35] On the traditional agency front, a 2019 survey of advertising and marketing agencies found that among those offering the full scope of content marketing services, 79 percent included social media marketing.[36]

All of this might make you think anyone new would run scared from entering the shark-infested space. But quite the opposite is true. Social Media Marketing training services have popped up all across the web, promising aspiring young freelancers the chance to live their dreams of owning self-run businesses. One 30-day course, *Choose Pristine*, promises 'SMM' training whereby you can launch a social media marketing business by simply watching online videos. "This Is THE ONLY Way to Make $10K in the Next 30 Days Without Any Experience. Period," they claim.[37] Such offers are today's Get Rich Quick schemes. Google them sometime: *Our Proven Step-by-Step System for Reaching Out to Businesses and Getting Them to Give You a Shot... How to Get ANY Business to Say YES, Even If You've Never Sold a Thing Before... How to Create a PROFITABLE Facebook Ad in 10 Minutes... How to Use LinkedIn to Get New Clients at Will.*

Choose Pristine is founded and run by two guys dripping with stereotypical FIRE (financially independent, retire early) tropes and who make promises of breaking free from the grind of traditionally-employed situations that are hard to resist. Quentin Chad and Jovan Stojanovic, complete with man buns and wood bead bracelets, serve up their promotional videos from places like an outdoor coffee shop in Thailand to sell their "digital nomad" lifestyle.[38] You, too, can take advantage of marketers who're spending on social media marketing without any evidence of return. No experience required. The demand is that strong.

As Augie Ray did before me, I'll summon Upton Sinclair to help us understand one simple reason why marketers tend to deny the data surrounding social media's effectiveness: *It is difficult to get a man to understand something when his salary depends upon his not understanding it.*

So what are we to do about all of this?

First, as marketers we have to embrace the fact that we, too, have cognitive biases that cloud our perception of social media. Mitigating these biases starts with the simple fact supported by Dr. Lieberman's research: we don't interact with social media the way consumers do.

We see promises of friend-to-friend marketing, of exciting and new campaign possibilities, and we watch with goosebumps and spine chills when a brand uses the platforms in creative ways. This simply does not align with how non-marketers interact with the platforms. Non-marketers don't view social media as channels for influence opportunity. They see opportunity for reciprocity and connection.

This is hardly a new issue, yet it persists. You'll remember my boss' advice about never using your marketing mind as evidence. Marketers: *we are unreliable data points.*

Second, we need to come to terms with a tough reality: when you really evaluate the success stories in social media marketing (setting aside customer care for a moment), the vast majority of the more thriving social media communities tend to be built in three relatively narrow contexts. As marketers we don't very much like to admit this because we want social to work in all contexts, especially those for which we're pressured to drive revenue. But time and again we see three types of organizations building communities on social media and we're seduced by the case studies and blog posts that ask us to learn lessons from them. In reality they're outliers, not standards:

1. **Brands with inherent and unusually powerful scroll-stopping content or what I like to call Remarkability (think GoPro, ESPN, and celebrities).** Your B2B office furniture reseller has to compete with heliskiing front-side spins and Zion Williamson 360 dunks on social media. In HD.

2. **Brands with cause or purpose built in, like nonprofits, issue or political campaigns, or the very rare corporate brands that contrive it (think Charity: Water or Obama for America).** Manufactured cause marketing, a call to action among many social media marketing consultants, is tricky and can backfire: bait-and-switches kill the value in social groups as we'll explore in following chapters. If purpose and cause aren't built into your brand already, you run the very real risk of damaging sales trying to contrive it. Also, if you're looking to examples like Dove's *Real Beauty* to guide

you, good luck teasing out what results Unilever's behemoth marketing machine realized from social vs. traditional media.

3. **Brands that follow tried and true marketing principles and have built global, hardcore support over time with unique, solid quality in their products or services (think Harley-Davidson or BMW).** Nike and Taco Bell were a thing long before social media. Their audiences found them, not the other way around. Remember the *Journal of Marketing Research* study with its compelling evidence that not only do consumers like brands they already have a fondness for on social media, but "the mere act of 'liking' a brand has no positive first order effect on consumer attitudes or purchases" and its two meta analyses suggesting that "if anything, its effect is detrimental." Social media engagement is a consequence, not a cause, of brand affinity. Moreover, like Dove, such brands also integrate their social activities with well-funded traditional marketing activities making it difficult if not impossible to tell what's responsible for what.

A culture of using pot-of-gold case studies combined with marketers' biases make us believe that we can apply what we see from GoPro, Obama for America, and Harley-Davidson to our restaurant and accounting firm brands, and that's just fantasy. The lens of these categories illuminates the important concept we touched on in Chapter 1: *appropriability*, the degree to which the value in one social construct is able to be used in another. This is a barely-studied dynamic in marketing, one that's found more commonly in the finance and leadership disciplines. Developing the acumen to understand and recognize degrees of appropriability would be of tremendous value for marketers when evaluating whether effective social media marketing is possible in our various contexts.

The third thing that needs addressing is specific to agencies: we need to stop making promises we can't keep, and stop supplying clients with data that doesn't measure business outcomes. The more we claim social media marketing will generate business returns for our clients—as opposed to billable hours for us—the more entrenched we all become. We need to encourage clients to consider social media as a tool for other areas of their business, like customer care. Asking clients about how they measure that side of their business, and how you can align social media efforts with it instead of sales, can open up valuable conversations that build value as a trusted partner in their business as opposed to a billable hour-grabber. Conversations about social capital as a learnable skill that will help organizations well beyond their social media activities will build similar value as well.

Fourth, we need to stop—once and for all—thinking of social communities as channels. They don't work the same way. They have social norms and ties that are very different from marketing channels. Driving conversions is an entirely different pursuit to facilitating opportunities for connection. We'll get to how and why later, but channel thinking among marketers in social constructs is a serious problem.

If you need evidence of how utterly incapable we are of untethering ourselves from channel thinking, look no further than the seemingly intractable desire to use fans and followers as measures of social media success. Networks don't act. The people in them do. Measuring the size of a network is to completely misunderstand how social constructs work. Remember the 2017 University of Maryland study that found the larger the following, the more likely word-of-mouth is to be negative, and smaller followings lean more positive. To reiterate: think about that study the next time you report social media follower growth to your boss, your client, or demand it from your staff.

It's time to face a few truths. Most of us marketers aren't very good at measuring our work, we're not very honest with ourselves (or our clients) about not being very good at measuring it, and most of the people trafficking in the data that purports to demonstrate social media marketing effectiveness stand to gain from promoting it. Meanwhile, we continue performing marketing and conversion-oriented activities that aren't returning clear results while ignoring those activities that do, like customer care.

Moving people to act in online social groups and realizing lasting value from these communities can be done. We have many examples of people and organizations doing so successfully. A few are marketing success-story outliers, but most—and the most helpful ones for our purposes—are examples of leaders who know how to build and use social capital decidedly outside of a marketing framework. We'll take a look at some of these pathways as we go along, but it's important to return to the notion that building and realizing value in social groups isn't a marketing function. It's a leadership one.

So it's time to ask and answer the most serious question of all: What is social capital, anyway?

Chapter 4

TRAFFICKING IN RECIPROCITY: SOCIAL CONSTRUCTS AND SOCIAL CAPITAL

Aakash Mittal is a jazz musician and composer living in Brooklyn and his is one of those special brains that can articulate the creative process. Often people who are really good at something just do it. They aren't inclined to talk about it much. The classic Miles Davis quote "I'll play it first and tell you what it is later" is never followed up with the observation that he hardly ever did.

The ability to bring the creative mind and the creative process to life makes Aakash a wonderfully effective teacher and he has crossed over into the business world with remarkable ease as well, helping businesses increase the creativity in their organizations. I've been lucky to work with Aakash in both spaces. He led some ensemble arrangements and performances I put together for an Indian dance troupe show (playing in an ensemble and accompanying him on dhol during one of his sax solos is a personal highlight of my music career), and he let me interview him about the creative process for a client blog that my firm managed. We're also friends, which means I can have safe conversations about either of those worlds with someone who is always down to hang (as he likes to put it), and just explore the crossovers between creativity, influence, marketing, and business. It's an incredibly valuable relationship for these and many other reasons.

Why start a chapter of a business book dealing with leadership and marketing by bringing up a jazz musician? Well, as Aakash will tell you, the creative process is largely about synthesizing apparently disparate data. Taking inputs from one area of life and expressing it in another. Seeing connections and deriving unique meaning from them. The creative mind swims metaphysically and freely between streams of perceived domains until the streams merge. It's how creative minds process things others don't: by exploring intersections and making connections. The goal, of course, is for these explorations to gel as some kind of expressive, creative work.

Creative minds tend to practice this. A lot. People with strong creative minds always seem to have some side thing they're pursuing. Not just skimming. *Learning.* Polymathic thinking is nourishment for the creative mind. We crave it, need it, and can't help but act on it. Think about the creative people in your life. No matter what discipline they're primarily focused on, creative people are always tackling a new instrument, are obsessed with some new theologian, running their first marathon, mastering the perfect coffee roast, or perfecting a barbecue slow cook. It's what Anthony Brandt and David Eagleman in their book *Runaway Species* liken to scout bees flying away from the hive to find new nourishment. They call it *distancing* and it's both a characteristic of creativity and a strategy for creatively solving problems: "an optimal strategy is to generate a range of ideas, some of which stay closer to home, while others fly further."[1]

As we explore the intersections of leadership, building online communities, and branding in this chapter, try to think about lines-of-sight between your discipline and how learning from one area will make you a better marketer and leader in another. Connections and alignments, polyrhythmic meaning. Maybe this approach will even help you become a cross-disciplinary polymath who understands broader concepts, helping cement you as an indispensable employee in your organization.

With that as a backdrop, let's fly from the marketing hive for a bit. Distance ourselves from marketing, away from what we think we know about customer behavior and what we think we need to know about conversions. Let's explore a different sphere and see what kind of connections we can make.

In this context, it won't be easy. As we've explored, it's safe to say that the social media marketing world is deeply calcified by its biases. The social mind is at odds with the marketing mind, and we as marketers view social constructs quite differently to the non-marketing people participating in them. Adding to this calcification is the fact that social media marketing is a huge industry and as marketers we've made some big bets: A CMO would have a lot to answer for if they decided to foreswear today the justifications for social media budgets and staff they made yesterday. And of course the tide of behemoth advertising platforms and their pick-and-shovel associated industries is huge and powerful. A status quo is hard to change for a reason.

If we once again summon Upton Sinclair—"It is difficult to get a man to understand something when his salary depends upon his not understanding it"—it's no surprise to discover that very few marketers take the time to consider social capital, let alone learn how to build and use it. Still, the word 'Social' is in the name of the social media marketing discipline. It's staring us in the face.

It's worth repeating that with workplaces, teams and groups dispersed in entirely new ways today, learning to build and use social capital is the pressing issue of our time. Leaders who understand how to build and use social capital across a variety of media—in person or virtually—will thrive. The pandemic has forced a dramatic acceleration of other technology and business model transformations that were underway before the virus hit us full bore. The timeline for our need to fast-track our understanding of social capital and how to build and use it while physically distanced from one another is no different. Add to this the fact that the web is always finding new ways to be social as it evolves like the species that drives it. Yesterday's TikTok is today's Clubhouse is tomorrow's MySpace, and savvy leaders (and managers of brands) don't chase their tails learning tactics associated with platforms. They look for the concepts and the disciplines that span the fleeting tactical areas and build sustainable skills that transfer to any context, be they bull markets or stay-at-home orders.

Our concern as business leaders and marketers, then, should be to build our skills in social capital, not the technical capital associated with social media tools. All the claims about the effectiveness of social media marketing, and the resulting resource allocation dedicated to tactics, represent a huge distraction from the fundamentals like trust and community-building that have always distinguished the best leaders, organizations and companies from the crowd. We need to approach online social groups as leaders, not marketers. It's a far better use of our time to learn the principles of social ties, how networks operate, and what is exchanged between them. Content creators, clickbait experts, and follower generators have limited value in this world of ever-changing technology and ever-evolving social connections.

The interesting challenge in making this shift from marketer to leader is to recognize the water we're swimming in. Meaning, as humans we're surrounded by social connections and we intrinsically see the value all the time, every day. It's "hidden in plain sight," wrote leading social capital scholars Don Cohen and Laurence Prusak in their book *In Good Company*.[2] Social capital is so much a part of our lives (and our hardwiring, as Dr. Lieberman teaches us) that we take it for granted. We swim in social interactions like a fish swims in water, hardly noticing it. Sometimes it feels odd—unnatural—to take the time to dissect something we inherently know is, well, *there*. But in order to intercede in social constructs it's important that we understand the rules and dynamics of social groups beyond our intuitive understanding. If we don't, our marketing minds might take over and we could end up breaking them.

Cohen & Prusak quote Arie de Geuss of Royal Dutch Shell as saying "Whereas the management curriculum had no place for human beings, the workplace was full of them."[3] We can modify his quote to help us understand why we need to move into the leadership sphere to better understand social groups: It would seem that the marketing discipline has no place for social capital, but social media is chock full of it.

Social capital requires quite a bit of mental flexibility when trying to get your arms around it. It's another ouroborus-like dynamic: what's required to build social capital can often be its resulting value. Prusak & Cohen put it less portentously. Some elements of social capital are both cause and effect, "simultaneously its underlying conditions, indicators of presence, and chief benefits."[4]

They illustrate this concept by examining trust. Trust is absolutely foundational to building social capital. An organization can't begin to see the benefits of social capital—on the social web or in itself—until it establishes some modicum of trust. But trust is also how we measure strong social capital efforts. It's an outcome. Trust can lead to organization and online value in such areas as collaboration speed, knowledge transfer, and speedier, customer-driven customer service results. When you dive into the body of academic work on social capital, this tautology rears its head much more than it probably needs to, or at least more than those of us using social capital care to consider. Reading some of the academic papers you get the sense that academics hate the kind of tangled reality social capital presents, and reading their hand-wringings about it can get a bit dizzying. Sociologist Nan Lin in his book *Social Capital: A Theory of Social Structure and Action* gets so spun around the axle on this issue that it becomes more interesting to watch him try to unwind it grammatically than to divine his message. Ultimately, he plays a *parsimony* card ("A theory would lose parsimony quickly if the conditional factors become part of the definitions of the primary concepts") against a royal straight flush of humanity, relationships, emotions, and evolution driving the disorder.[5] When exploring social capital, you simply have to start by taking comfort in the cause-and-effect interweavings of social capital.

If we zoom back a bit and consider where the notion of social capital comes from, it's fun to dip our toes into the pool of Bruno Latour, a mind-bending philosopher, anthropologist, and sociologist. He's written extensively about social sciences, and is refreshingly honest in his appraisal of the discipline by calling it more a phenomenon than a science. Social, Latour reminds us, is used in front of *science* as if it's a helpful adjective describing a material (a bit like we do with *social media*, actually). 'Social' isn't the same as noisy, or wooden, or pungent. Using it as such "shrinks" the definition of social for Latour, distancing us further from an understanding of it by "adulterat[ing] what was productive and scientific" in it.[6]

In reality 'social,' like social capital, is best described than defined. It's a "very peculiar movement of re-association and reassembling"of everything.[7] Social isn't an adjective. It isn't even a frame. It's the constantly shifting and changing relationships of all things human. It's the water we're swimming in. I've found that embracing the ambiguity can actually help understand social capital better if you're willing to let go and just swim in it. As one social scientist put it, when it comes to understanding our social world "paradoxes are a welcome antidote to theories."[8] Understanding social capital in this way introduces elements of spontaneity and unpredictability that are exciting for some but may discourage those with a tendency for planning and categorization from wading into such waters.

One way to think about social capital's rather amorphous nature is to break it down into Substance, Sources, and Effects. Back to the idea of trust—a durable, measurable confidence among relationships—as the substance of social capital. Without trust there's no social capital. In fact, it's the source of social capital and its effect. One way to find and measure social capital is to find and measure trust, which occurs in varying degrees across a multitude of connections, and it's also social capital's effect (the value trust brings to an organization, be it in real life or online).[9]

So studying and reading about social capital isn't for the rigorously categorical mind. You have to be willing to wade in and out of shared concepts, feel the weight of the concepts in totality and break free from them as you map them back to common sense, constantly thinking contextually even if I or other authors don't draw those lines of sight for you. This shouldn't come as a surprise, really. Social capital is a deeply human reality, derived and built by emotional beings seeking connections to satisfy physical, physiological, and even moral needs. As Actor-Network theorists like Latour will have us believe, it might even be rooted in what makes up all of reality itself. The gray area, as Cohen & Prusak put it, "reflects the organic and self-reinforcing nature of social capital and not (in this instance, at least) the sloppy thinking of the authors."[10]

I'll take that excuse as well as we continue to explore what social capital is.

Academics, who tend to hate excuses like that, have researched and written extensively about social capital as a leadership skill. Much of this academic material is helpful, even if some of it comes across as written in total isolation. It seems as if many of the academic thought leaders in the social capital space haven't ever had to actually use it, in stark contrast to those of us who rely on networking for our livelihoods. Academic studies can, oddly, feel like learning from an amateur and a professional at the same time.

Still, academic studies provide research and focus that businesses can't. They can look across many organizations and see connections in ways that myopic businesses never can, and they have access to more disciplines with which to coordinate research and connection points than businesses do.

Academics provide value for us in another way. Because of its everydayness, defining social capital can seem like an exercise in banality, but that's never been something that's discouraged academia from giving something a shot. When you dig into social capital, the nuances and sophistication can actually impart a layered effort, and in fact, a topic in and of itself. University of Southern California professors Paul Adler and Seok-Woo Kwon have published extensively on social capital, including on the question of defining it. In their *Academy of Management Review* paper titled "Social Capital: Prospects for a New Concept", they set out to "clarify the concept and help assess [social capital's] utility for organizational theory," and to "synthesize the theoretical research and develop a common conceptual framework that identifies the sources, benefits, risks, and contingencies of social capital."[11]

Pretty heady for something we're hard-wired to understand at a primal level. Their paper categorizes social capital into some helpful frames, and they do a remarkable job of collecting and synthesizing over 20 social capital definitions from fellow academics and authors. In the end, their attempt to create an umbrella conceptual framework for social capital across all disciplines ultimately left them "cautiously optimistic" that it could actually be done, so we still don't exactly have one go-to definition.

I find social capital to be more like a puzzle. The first task in putting it together is to choose an area—a discipline—to drop an anchor into. Social capital has its place in everything from neighborhood communities to investing to politics to immigration to religion. Sociologist Nan Lin's *Social Capital: A Theory of Social Structure and Action* walks through a complete history of it from Marx to Putnam, if you're interested in going way down the rabbit hole. Since we're primarily talking about marketing in this book, we'll simply focus on social capital in the discipline of business (and similar organizations).

In business, there are various forms of capital that leaders account for and manage. I'll take a shot at defining three of the most common:

- Physical Capital: Created by investing in and managing tangible materials and tools that result in production value,
- Human Capital: Created by investing in and managing people that result in better decisions and action-derived value, and
- Intellectual Capital: Created by investing and managing a combination of people and ideas that result in conceptual property value.

A business leader's job is to intervene in these value-production processes and maximize their return. Social capital (if for the time being we accept that it is indeed capital) is similar. Its value can be managed, measured, and multiplied. I find the business anchor most helpful for understanding how social capital works in the marketing and social media sphere because marketers seek to extract value from their online groups, like a company wants a return on its investment in social capital. Plus, understanding it through this frame helps in a leader's never-ending pursuit to be a better working professional. You can take this stuff and apply it in all kinds of places in your work and life.

Another important anchor is social capital's primary substance: the value it returns to those who invest in it. For our purposes of understanding social capital through a business lens, we can start with the business notion of goodwill—which we'll define as an intangible asset —as the primary substance, and its effects flow from the information, influence, and solidarity that goodwill makes available to those participating in the social group.[12] Relational wealth, as one academic paper puts it, is the value extracted from access to privileged information, networks, and opportunities.[13]

For our purposes a decent working definition of social capital, then, is a resource of relational wealth for individual and collective working professionals, created by investing and managing the configuration and operation of networks and their durable social relationships.

The Capital in Social Capital

We'll get to the value of social capital shortly, but right now we need to return to an assumption we made earlier and ask: Is it capital? Could social capital simply be a resource instead? Does it matter? I think it does. A resource (say, land) is measured and managed differently to capital (the oil rig built on the land).

Some economists claim social capital actually dilutes the term capital in the larger sense. Not that that should hold us up: I've read enough Nassim Taleb to believe that economists are not exactly in unassailable positions when it comes to defining and valuing common sense. But a fair degree of skepticism about the notion of capital helps us dig a little deeper and become more sophisticated managers of social capital, capable of moving beyond SMM training scams and click-bait-follower artists.

Following the work of Adler & Kwon, I'll put the value of social capital through a Q&A session with the finance side of my brain (not turned on much since my MBA days if I'm being honest), see where we land, and maybe learn a bit more about what social capital is along the way.

Q: Is it measurable?

A: Somewhat. In many cases, social capital may be difficult to measure and manage, casting shade on the concept of capital right off the bat. We saw how difficult if not impossible it is to measure social capital from a social media perspective. Marketers have practically thrown in the towel trying to measure it in any kind of substantive way. The benefits of social capital can be measured, but in a highly contextual way. Southwest Airlines saw value from one social media campaign by way of a "virtual focus group," which is very different from a small pizzeria seeing a bump in sales from Twitter referral coupon offers.[14] It also depends entirely on the entity opting to do the measuring (see SMM training scams and shingle-hangers, above). Still, companies do measure their social capital. An online payments company my marketing firm helped rebrand measured a new management technique intended to build trust and a culture of collaboration—very much hallmarks of social capital. They tracked and measured productivity down to the last hour and found the new technique was responsible for an increase in productivity and hours worked. Measuring social capital is difficult, very specific to the organization, requires discipline and usually a very long lens since building social capital and cashing in on it is not at all punctual.

Q: Does investment in social capital return value?

A: Yes. If this isn't an intuitive truth to you, you'll have to trust me on it for now. The entire second half of this book explores how it's done.

Q: Is it constructible?

A: Somewhat. Much more on this later, too. But think of social capital in contrast to legacy university admissions, or family wealth. While not something like a factory that can be built to generate physical capital or a training program to create new human capital, we can construct social capital under the right circumstances and environments using a defined set of skills.

· · ·

Q: Does it yield losses (disutilities in finance parlance) and gains?

A: Yes. Like other forms of capital, both counterproductive outcomes and value can be generated for the group or groups building and using social capital, as well as generated for others. In 2010 the food and drink conglomerate Nestlé found itself in the middle of a firestorm when Greenpeace decided to launch a social media campaign against its sourcing of palm oil, which destroyed orangutan habitats. When the dust settled, Nestlé's social capital was severely damaged (measured mostly through negative PR when they had to issue a change in policy that was dictated to them as opposed to by them) while Greenpeace's grew (nonprofits measure 'actions' such as new contacts as important assets, and the digital manager I spoke to about this campaign told me they added a significant number of names to their rolls during the Nestlé action).[15]

Q: Is it appropriable?

A: Yes. The simplest examples of appropriability in business are patents. Patents, unlike the knowledge that created them, are capital that can move with and be transported in and out of businesses. Social capital can be used for different purposes and can be moved from one area of an organization to another or from one domain to another. As we also saw from Erik Proulx's efforts in Chapter 3, building online social capital through marketing efforts is most often achieved when it already exists in other constructs and moves into social media channels. By way of reminder, this tends to occur in (1) brands that follow tried and true marketing principles and have built global, hardcore support over time with unique, solid quality in their products or services; (2) brands with purpose and cause built in; and (3) brands with inherent and unusually powerful scroll-stopping content or what I like to call remarkability. In reality these are the exceptions in the social media marketing world, but they illustrate the point of social capital's appropriability.

. . .

Q: Is it convertible into or complementary with other forms of capital?

A: **Yes.** Like we saw with Erik Proulx who used social capital to finance a film, it can be used in lieu of financial capital. But more often it complements other forms. Studies have demonstrated, for example, how social capital decreases transaction costs in companies.[16]

Q: Does it require maintenance?

A: **Yes.** Like human, physical, and intellectual capital, those building and using social capital must continue to provide value to the social construct in order to receive value from it. This is another intuitive notion to those of us who network regularly, and it's the substance behind the idea of 'durable obligations' mentioned in passing earlier. If there's an immutable law of networking that applies across real life or online, those who get the most from social constructs give the most to them. And they do it with intention and by understanding the varying power and influence of the individual players in the network.

Q: Is it a collective good?

A: **Yes.** Meaning that it's not always the private property of those who build and benefit from it, and when it's consumed by one person it's still available to another. Put another way, it's nonrivalrous: a fancy-pants economics term that points to the fact that one person's use of social capital does not diminish it for others. This attribute makes social capital susceptible to free-rider exploitations, but on the flip side outsiders can be excluded. This dynamic makes it a collective good, not a pure public good (like a clean environment). From a social media perspective, a company like Ann Taylor LOFT has reported value from their social media efforts by way of customer service hours saved because, as one of their marketing managers once told me, members of their social media community jump in to help with inquiries. This benefits LOFT, but also benefits the community because the responses may be quicker and based on earned experience. Ann

Taylor's accounts surely have ghost followers, meanwhile, who don't contribute to the community but who benefit from this value.

Q: Is it a network good (dependent upon the actions and connections between the people building and using it)?

A: Yes. Some scholars argue that social capital is not capital because if one person withdraws from or poisons the network, the capital is diminished or perhaps even destroyed. But this is very much like the capital found in network goods like co-ops, Facebook, smart phones (the number of apps developed for a phone platform increase its value), or Uber: value increases and depends on the number of people who participate.

Q: Is social capital capital?

A: Yes. Ultimately, social capital is capital in my view, and should be managed as such.

Much as we try to apply definitive constructs like those in the financial world to social capital, social capital keeps us on our toes. It's used (confusingly) as a concept, sometimes as a metaphor. Sometimes we refer to it as an outcome, sometimes we refer to it as the thing generating the outcome. I've become comfortable wading in and out of these waters when teaching and consulting about social media, and I encourage you to go with the contextual flow as well.

Digital Relationships

The next piece of the puzzle: What constitutes a durable social relationship, and, equally importantly, can it exist digitally? This will be unsatisfying, but the answer is *it depends*. I'll make the case that social capital can and has been built online, but there's ample argument to the contrary. There are generally accepted rules based on research that social networks tend to adhere to. Rules, it's theorized, that have been made over millions of years of evolution and are hard-wired in our brains. Some of these rules are broken online, leading many social scientists to doubt the verity of online social capital formation.

For instance: in their book *Connected*, Christakis & Fowler find that the chance one friend in your social network knows another is about 52 percent. This structural "rule" for tight-knit groups is necessary for influence to occur within them. Ideas and behavior spread more effectively in groups with high degrees of so-called transitivity (overlapping connections). What are the implications of this rule when applied to online social groups? Are online groups less transitive because they're more physically distanced, or more transitive because the internet has brought them together in the first place? In addition, less transitive ties—so-called weak ties—actually generate tremendous value. So do we need to consider (and manage) online social groups in terms of tight network groups or bridges between network clusters? The majority of what we know about how influence and value are generated socially is, currently, confined mainly to our knowledge of social groups in non-digital places, an important point moving forward as we apply the science to online spaces.

There are plenty of skeptics questioning the existence of social capital online. One stunning academic paper I ran across challenges the notion that marketing communities exist online at all, let alone social groups that generate more obscure value. The paper feeds into those moments of existential dread that keep us marketers up at night. We've all had these moments, haven't we? What does this *marketing* thing even mean? Am I making any difference at all? Well, add this to your waking nightmare: "We propose," write the authors, "that marketing's fantasy of the customer community as a wild and communal space of radically creative social production is conjured" and that as marketers "everything we do, even our acts of resistance, appears to always end up in the great vortex of promotional culture."[17]

Sleep well.

It's certainly true that there are some in the marketing thought leadership space that have conjured up a fairly unrealistic, utopian notion of a communal place without institutional control when describing online social spaces. But we can certainly agree that institutional control is different and at least somewhat democratized thanks to online social spaces, changing the transactional relationship from *buyer beware* to *marketer beware*, and this new reality has necessitated new acumen and skill sets. As illustrated throughout this book, marketing and marketers have little to no skills for measuring value in the online social world, let alone an appreciation or knowledge of how to actually build it. This is largely because marketers are typically trying to build consumption-based brand communities and measuring the effectiveness through that lens, versus building and measuring the value of groups that demonstrate social capital. Driving conversions and building community are very different. No more so than in the customer care world.

Before social media was used in customer care the most commonly social media-generated social capital was the creation and use of peer-to-peer-to-place (P3) communities, leveraging their ability to build and exchange value. This has been studied. Virtual P3 communities are self-organizing 'networks of practice' that come together to solve problems related to their shared consumption experiences. Which basically describes the social web (outside of a marketer's lens) even if the 'problem' they're looking to solve is finding the latest Kpop video. And at least one study that "empirically tested [...] the conditions under which social capital is transformed into commitment to a virtual P3 community" found that social capital does indeed exist online: "Empirical results support the conceptualization of social capital [as evidenced by] voluntarism, reciprocity, and social trust."[18]

Social capital can exist and be exchanged online, but what should be glaringly obvious to marketers is that building durable social relations starts and ends with credibility and authenticity. Hypocrisy, as Cohen & Prusak point out, kills social capital. This is another intuitive truth for anyone who has experienced the severing of any kind of durable social relationship. We cut ties with those who bait-and-switch us, effectively hanging up the phone on the telemarketer when we feel like the shine has been put on us for some ulterior motive. Like when a brand starts selling to us in what we thought was a P3-oriented virtual community. And remember: our minds are wired to sense such baits-and-switches, as we learned from Dr. Leiberman. Our senses tingle when we, say, receive that email from someone in our network, someone we haven't heard from in a while, who begins their email with paragraphs of nostalgia and regrets for not keeping in touch. We see the ask coming from the moment we recognize the 'From' field in our inbox. The same is true for brands that use social media as a marketing tool with a value-add wrapping: We know what's underneath, and it undermines credibility. This dynamic is one of the more common reasons why social media efforts flail or fail in business. We act like we want to add value but our motives are entirely different.

We'll meet some folks from Zappos a little later, and learn that their approach to this dynamic is a separation of activities, like a newspaper separates editorial from ad sales. The teams communicate—the customer care team telling the more marketing-centric one what's resonating and what's trending—but the business objectives and the skills required to achieve them are very different.

Social capital is built with all kinds of relationships between ties: strong, weak, transitive, bridge-and-cluster, closures, and more. Social capital doesn't necessarily come from intimacy. It comes from credibility and authenticity. When we're all aligned and when we believe, we connect. When repeated actions demonstrate the connection, we trust. Trust builds relationships and commitment, which leads to a durable social relation.

This is a difficult thing to measure *en masse*. We don't know how many companies feel they've built durable social relations online because no one (that I've found) is really measuring it that way. Given the level of confidence marketers have in measuring much of anything on the social web, this isn't the least bit surprising. There are anecdotal instances to point to, though, and maybe that's enough to demonstrate that durable social relations can, in fact, be built online in a brand-and-consumer relationship. It's most effective in customer care situations, like those at Zappos and Xbox, but there are instances in more commercial settings as well.

Or at least there used to be. A classic example comes from Ann Taylor LOFT, a brand I mentioned earlier, that launched a multi-channel marketing approach in 2010 and more than doubled their e-commerce sales as a result.[19] This had come after hard-earned trust-building, best illustrated by what I call *The Legend of the Cargo Pant.*

This case study is widely circulated and 10 years old now, but 10 years ago we were still thinking like community-builders on the social web and less like marketers. So while *The Legend of the Cargo Pant* may be a dinosaur from a technical capital standpoint, it remains a nice example of social capital-building. (In reality the digital marketing managers on the account used the same technical levers anyway—not much has changed on Facebook other than the algorithms determining which of a brand's posts users see and to what extent they see them.)

At the time, LOFT was adept at building social capital, and was considered a leading brand on social media. LOFT as a whole had seen a 16-percent increase in sales during the period in which they were aggressive with their social presence.[20] As a brand, LOFT was (and is) Ann Taylor's brand for the 'Everyday Woman,' so when LOFT posted photos on Facebook of a particularly thin fashion model displaying a new cargo pant, it raised the eyebrows of more than a few of their customers. "They are cute on her," one Facebook commenter wrote, "but on someone who is only 5 ft 4 inch and not itsy bitsy?" Many such comments followed, enough to catch the attention of social media watchdogs and others interested in how LOFT would choose to respond.

Listening to their customers, LOFT offered not so much an apology but a remedy:

> Thank you all so much for your comments and feedback. One of the requests we received was to show how regular women would wear these looks. Our Manager of Digital Programs (otherwise known as the woman who answers you on Facebook) has posted a gallery how she (me) would wears [sic] the pant at work, at night, and on the weekend. We hope you will take a look. And please stay tuned as we will be posting images of women at LOFT wearing the pants throughout the day!

And they did, posting images of the women in the office, 'everyday women,' wearing the cargo pant. The comments from their Facebook fans that followed generally praised the move while not holding back on their distaste for the pant itself: "Hideous retro-pants, but a fabulous idea....more real-life pics. Love The Loft."

It was clear that LOFT's social media managers were tapped into a few key dimensions of what it takes to build durable social relations, whether they knew it or not. First, they were leading their customers by democratizing the relationship with them. Creating, as social capital stalwart Robert Putnam puts it, horizontal relations of reciprocity and cooperation, as opposed to vertical relations of authority.[21] Second, they honored the social contract inherent in the relationship, and they pulled back the transactional curtain to connect on a human level. Third, it was their actions that made the biggest impact. We tend to follow leaders who walk the walk ('modeling the way' as leadership icons Kouzes & Posner call it), a cornerstone to building trust. They were vulnerable to (and received) continued negative comments about the pant itself as the cost of listening and responding. That's walking the talk, the kind of action-based activity that transcends 'we listen to our customers' manifestos into bona fide relationship-building. Into durable social relations.

To me it's clear that, just as texting hasn't broken language but rather added to it, social media practices have added possibilities and dimensions to traditional notions of building social capital, and doing so online.

Generating Value

The next question, another nuanced puzzle piece, becomes: Can it be turned into action? Can entities like brand managers intercede in online social groups to encourage action toward a collective goal, something that adheres to the benefit of the entire group?

Considerable intellectual effort has been put into understanding why we set aside individual goals in service to a collective good, so we have a plethora of studies across every imaginable discipline to draw conclusions from. I think it can be persuasively argued that Dr. Lieberman's work puts much of these speculations to rest. You'll remember him quoting philosopher Alain de Botton: "Living for others [is] such a relief from the impossible task of trying to satisfy oneself." When we participate in social settings we're simply following the mandate of our wiring to harmonize with a group.

So maybe it should end there, and yet maybe it's just a beginning. If we're to intercede in social groups in order to move them to action, understanding the hardwiring should be combined with the mechanics. What are the mechanics involved with social groups moving to action? To participate in the common goal of the group? If there's a tangible return—when it's obvious that you'll get something from participation in a social group—it seems fairly obvious. But most social groups operate without this type of contract. We participate without a tacit understanding that we'll see an immediate return, or even any return at all.

Even participating in social groups is ambiguous. Deciding to participate in a networking, religious, book discussion, or meditation group flies in the face of rational actor theories that would have us making decisions on joining and participating in such groups based on factors that, on their face, the group makes good on. What social group can demonstrate a maximum gain with a minimal loss? Or that its options are better than alternatives?

At first glance, a social group typically has very little tangible value to offer someone who's rationally evaluating whether to join it or not. Its ties are probably the most obvious: Countable nodes in the network, in various places with implied connection-making value. But ties do not act. People do. This is a central concept for social capital and something marketers still don't seem to have grasped. Networks are a context for action, and there's no value unless they act. It's the collective action that drives outcome and value, that creates social capital. Networks require synergy to activate and some glue by way of norms and values to adhere and move toward a collective action.[22]

For marketers operating the levers of social media, I find it downright insidious to value online social networks by measuring fans and followers when viewing such activity through this lens. To measure the network, and make evaluations about its value based on the number of ties of which it is composed, is to misunderstand social capital almost entirely, to say nothing of the negative biases in large online social media groups uncovered by the University of Maryland study.

Maybe misguided measurement practices are a part of why economists and finance experts have a hard time valuing social capital and why marketing-centric professionals find themselves completely lost when trying to navigate it. Norms are defined and dealt with rather differently in finance and economics universes from how they take shape in social groups. Take the social capital norm of reciprocity, for example. One of the few social capital norms that crosses virtually all contexts, its meaning is entirely different in a transactional, economic setting.

Princeton professor and author Alejandro Portes points out a few of the salient differences between social capital and transactional capital, underscoring its irrational appearance to rational actor theory zealots. Social capital is built on unspecified obligations, uncertain time horizons, and a very real risk of zero or unbalanced reciprocity.[23] What we pay into social systems usually looks entirely different from what pays out, and regardless of the difference we usually have no idea what the payout will look like when we sign up, or even if or when it will come to us. Try convincing your CFO to invest in a reciprocal arrangement as vague as that.

Consider how Christakis & Fowler put it in *Connected*: "Social networks generate behavior that is not consistent with the simplified, idealized image of a rational buyer and seller picking a price to transact the sale of goods." It's clear that we're not in marketing-segment Kansas anymore.

Portes and others point to ideas such as "enforceable trust" to illustrate the idea that what social groups lack in formal contracts they make up for in moral imperatives. Other ideas like "we-ness" or "practical reciprocity" are terms arrived at by economists' athletic maneuverings to derive a utilitarian meaning, thus satisfying the Rational Actor devil on their shoulders.[24] But after spending time with Dr. Lieberman I've come to simplify things. I think we take the risks to join social groups, as irrational as it may seem, because we have a hard-wired belief in the value of what an accumulation of obligations, as Portes puts it, brings us. It satisfies our primal need to connect. How to go about demonstrating that is a complicated proposition, but why can't the reason for joining social groups be that simple?

As if 'reciprocity' wasn't clinical enough, Putnam refers to it as "generalized reciprocity," a term dripping with so much academic rigor when describing something so innately human that it pegs the irony meter every time I hear it. Putnam defines it this way: "Not 'I'll do this for you, because you are more powerful than I,' nor even 'I'll do this for you now, if you do that for me now,' but 'I'll do this for you now, knowing that somewhere down the road you'll do something for me.'"

Which is close, but as those of us who rely on networking for our livelihoods know, it's even murkier than that. When it comes to participating in social groups you might say it works more like this: "I'll do this thing for this group—what the thing is depends on what the group wants—with the understanding that the act of doing it will have to be good enough as a return to me, and it might result in something coming back to me in an entirely different form someday maybe."

After all, if you find yourself in a group built on clear *quid pro quo* norms, you're probably in a leads group, not a social group. Or you've been duped by a marketer.

Social capital isn't a balance sheet. There's no such thing as putting in a certain amount of value in order to receive a certain amount back. It's common for people managing social media accounts to plan their tactics using some version of this misguided, fantasy quotient: "Post 60-percent content that purely adds value to earn the ability to promote with 40 percent of your posts." Forswear these equations, social capital *littérateurs*! The correct answer, when asked how much value-added content should be published on your social media accounts in order to build enough credits to sell, is always "However much is necessary."

Those driving social media at Zappos know this. The online retailer has broken all kinds of barriers when it comes to business and social media, and their formula of customer-centric activity on social media to marketing activities, if you can even call it that, will clarify this point perfectly when we get to it later. Xbox and the debt assistance nonprofit CareOne we'll take a look at will also help illustrate this concept.

However much is necessary is the answer because to build and use social capital intentionally, online or in real life, requires more than simply bringing a group together around a common interest. Social capital scholars call this *sociability*, which may be a first step in building social capital but is hardly sufficient. It's the value that's exchanged between the ties that matter.

Connected explains social networks in groundbreaking ways, revealing their structure and function for those interested in inter- ceding in them. In one small example they ask us to imagine a bucket brigade working together to douse the flames of a burning house. Working together in a line, passing buckets from the stream to the house, works more effectively than each person individually running to the stream and back. But if no one actually passed along the buckets, standing in a line wouldn't douse many flames. "Ties," the authors emphasize "and the particular pattern of these ties, are often more important than the individual people themselves [...] The ties explain why the whole is greater than the sum of its parts."[25]

The goal of leaders interested in building and using social capital should not be sociability. It should be associability: generating value by encouraging groups to act together for a collective purpose while putting individual desires and goals in an ancillary position. This isn't exactly a typical goal of marketing departments, and presents a signifi- cant challenge in terms of the mental shift marketers need to make. But groups that stop at sociability fail to establish norms and trust, and thereby fail to move beyond a simple, interactive social gathering.[26] This should sound familiar to most marketers building social media communities. Sociability online looks something like this: We have a bunch of people following our feeds, some liking some stuff and a few even sharing it. But what is it doing for us? What are we doing for them? What's the point?

If you've built something like this on social media you've constructed a group. And if your advertising is good, or your coupon offers are compelling, you might move them to transact, temporarily. But it's hardly the sustainable, capital-intensive stuff that *can* be, and *has* been, built online. And as we saw in the WARC reports, you may be risking long-term damage for your short-term sales.

Associability achieves cooperation and care for the welfare of the group. Groups that achieve associability have a willingness to agree and act on collective goals and the skills to coordinate, act, and achieve them. Associability is a beacon of social capital, and an important differentiator when building social groups.[27] Associable groups online, like those of Xbox, CareOne, and Zappos, exchange ideas freely, give access to each other's networks, troubleshoot problems for one another, and advocate for causes (and, yes, brands). When social media efforts stall, it can often be traced to a manager of the network stopping their efforts at sociability, possibly because that's where their understanding stops, too. Or perhaps because the draw of immediate returns is too strong and their patience has run out.

Building social capital is a learnable leadership skill. Understanding concepts like associability is important for leaders intent on realizing social capital in their organizations and, I argue, leaders in social media constructs looking to do the same. It's helpful to have a model when going about the work of leadership, an area where leaders can focus their efforts. Leaders can find themselves wandering around the swamps of people, relationships, and culture and never really get anywhere, especially when dealing with a discipline as humanly mushy as social capital. The areas between sociability and associability are clear examples of this.

So now we have a working understanding of what social capital is, and have become comfortable with its beautiful sophistication and paradoxes while finding confidence in bobbing in and out of them while relying on our intuitive sense of things to stay oriented. In the following chapters we discuss the learnable leadership skill of building and using it, including the three areas of focus intentionally managed by social capital-savvy leaders in organizations. By way of reminder, these areas of focus—relational, cognitive, and structural bonds—should be the focus in social media constructs as well.

So far I've tried to convince you that social media marketing is fool's gold outside of organizations with existing, appropriable social capital situations (mostly cause-based organizations or those with unicorn remarkability). I've also focused on why marketing in social constructs runs counter to how and why social groups exist.

So in what setting can social media drive value for organizations? Based on what you've learned, can you guess?

Chapter 5
SOLVING MUTUAL PROBLEMS: SOCIAL MEDIA AS A CUSTOMER CARE TOOL

If you own or manage a marketing firm you're familiar with the legion of marketing agency lead gen sales reps that assault LinkedIn inboxes on the regular. Good God, they're like gnats. You just can't get rid of them. It isn't an exaggeration to say that I get a daily sales pitch on LinkedIn and as many in my email inbox with promises of piles of leads, without disrupting my day or brand's reputation no doubt, from companies actively seeking my services, just like my competitors are mining. Like social media marketers are in danger of killing what sustains them, marketers for these companies are overfishing the LinkedIn waters and are about to (if they haven't already) exhaust the carrying capacity. I have a feeling I'm not alone in my practice of ignoring, without exception, a LinkedIn request from any kind of person with a hint of lead generation in their company or job description.

It might have been this bias against overfishers that gave me such pause as I reached out trying to persuade the people I had discovered in my research to give me some time by way of an interview for this book. Here I was, out there without any prior book or much general publishing credits to my name at all, making an ask that could easily come across as a bait-and-switch. I get it. If a complete stranger hit me up on LinkedIn saying they had found me in a case study and would *really* like to talk to me, trying to sound genuine, asking for my time as someone who owed me nothing and saw nothing in it in return, I'd be skeptical to say the least. Despite all this, there were kind introductions in my network that facilitated an introduction or two, a few kind declines, some straight-up ghosting, and of course a few kind and generous souls who did take a flier on me. As a side note, the entire process has inspired me to make this promise: if you're writing a book and for some reason want to talk to me, you got it. Hit me up. (There you go, agency lead gen hawkers. You have your in.)

In the midst of all of this outreach and contact soup I sent a request to a generic PR channel at Zappos. Zappos shows up in countless studies and articles on the topic of social media and social media used as customer care, as well as in leadership studies trying to understand how those at Zappos are able to build such a unique culture. Zappos is a pioneering place on many fronts, and their approach to social media and its use in customer care has grabbed the attention of many. Zappos rose to prominence ten years ago in part by famously using social media to give the world a sense of "who [they] are as a company rather than what [they] sell," to simply "build emotional connections with people and their customers" and let the sales chips fall where they may.[1] As all the studies and interviews will transparently tell you, customer care isn't a department at Zappos. They've holistically built a customer care-first organization and brand—"an intense, even obsessive, focus on adding value to customers"—and pioneered social media as a tool to connect and engage their customers rather than push messages to them.[2]

So I reached out, hoping to put some social capital texture around what we were finding in our secondary research.

It couldn't have been a colder and more impersonal way to ask for a favor. It was one of those things done in a brain fog, in the midst of distilling some research and thinking about a certain passage in my manuscript. I thoughtlessly shot off a random request to one of the first *Contact Us* links I found on the Zappos site. Honestly, and as it turned out, it was even insensitive: Zappos was heading into their holiday rush (could I have been more thick-headed?) and right around the time when, tragically, Tony Hsieh, the Zappos CEO who took the company to the heights of their success, passed away. So needless to say I wasn't terribly hopeful to connect with anyone from Zappos, and after reflecting on it, a part of me hoped *not* connecting with them might save me some embarrassment. I basically put the idea on the back burner until I could find someone in my network who could make an introduction somewhere down the road.

Then a note popped into my inbox from Laura Davis, a Zappos Public Relations manager. Apologizing.

"Apologies for the delay—we're in the midst of our busy season. With that being said, we do have a Zappos social media expert who'd love to speak with you for your book." She offered a time frame after the holiday rush, gently reminding me "that will be best on multiple fronts."[3] In the weeks that followed, Laura gave me her time scheduling multiple interviews with Zappos social media team members, facilitating follow-up questions, and putting up with my (notoriously) poor calendaring skills. I remember actually mispronouncing Zappos in my first interview with social media lead Amy Gilmer. I'm probably the only person on the planet who didn't make the connection between Zappos and the Spanish word for shoe, *zapato*. So I clumsily bounced about in my white bubble calling it 'Zay-pos', instead of 'Zah-pos'. Amy corrected me by taking it on herself, saying "I'm going to let you know that I choose to pronounce it 'Zah-pos' because of its roots in the Spanish word *zapato*."[4] I'll never forget that. Amy owned my error, keeping our relationship leveled, keeping us connected. No one was right, no one was wrong. It was a small, beautiful way to build a connection and is actually a key element in building social capital.

Amy, two other social media team members, and a PR manager, in the midst of mourning the loss of Tony Hsieh (rest in peace), during the holiday season, taking the time to help out an unknown, rather bumbling, aspiring book author. We'll talk more about Zappos and their use and approach to social media and customer care along the way, but it immediately became clear that all I was reading about—and all I'd soon hear about in my interviews—in regards to Zappos' focus on making emotional connections with people, about going above and beyond, truly is a core value that permeates all they do and reflects the value they place in building social capital. It isn't a marketing or customer care tactic kept within various silos. Zappos wants to share their culture as a way to engage the external world, and make emotional connections with people. My problem was needing insight for a book. Your problem may be returning some shoes. Interacting with Zappos is an experience, not just some reaffirmation of talking points. So right from the start, the answers to my questions about Zappos' approach to social groups were answered. Zappos is about realizing the kind of reciprocity—unknown, generalized, and the opposite of *quid pro quo*—from their interactions in online social groups that social capital-savvy leaders understand.

From a customer care perspective, the nuts and bolts behind emotional connections, as those in charge of effective customer care know, is this: you solve a problem together for mutual wins. It isn't promotional, it isn't about sales lifts. Of course organizations measure the commercial benefits of their customer service efforts, but shining customer service cultures recognize that it's an outcome, not a goal.

Perhaps even more famous for their customer care processes than Zappos is Nordstrom—an almost trite reference to customer service at this point. They tout that their primary business goal year in and year out is improving their already peerless customer service. How do they measure the outcome? What kind of metrics and KPIs do they use across their staff, stores, and online and offline properties to determine a return on their customer service investment?

They don't. They just look at sales. "Sales are the truth" to Nordstrom.[5] Their driver—their mission, vision, *and* goal—is "to provide a fabulous customer experience by empowering customers and the employees who serve them."[6] So convinced that sales are inexorably tied to exceptional customer care is Nordstrom that they skip the leading indicators.

Zappos and Nordstrom are our foundation for exploring social media as a tool in customer care because social media in a customer care setting stands in stark contrast to social media marketing, and we need to build from that foundation. Customer care is driven by the customer and the community, not by the brand and sales. And guess what? Customer care operates within the same creator and benefit of social capital: reciprocity. You solve a problem for me, I may thank you publicly for it. You go a bit beyond expectations, and maybe I'll tell others about you. You exceed expectations and I might actually help you solve other customers' problems. Care about me this much consistently over time and you've got a lifetime customer and advocate. (Or a gushing callout in a book.)

Conversocial's *State of Digital Care* put it this way: "A digitally mature brand will execute a well-crafted customer service approach [...] focused on building positive and genuine connections. Every customer wants to feel valued and if a brand can do this, it will mean the customer is more likely to come back to your brand again and again and spend more in the process."[7]

Your customers are clamoring for you to engage them in social media channels in this way, but marketing biases are strong and marketers aren't receiving the signals. Or aren't willing to. Perhaps this is due to our years of training and conditioning to look at pools of customers and potential customers as 'audiences' and 'target markets' and 'market segments' instead of horizontal cooperatives which drive value through reciprocity. Or, as Nordstrom puts it, by "constantly putting the customer at the center of everything we do. If something is important to the customer, find a way to deliver. If it's not, [...] question if it's worth [the] time and focus."[8]

Zappos Senior Director of Customer Loyalty Rob Siefker told me that Tony Hsieh called him into a meeting room one day and said "Hey, I want you to create a corporate Twitter account and start interacting with customers online and helping them out." It was that simple. He didn't ask Rob to tell stories, engage people, or disrupt how marketing is done in online retailing companies. He asked Rob to interact, build relationships, and solve problems.

Maybe marketers don't have bosses like Tony Hsieh who see this dynamic intuitively. Or maybe we don't want to lose the billable hours, budget, or responsibility that social media brings our agencies and departments. Or maybe we don't want to face the fact that we need to invest in retraining the talent we've put in charge of social media marketing. (You'll recall that Zappos told me they don't look for social media skills specifically when hiring social media talent because "everyone knows how to do it.") Nonetheless, the challenge for marketers entrenched in social media marketing is this: instead of clinging to an ideal, hand off the social media to the customer care team. Recognize what marketers are good at and what we're not, and either unlearn, relearn, train up, or delegate.

Moving social media out of the hands of marketers into those of the customer care teams isn't at all a new idea. In fact, the discipline is maturing from what used to be called 'social care' into 'digital care,' and the standard is moving toward nothing less than 'effortless care.'[9]

The evolution makes perfect sense. Those executing top-shelf customer care understand that the primary driver for customer retention is ease of access—not necessarily achieving some level of excessive delight. A *Harvard Business Review*/Customer Contact Council study throws shade on our intuitive notions of solving customer service issues with some kind of pot-of-gold, downstream resolution for customers.[10] Turns out that some of the typical resolution tactics of the customer care interaction—a refund, a replacement, a nice bump in miles or loyalty points—make marginal differences at best in customer loyalty scores. Not only that, but despite the sometimes backbreaking (and expensive) work brands put into resolving customer care interactions, customers are still *four times* more likely to leave disloyal when their issues have been resolved this way.

As Zappos and Nordstrom know, and what the data shows, what really moves the needle when it comes to creating loyal customers through customer care is easy and quick access. The upstream ease, not the downstream offers, are the primary drivers for customer loyalty. And what can be quicker and easier (for the customer) than social media? The platforms are ubiquitous and free, and serve multiple functions for customers so they use them all day, every day. Tag a brand in a tweet, click send, *boom*. Do it on the toilet or the subway. Middle of the night when you can't sleep, at breakfast when your kid reminds you. Brands that invest in social customer care recognize that investing in 'quick and easy' via social is less expensive and more effective than costly 'exceed expectations at all costs' downstream efforts.

"Zappos customers use it," Rob Siefker told me. "As Tony and I thought through [using Twitter to connect with customers], we realized that we don't invent the communication channels that customers use. All we do is decide if we want to be in that space. Customers called us, but we didn't invent the phone."

Social customer care doesn't just drive loyalty. A Twitter/Applied Marketing Science study found that airline customers were more likely to recommend the airline and showed willingness to spend more to use it when responded to on social media.[11] What's more, the faster the response time (*quick* and easy, remember) the more potential revenue. To check against a potential bias by way of Twitter's sponsorship in the report, consider these findings from a similar *Harvard Business Review* study of airline and wireless carrier social customer care.[12] Those with positive interactions on social media would be willing to pay $9 more per airline ticket and $8 per month more for a wireless plan. (That may not seem like a lot, but the point is measuring a change in behavior, not necessarily revenue.) The study also uncovered a significant bump in Net Promoter Scores among those with positive interactions: up 37 points for airlines and 59 points for wireless carriers among those with positive social media customer care experiences.

Some 51 percent of respondents in the Conversocial report said they were "very likely" to repeat a purchase from a brand that responded to their customer service questions over social channels, and 41 percent were "somewhat likely."[13] Look at those numbers through a Net Promoter Score lens. What are you doing today that could potentially bring you a 94-percent NPS? What would you be willing to do? Meanwhile, a full 57 percent of respondents said they've stopped doing business with a brand due to poor digital care. How many of these actively disengaged customers has your organization lost with a marketing-and-sales approach to social?

A Microsoft study agrees with Conversocial's report when it comes to social media's ability to deliver value as a customer care channel, and finds it to be true across age groups (lest you think digital natives somehow have a unique perspective on how social constructs should operate).[14] Consumer use of social media among those 35 and over doubled between 2018 and 2019. "No longer just an important option for millennials, social channels are fast becoming a standard for all demographics," the study found.

It's not just that customers flat out expect organizations to use social media channels for customer care. The bar is extremely high:

- The Convince and Convert agency published a report that found 32 percent of customers expect a response from brands on social media channels in 30 minutes and 42 percent expect a response within an hour.[15]
- Some 57 percent of Convince and Convert's respondents expect the same response time to social media customer care posts submitted at night and on weekends as those submitted during normal business hours.
- A SmartInsights report found 63 percent of customers actually expect companies to offer customer service via their social media channels, and 90 percent of social media users have already used social media as a way to communicate with a brand or business.[16]
- Of the 2,000 respondents in Conversocial's *The State of Digital Care Report*, 81 percent indicated that their expectations for digital customer service are higher in 2019 than they were in 2018.
- The study also reported—wait for it—100 percent of the respondents saying an "issue being resolved in a single interaction" is a must-have for digital customer service.

Still it seems marketers are struggling to break through the volume of our biases to see this data and make the shift. You'll remember the Sprout Social content marketing report that claimed a 146-percent rise in social messages that require brand responses over three years, but in the same time frame, brands' response rate has actually decreased (on average they respond only 1 time in 10). There's more:

- The SmartInsights study finds similar response-time expectations from customers, even finding as many as 18 percent of customers expecting an immediate response. Still, brands with digital customer care processes average a full five hours to respond to inquiries on social media.

- The report also found 63 percent of customers actually expect companies to offer customer service via their social media channels, and 90 percent of social media users have already used social media as a way to communicate with a brand or business.
- The same report also found 80 percent of companies think they deliver exceptional social media customer service; 8 percent of their customers agree.

As I mentioned in Chapter 3, Zappos has two distinct social media teams. One team, 15 members strong, is purely focused on customer care (they're a part of the Zappos Customer Loyalty Team, or CLT) while the other focuses more on marketing and promotion-related activities.

It's important to point out that marketing and sales look very different to Zappos than it does to companies. It's hard to even type those words when trying to explain it. First of all, their activities, as Amy Gilmer told me, are more about sharing the Zappos culture than they are about pushing offers. Making emotional connections supersede promotions, and they seek conversations as much as create original content. "It's their space," Amy told me. "We're just on the bus."

Secondly, using 'marketing' when describing Amy's team is dissonant with our notions of the term because, as you'll recall, at Zappos everything is in service to their intense, even obsessive, focus on the customer. So in Rob Siefker's words, Zappos marketing "builds relationships and builds a fun brand. It [marketing] is a part of our service model, too."

As conceptually blended as service and marketing may be to Zappos, the separation of the customer care team from the 'marketing' one is sharp and intentional. The structure serves many purposes, the most obvious of which is separating the selling from the problem-solving. Zappos can focus on service without their CLT social team being doubled up trying to sell. The separation works the same way for Amy Gilmer's marketing team: they can do their thing away from the problems and challenges that necessarily surface in customer care situations. Amy's team "tells stories" and entertains as a way to get back to

Zappos' ethos of engaging customers with their culture and making emotional connections. This is a democratic flattening of the relationship which, again, is a marker for social capital. Zappos understands that with the trust built on the customer care side, Amy's team can focus on connection. "Part of what we do is to create weirdness and have fun," she told me. "That's our brand. Don't take it too seriously. We have the space to play and have fun [thanks to customer care happening elsewhere] and it opens up a lot of doors to do a lot of things. It's about building this brand, genuinely."

In other words, Zappos can promote, tell corporate culture stories, and perform the kinds of activities social media marketers drool over *because* of the trust and democratic relationship they build on the CLT social team. It's hard-earned and intentionally managed. Each team lead told me that they collaborate with one another to share information, constantly interacting to understand which messages are resonating and which aren't. And while neither claimed to lead the other (in keeping with Zappos' flat structure, something we'll touch on later), it was clear to me that the CLT social team owns the online community. Zappos Customer Service Manager Kelsey Walsh said her "team spends 99 percent of their time online. We see trends, challenges, and send it to the marketing team."[17] Amy told me her marketing-focused team "is constantly checking in with the CLT social team, on a daily basis. They bubble up commentary and themes from customers so what we put out there resonates. The CLT social team has feet on the ground."

Stripped down, Zappos' separation of customer care and marketing social media efforts might not seem breakthrough-inventive. Many organizations have multiple social media teams in different organizational units. Zappos' arrangement is unique in two ways. First, it *started* with adding value and by connecting socially has become the foundation. The second is that CLT social team *leads* the other Zappos markets only to the extent that it isn't at the cost of customer care. And the exemplary customer care, driven by an authentic and core desire to put the customer at the center of all they do, generates the social capital necessary to promote and connect their community to the Zappos culture.

Oh, and they respond to everything. *Everything.* Even on the marketing side, as their willingness to engage with me demonstrates. "We have extensive conversations on social media," Amy told me. "And when it's a customer issue, CLT responds." And, as CLT Manager Kelsey Walsh pointed out, they "respond to everyone, no matter the issue. Big or small. We don't choose who we work with, who gets priority, and the channel doesn't matter. We are consistent with this." And they have been over the years. Consistency is a major focus of social capital-savvy leaders, and it's clear that consistency in customer care has been a large part of Zappos' ability to generate social capital—real value—from their social media communities.

Most marketers and leaders are charged with measuring the value of social media-based customer care across more business imperatives than just "emotional connections" as Zappos does or "sales up or down" as Nordstrom does. To those ends, we know that effective customer care can result in many business outcomes like reduced customer churn, enhanced customer lifetime value, and increased re- and upselling rates. But, again, the most effective customer care cultures use these organizational-centric measurements as outcomes to a customer-centric goal.

It was hard, measurable numbers like these that motivated British Telecom, the United Kingdom's largest broadband, landline, and mobile provider, to funnel resources into their social media customer service channels. BT was noticing increasing demand for social care— 74 percent of their customers were beginning to use a multichannel approach to seeking care, and 50 percent preferred live chat or social media—and social media was checking all the boxes for their customer care strategy:

- A wide footprint that was easy and cheap to access
- A means of reducing expenses by way of reduced demand on the more expensive traditional channels
- Multi-touch communication opportunities which could reduce the number of individual contacts, and
- The potential to create user-generated support, again saving costs but also creating a peer-to-peer problem-solving

platform which is always a more effective way to provide customer support.

Social media was also starting to outperform other support channels on BT's Net Easy score: an internally-created, leading indicator metric that helped BT predict churn, and increase spend and repurchase rates. For example, BT was able to correlate higher Net Easy scores on customer care interactions with reduced customer churn by as much as 40 percent.

With a focus on four social channels (Twitter, Facebook, YouTube and a support forum), BT measured their social media customer care effectiveness by separating the social channels and calculating the number of unique customers, effectiveness of resolution rates, and the operational cost per channel along with some other typical social media metrics.

The results? BT lowered the cost of their customer service operations by £2 *million a year* (approximately $2.6 million). About 600,000 contacts are now handled via social media every year instead of through expensive traditional methods. And they've seen live chat and social media channels *both* register a 44-percent increase in preference scores while traditional methods decline.[18]

Other case studies with specific ROI numbers like BT's are hard to find. Perhaps this is because organizations haven't built their Net Easy scores and correlated their bottom-line numbers. Perhaps organizations view their social media customer care as a competitive advantage and like to keep it to themselves. Or perhaps the social media customer care industry is still maturing while marketers, who clog up the case study bandwidth, don't yet know what to do with social media customer care data.

Still, it's clear that organizations are taking note. For instance, Microsoft launched a branded online community to support its quickly overwhelmed support team during the launch of its Power BI product. It built and cultivated a branded online community forum to generate user support, and claims a $1 million *per month* savings in support costs.[19] The Intercontinental Hotel Group, with its 20 social media customer care agents, reported that they're keeping "remediation lower than we initially forecasted" with social media customer care, and planned to increase their investments in it.[20] When a Starwood Hotels and Resorts team member was asked if their social channels are deflecting traffic away from traditional, more expensive channels, they answered "Absolutely. Instead of emailing or calling, customers are reaching out through social media channels. In 2014, approximately 1.1 million messages came through our brand channels alone."[21] Adobe, having made a monumental shift from the boxed software days of Creative Suite to the online, subscription-based Creative Cloud, put social media customer care at the center of its support strategy. "Social plays an important role in that it allows Adobe to meet our customers where they are at versus insisting they come to us. One of the unique support options we've been able to provide through social media is facilitating customers to help other customers [...] they crave the social validation." For Adobe, social media customer care facilitated "new solutions that [...] make it easier for new Creative Cloud members to learn from more tenured community leaders."[22] Adobe's Madison Leupp told me Adobe has expanded their social media support from a North American focus with groups in India, Ireland, and Scotland using native speakers in French, German, Portuguese, and Spanish.[23]

From a business perspective, the promise of social media has always been that a collaborative community could add value to an organization's bottom line—basically the next evolution of the P3 communities we looked at in Chapter 3. It's easy to see where business took a wrong turn by assuming that value would be in the form of word-of-mouth advertising and sales, and that it could be generated by engaging customers in traditional marketing and sales methods. The promised value of social media is social capital, and it simply isn't built that way.

One of the key reasons customer care through social media creates social capital is because it's user-generated. This stands in clear contrast to conversion and sales-driven social media marketing. The fact that organizations seem to have been (and arguably still are being) drug kicking and screaming into social media customer care is a clear indication that marketers, by-and-large drivers of the social media bus for organizations by way of ownership over it in marcom departments and agencies, either aren't willing to let it go or flat out don't understand how social constructs work. It's only recently that organizations have started to catch up with user demand as they prise control away from the marketing mindset of sales figures and lead gen metrics, distorted by stars-of-grandeur in marketers' eyes. I suppose a less cynical view about this reality is that it isn't at all a small challenge for leaders and change agents within organizations to up and realign their teams, budgets, and the missions of those teams to this data. Change leadership is challenging stuff (another compelling reason for marketers to spend more time developing their leadership chops).

Customer care communities stand in contrast to conversion-driven social media marketing in two other ways. As mentioned, in a customer care context, value is derived *because* community members are driving it. By its definition brands are forced to play by the rules of the customer as they come to the organization with a problem in need of a solution. It's not the other way around. Brands are forced into a democratized relationship with their customers—a position of responsibility to a diverse range of stakeholders.[24] This is a leadership-style hallmark among social-savvy leaders we saw in action with Ann Taylor LOFT's *Legend of the Cargo Pant*.

Second, we know that social communities are built over time and in stages. This no doubt presents another deterrent to organizations moving social into customer care departments as so many of us operate in contexts that are obsessed with immediate returns. Online problem-solving communities have to mature toward building norms of reciprocity, and they start with building social trust. This happens in stages, over time, and it depends on patterns of behavior—not promises—as the community demonstrates that they are there for each other and that facilitation of things by the organization is a part of this social contract. And that it won't be interrupted by marketing. It's the importance of consistency that Kelsey Walsh of Zappos recognized in my conversation with her, a hard-earned and long-term investment Zappos made that Amy Gilmer and her team are now able to build upon.

What this process looks like is different for each and every social group, so it's difficult to articulate how this unfolds for each unique situation. I provide a few rules a little later that can be used as a kind of scorecard to determine where your organization stands.

In any event, a lack of demonstrated consistency represents a 'magnified risk' (as social scientists put it) to potential social community members as they begin to feel out social situations, and it's why social communities can be difficult to build. If authentic conditions exist and trust is established, the community will move to the next stage—reciprocity—relinquishing power and control even to strangers in return for affiliation in the group. And "as the norms of reciprocity, voluntarism, and social trust strengthen, the [value] will increase."[25]

But it doesn't come easy, and should send up the most obvious of warning flares to brands trying to build social communities online. Seeing the kinds of returns BT was able to achieve came from a dedication to solving problems, and being true to that promise. Zappos reflects their dedication to service everywhere and all the time—even with unknown aspiring book authors who don't know how to pronounce their name. Bait-and-switches kill the value in social groups and the pressure to act against this truth is omnipresent in marketing. How many times have you as a marketer bent to the directives of a boss or the pressure of a client to promote something in a social channel where you've been trying to add value in order to build trust?

The evidence is solid: the formula of added-value-to-promotional-content is a myth. Communities require unwavering consistency, over time, in order to build trust that converts into value, aka reciprocity. And remember: it's a fragile trust. Even a whiff of a bait-and-switch spoils it.

You'll recall that a social construct itself is not capital. It isn't the followers and fans that create value. It's the function of the group that does. Only when the function of the group is facilitated to actually achieve social capital—through a consistent history of trust-building that facilitates collaboration and reciprocal problem-solving—can the result be an "achievement of ends that would be impossible without it."[26] Otherwise, you're just building networks. Or maybe even tearing down brands, as the University of Maryland study demonstrates and as Avinash Kausik warns.

Realizing the value of social capital from online customer care communities requires a specific set of rules, very different from sales-and-marketing frameworks. Here are the keys, synthesized from my experience with clients, years of social capital research, and digging into effective online customer care environments like Zappos, Xbox, Adobe, and CareOne:

1. **Figure out what the customer wants, and let them lead.** Democratize your relationship with customers, listen to them, and let them drive the kind of value and ultimately the kind of community they wish to see. You aren't in charge. You're in collaboration.

2. **Appreciate online communities as people with various life experiences and levels of expertise all coming together to build value.** They aren't target markets, audiences, or segments. They're social beings called people, putting their time, energy, and to some degree their sense of control at risk in order to participate. They aren't there for you. They're there for them. For many marketers this will run against every fiber of your *Control the Message* being.

3. **Think democratized and horizontal.** Social groups demand equality and despise hierarchies. Like a leader adept at building and using social capital, think of yourself in service to a diverse set of stakeholders. Not at the top of some kind of pyramid with power and prestige.

4. **Extend this to 'newbies' and actively stick up for them.** Studies show that attacks or even slights against newcomers to social communities erode trust because it reinforces rank-and-title systems that are antithetical to building social capital. Step in and moderate that stuff, fast.[27]

5. **If you don't understand customer care, or don't care to understand it, learn up or hand off social media to a different team.** It's perfectly possible—and acceptable—to be a kick-ass marketer with no sense of or even desire for customer care skills. Embrace the truth in your team and adjust accordingly. As Jim Collins taught us, confronting

brutal facts always makes us better professionals and organizations anyway.

6. **Make adding value to the community the goal and view commercial returns as outcomes.** If you're putting pressure on a social community to drive leads and sales, take a look at how you can create or improve other tactical areas in your digital marketing mix to accomplish that. Social communities sniff that stuff out accurately and quickly.

7. **Reframe commercial return expectations as bottom-of-the-funnel value, not top or middle.** If you're skilled enough to create a social system of reciprocity the returns will, more times than not, be found in customer lifetime value, brand advocacy, upselling, and re-purchasing as opposed to leads, sales, or conversions through the decision-making process. So get ready to measure that.

8. **Create your Net Easy score.** Remember: It's fast and easy that matters in customer care. Social is a terrific tool to meet customers with Fast and Easy. Stop assuming that a downstream 'satisfied' customer is a loyal one, put less weight on customer satisfaction scores, and more weight on quick and easy (upstream) metrics to measure the return on social media customer care investments. The *Harvard Business Review*/Customer Contact Council study I referenced earlier suggests that organizations put far too much weight on customer satisfaction scores. A full 80 percent of the organizations in the study said that customer satisfaction scores are their primary metric in determining customer experience. But 20 percent of the measured 'satisfied customers' said they intended to leave the brand for an alternative.

9. **Declare your intentions, gain alignment from your organization, and hold everyone to it.** Inauthenticity breaks trust, especially at the beginning of the building process. Bait-and-switching destroys durable social relations, and puts an end to social communities. If your organization doesn't have the appetite for something more in line with

customer care, find a non-social media marcom tactic to accomplish what you're looking to accomplish.

10. **Get ready for the long haul.** Building social capital is not a short-term investment. Communities take time to develop, and they move through stages before actually creating social capital for organizations. Manage this expectation from the jump among your team, agency, client, boss, and stakeholders. If things are too urgent and resources can't be allocated to longer-term investments, look to another tactic area for your resources.

11. **Evaluate response rates and be honest about your ability to meet demand.** We've seen the data and it's clear: customers expect prompt responses on social media, and the faster the response, the more value returned. So be prepared to set a non-negotiable standard of fast response times, even if it's to say "I don't know, but I'll get back to you."

12. **Put yourself in the capital creation and exchange.** Value from social reciprocity may be your goal. But you're going to have to be a part of it *at least as much as* you expect to receive from it, maybe more. Individuals join social communities with an understanding of risk, that they will likely give value with little more than a vague sense that value will be repaid at some undefined point down the road. You're going to have to be comfortable with that arrangement, too. What exactly do you think Zappos expects to receive in return for helping an unknown author? Do you think they even know, exactly?

13. **Be human.** Social communities are not the place for corporate, risk-averse, stuffy-apology talk. Leave that to the crisis communications and legal teams to distribute through their channels, and have a personality—someone who 'gets' internet culture of the type Madison from Adobe strives for —that connects with people in your social communities.

14. **Finally, be ready to make mistakes, own them, and improve.** Vulnerability is a human trait, one that's necessary to build meaningful relationships, and is one brands can

exhibit through interactions with people in social groups. Despite a reputation as preeminent experts in the domain of customer service, Nordstrom famously eschews any such accolades probably because they realize social communities are living, dynamic, and always-changing entities. Karen McKibbin, president of Nordstrom Canada, said "Please don't think that we think we're experts (in customer service). It's something we work really hard at every day."[28] Staying focused on the goal of adding value to customers to realize social capital returns for your brand means staying humble, listening, and adjusting. Like Erik Proulx, a Jim Collins Level-Five leader. And a lot like Dr. Brené Brown's approach to leadership, into which we dive later.

These guidelines to building social capital through social media customer care lead us into Part Two of this book in which we'll explore frameworks used by leaders who are effective in building social capital. We'll get creative with our approach to building social groups online by looking at leadership techniques—not marketing ones—that will help you become more social capital savvy, a better builder of online communities, and maybe even a better branding expert, too.

That's a big claim. Let's see if I can back it up with the help of a Dead Head business school dean.

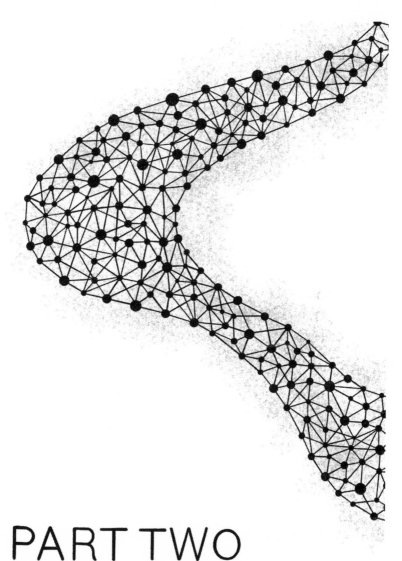

PART TWO
Learned not Made: Social Capital
Development as an Acquirable Skill

Chapter 6

THE SECRET LIFE OF SOCIAL CAPITAL, PART ONE: A DEAD HEAD IN A BUSINESS SCHOOL

I can't remember exactly how long it was into my stint as a marketing coordinator at a business school's executive and professional programs department when I was exposed to Bill Silver's leadership model, but it was early. I had come to the job with a vague notion that people were in positions of authority, that there were people who were in charge, people who gave the orders. But that was about it. Mine was clearly a beginner's mind, a burgeoning awareness of leadership as a discipline, when Bill, my boss's boss and the dean of the department, asked me to sit in on a leadership lecture he was giving to an executive MBA cohort. He and some colleagues had developed a new leadership model that would be the centerpiece for the programs we offered, and as one of the people charged with marketing these programs, I should probably understand it.

Bill was something of a rare bird in the flock of business school academics. He told me that he ended up in business academia after facing a crossroads in his life: enroll in the PhD program he had been accepted into, or follow the Grateful Dead for a year. He was into Zen philosophies (I'm pretty sure he introduced me to *Tao Te Ching* and would no doubt be proud that I just used the *beginner mind* phrase), and employed samurai allegories freely while keeping a samurai sword hung proudly in his office. Ultimately Bill left the college where we worked to move to another college in California wine country where among other things he built out a wine business program. Now he's leading his second cannabis company. Bill was one of my first clients when I launched my company. Bill is good people.

I'm telling the story of Bill now because Chapters 6 and 7 will explore academic and practitioner-based, professional studies and books published across several decades that uncover how leaders build and use social capital. We're flying from the marketing hive again, but remember: building social capital is a leadership skill, not a marketing one. Learning to lead by building and exchanging social capital will also help you market better if you're willing to make the connections across the two disciplines. There's a nice symmetry to the fact that many of these connections were first made for me by a would-be Dead Head running the executive education unit in a business school.

As I sat in the back of the tiered classroom that day to hear Bill's presentation on the new leadership model, I wondered, like the cohort of Executive MBA students waiting with me, why Bill had set up fifteen, maybe twenty leadership books at the front of the room. When he started his presentation, he picked one of them up and launched in. I can't remember the authors' names or titles of the books, but the gist of what he had to say went something like this:

"There are thousands of leadership books out there, and as many people who'll tell you how to lead based on their experiences. Here Wes Roberts will tell you how to lead the people in your organization using lessons from Attila the Hun. Is that how to lead? Like Attila the Hun?"

Laughter.

"Attila the Hun certainly accomplished some things. Was one of the most feared enemies of Rome."

That's an actual leadership book, by the way.

Then Bill picked up another.

"Here's one about leading the Navy SEAL way. Good stuff in this one. Ownership, emotional intelligence. It all centers around rather extreme goals and vision, and the need for burning platforms, as

Nokia CEO Stephen Elop put it." Bill called out one of the students. "Gerry, you're the director of HR for a wellness company. How will leading like a Navy SEAL work with your team?"

Not well, Gerry said with a head shake and dropped eyes.

This went on for a while. I have a vague sense of animals being involved at some point, lessons learned from a dazzle of zebras or something.

Bill's point then was to establish a need for his new leadership model, the foundation of which was situational and contextual: effective leaders use emotional intelligence to flex and adjust to the many contexts they find themselves in. And it starts with a healthy dose of self-awareness to evaluate and apply appropriate leadership tools for the situation. It was a good model. As someone who had once studied jazz music I remember this striking me as intuitive and comprehensive. Reacting to situations, listening, and knowing when to lead and when to support (and what the difference is) was (and is) something of a core value of mine.

It wasn't the model itself that had an impact on me that day, and not so much the point of the story here. That day was pivotal for me for a number of other reasons.

The first thing I learned from Bill's presentation was to never underestimate a Dead Head. The second thing I learned is that when it comes to leadership, it's been covered. I don't have empirical, academic-level research for this but having been in this world of leadership books, blogs, white papers, academic studies, and classroom lectures for over twenty years, my sense is that almost all of the leadership concepts created today are basically repackaging of existing work. This book included. There's only rewriting, as Hemingway (or Graves or Brandeis or someone) said. What most of us in this field are doing is taking concepts that seem particularly relevant for our times and recasting them in more salient ways, with more timely examples. Even Dr. Lieberman's challenge to Maslow that we discussed in Chapter 1 has precedent. As James O'Toole mentioned to me when reviewing the manuscript for this book, "Aristotle beat (Dr. Lieberman) to it by 2,400 years ('man is a social animal') and stressed the shared need to be part of a community ('He who stands alone is an animal or a god')."

There are exceptions to this, and there are those who will take a leadership concept deeper than the person who pioneered it. But in my experience there's very little that's truly groundbreaking and new anymore, except the evidence of what the always-evolving field of neuroscience brings us, the technology unavailable to the pioneering thought leaders who preceded it. Still, I'd argue that we've had a pretty good understanding of human nature and what influences and moves us for a while now even without the brain scans.

The biggest impact Bill's presentation had on me, though, was seeding a simple awareness of leadership as a discipline and putting me on the path that has essentially guided my professional life ever since. It was my job, at that moment as a marketing coordinator for an executive education unit and later as the director of marketing for the college as a whole, to understand leadership well enough to put it into words for a range of people, from traditional students coming out of high schools to working professionals coming out of board rooms, with aspirations for leading everything from nonprofits in rural Colorado to hedge funds on Wall Street. Leadership was at the center of our college's brand promise then, and all of us marketing the college at that time, like any marketers worth their salt looking to value-position a brand, had to dive deep into leadership and its many forms, tributaries, and dimensions in order to articulate its value and how our brand's approach to leadership was differentiated in the marketplace. In other words, for several years I went deep.

Truth be told, it was the casual conversations and mentoring moments during my time at the college that had the largest impact on my thinking as it relates to leadership. It was an incredible opportunity to rub elbows with accomplished leadership practitioners in the executive and professional programs unit who had come to 'retire' to the business school as adjunct professors and pass on what they had learned as seasoned leaders. The students who came through the business school doors also represented a unique and rich pool of industry backgrounds and professional experience levels from which to learn. Obviously it was a place for academic thought leaders and researchers as well, and this cross-pollinated mix brought to life the academic research with real-world stories. I was submerged in it, in hallways and classrooms, common kitchens and bathrooms, team meetings and coaching sessions. I became as familiar with the leadership language and the key markers of leadership development as an immersion program abroad might do for learning a second language. For eight years I was surrounded by lectures, conversations, and debates about all the important thought leaders in this space. Along the way we were putting it to use in running our departments and school as well. It was a delightful laboratory.

And the reading. Enough to make Bill's book display look downright beggarly. So many—a legion—lining the shelves in every office of every dean and professor in the place. Propped up in staff offices and overflowing into hallway bookshelves. Mentioned in passing and required in countless syllabi we were packaging up in the marketing department. Then of course came the books and case studies in the actual classes and programs I attended while there. In binders and online modules. Peer-reviewed and commercial. Articles and white papers and books and blogs and reviews and critiques of the books and blogs and case studies and whitepapers.

At this point, just so we can all draw lines of appropriate transparency as it relates to reading books, I'm compelled to declare my alliance with author, literature professor, and psychoanalyst Pierre Bayard. I'm not much of a reading proselytizer, but Bayard's book *How to Talk About Books You Haven't Read* is a must (not-)read for everyone. As witty as it is honest, Bayard lays bare our hypocrisy when it comes to reading and claiming what we have read when we all know we haven't (and can't), and he creates a refreshing space for us all to appreciate where a certain book falls in a canon-opus-pantheon without actually having read it. Or, more precisely, the more-than-one way to read or not read continuum that Bayard wonderfully explores. Non-reading, he asserts, can actually be an activity very different from the absence of reading. We can absorb the importance of a contribution without having read something, and this position creates space for a more honest dialog about the practice, what he describes as a "whole range of gradations that deserve our attention between a book we've read closely and a book we've never even heard of."[1]

Business professionals, can we please come clean about this? Let's agree, as Bayard puts it, "that even a prodigious reader never has access to more than an infinitesimal fraction of the books that exist [and] as a result, unless [they abstain] definitively from all conversation and all writing, [they] will find [themselves] forever obliged to express [their] thoughts on books [they haven't] read."[2]

We all talk about books we haven't read. And that's OK if we're just honest about it. In fact, it may be better than OK. The mountain of leadership and business material is insuperable, impossible to conquer. You could argue, as Bayard does, that committing yourself to a thorough reading of one book actively engages you in the act of non-reading because you're denying yourself the opportunity to read another. A noble goal actually might be to raise our noses *out* of books to appreciate the perspective of where the material resides in the overall, and develop a better grasp of a thought leader's contribution in relation to other materials. I've found this perspective to be incredibly validating. To have the librarian's wisdom that significant knowledge comes not necessarily from knowing a book's content, but knowing its location, has been, for me, a treasure.

So let's declare, here and now, that we can contribute value to discussions about books when we haven't read them. And I won't hold you accountable for reading all the business books you're 'supposed to' read if you'll grant me the same courtesy. Not only is there no shame in not reading everything, there's actually real value in not doing so.

Anyway, all of this is to say that my immersion in the leadership world of the business school also gave me the gift of perspective. And since I was so deep in the leadership world, and my actual job was marketing, I started making connections between the two. I began to form a mental model where influence was at the center of two overlapping Venn circles of leadership and marketing, particularly the study and practice of influence without power. How do you move a group or an individual to action, to change behavior, when you have no power? When you stop to think about it, this is the essential question of both leadership and marketing. Enlightened leaders realize that the power in the relationship between leader and constituent lies not with the leader but with the constituent. After all, unless you have a gun to your head, you have the power to simply stop following. Leadership, we can agree, is decidedly not the practice of putting a gun to someone's head. That's just oppressive power. Marketers feel this reality, the pressure of needing to influence without power, every waking moment (and sleepless night) of our professional lives.

After nearly 20 years of exploring this issue, I can tell you I've learned far more about influence from the leadership discipline than I ever have from marketing. I rely on leadership research and best practices for everything from creating brand strategies to writing email subject lines. The fruitful fields of leadership research and experiments, practitioner memoirs and case studies, and perspectives from every imaginable industry and context are bountiful for anyone willing to fly from their marketing hive and make the connections.

Here's a quick example. When building a brand, would it be safe to say that you're essentially inspiring a shared vision? That as brand strategists we find the common values, needs, and ways by which a target market needs to be reached, and then we communicate in the ways, through the channels, and in the stages the target market needs to be communicated to? This is as much a concept straight out of *The Leadership Challenge* by Kouzes & Posner—an old leadership standby book we dive into in the next chapter—as it is a marketing one. Kouzes & Posner have researched the best practices of leaders and their constituents for the last 30 years and I think they're also showing us marketers exactly how compelling brands are built, so long as you're willing to fly from the marketing hive and make the connections.

Plenty of pollen and nectar can be found in the fields of social capital development that can help us learn how to engage and move people in social constructs as well. Curiously, there aren't many sources in the milieu with a direct and intentional focus on using social capital as a leadership tool, but most of the standard leadership material weaves dimensions of building social capital in and out of their other themes. Sometimes, whether the authors acknowledge it or not, they're talking about building social capital and calling it something else. Social capital is almost always there though, hidden in plain sight. And in this and the next chapter we'll go looking for it.

In this chapter we'll take a look at a 2009 study by Shelly McCallum and David O'Connell published in *Leadership and Organization Development Journal* titled 'Social Capital and Leadership Development' which synthesizes five leadership studies focused on human and social capital. This will provide a good foundation for leaders interested in building and exchanging social capital. We'll mix in some thoughts about coaching as leadership, as well as taking a peek at a hippy's treatise about question-asking as a means of gaining euphoria, truly some splendid thoughts on the power of good questions.

In the next chapter we'll dissect the work of few seminal leadership thought leaders, a range of authors and practitioners whose work spans five decades of leadership skill-building. Their minds and words will draw on everyone from Walt Whitman to Maya Angelou in helping us understand how leaders build and use social capital:

1. Robert Greenleaf and his treatise *The Servant as Leader* (1970)
2. James Kouzes and Barry Posner with their iconic *The Leadership Challenge* (1982)
3. Stephen Covey and his book *The Speed of Trust* (2006), and
4. Dr. Brené Brown with her astounding work *Dare to Lead* (2018).[3]

Chapter 8 is a little different. It primarily deals with the structures of social networks: how they operate and how social capital-savvy leaders intentionally use their knowledge of networks as well as the construction of their own to build social capital. This is new ground for marketers, and important for any working professional anywhere in an organization that is curating communities. I think it's the next frontier for those looking for effective ways to build value in their digital communities, and I'll do my best to convince you of that. But it's all fairly new to be applied in this context, so an open mind will help.

I recognize that the very notion of asking a reader to draw conceptual lines-of-sight from one discipline to another—leadership to marketing in our case—can seem like a leap. However, as we learned from Aakash Mittal, finding relationships in different areas and among different data is a highly creative exercise. So if you're looking for ways to boost your creative muscles, this is what it looks like. As an additional motivator I'll throw in some social media examples from folks who're working in this space to help illuminate the lines-of-sight. The fun will lie in stripping out the academic and making connections to day-to-day practices of marketing and leading. I spent eight years of my life translating this stuff into relevant and salient marketing messages alongside folks like Bill Silver, so we should be fine. Let's see what kind of pollen we can find.

Back in those business school days I lifted an old saying about leadership and reused it for a headline in an ad. It read:

Leaders aren't born. They're made. Here.

Here we go. Let's make some leaders.

━━━

We have an interesting relationship with personal debt in this country. It's not at all uncommon, yet we pretend as if it's a rarity and those who find themselves in it should feel ashamed. Is there anything else in our society that affects so many of us yet we hide with such vigor? Debt is pervasive—credit cards, student loans, auto loans, medical bills —but we act as if it's happening to someone else.

When Nichole Kelly took the marketing reins for the debt-relief company CareOne, she saw through the shame and realized that she was actually working with something special. CareOne had users registered on a social platform, sharing stories and advice and engaging with one another for getting out of debt and improving financial situations. "It was an opportunity to build community in a meaningful way," she told me. "You had people in very vulnerable positions in their lives, dealing with an issue that has a lot of shame around it, sharing and connecting."

These were people in debt looking for help on the platform, yes. But Kelly recognized something that no one else at CareOne previously had: people who'd made it out of debt were still participating, still helping those struggling with debt by offering their stories of inspiration and financial tactics to turn things around. "With a little support," she said, "this could be a powerful asset for our marketing efforts."

It wasn't long before Kelly had built a team specifically for social media efforts. She pulled the best direct response marketer in the company over to her team—"someone who understood the measurements"—and filled the rest of the slots with front-line, customer service talent—"people who wouldn't have to unlearn marketing," Kelly said.

They got to work with a dedication to building a community as their platform. They identified the nodes in the network who were creating the most compelling content and published it—with only grammatical changes—on their company blogs. They intervened in other social networks to share this content and encourage dialog around it.

Eventually, Kelly and her team realized that customers who 'touched' the social community were the most valuable customers they could find. They realized better form submissions from social community members (179 percent more likely), dramatically stronger return-to-form rates (680 percent stronger), and stronger sales from them (217 percent more likely to make their first payment).[4] Before long Kelly and her team had built a community over a million strong, most of whom represented some of the organizations' most valuable customers.

We stop and ask ourselves again: is this a marketing lesson? Do you think Kelly and her team realized those returns because of their social marketing savviness? That they know the secret to the most compelling Instagram photo compositions? How often it's best to post on Facebook? That they have all the social media secrets you and I don't? Did Kelly and her team have a better grasp of the technology than we do? A better technical sense of the digital tools she used and what makes these so-called marketing tools tick?

Kelly was (and is) a leader more than a marketer, and I'm not talking in the context of her team. She was leading a group of online constituents. Very different from the marketing construct of customers or clients, she knew (and still knows) that viewing them as such was the first step in building a community. When we spoke she called her work 'community building,' and even if she doesn't articulate it, she thinks of it in much the same way as what we're exploring in this book: social capital. To her, community building is literally "a flip on marketing." An effort where "you meet [constituents] where they are even if they aren't buyers [...] where you hold space for whatever they need from you. You provide encouragement, you answer questions, and sometimes you're just a person to listen and witness and say "I see you, I hear you, I understand, I connect."

These are leadership skills, not marketing ones. And they're social capital-building skills, writ large. We can find these skills fleshed out and taught throughout the leadership development world if we're willing to mine for them, and they have lessons for brand-building as well: a three-circle Venn diagram where leadership, online community-building, and branding meet.

Leadership is social, and leaders build communities: McCallum & O'Donnell (2008)

I'll come out and say it: leadership itself is a social exercise. It requires emotional intelligence, self-awareness, and the ability to build relationships by listening, coaching, and meeting the needs of others. It's the kind of skillset Kelly honed and used to build the CareOne community, and the kind of acumen all the leadership literature is steeped in.

This can be a challenge for many of us to come to terms with for several reasons. First, when it comes to improving a professional situation we all tend to lean toward the tactical. We immediately look for *things* we can *do*. We like tangible actions we can mark off on a to-do list. With constant pressure on our professional lives to achieve and grow, we all seek a tool or two we can use, a box or two we can check, right away. This is true for marketing communications as well. It's a lot simpler to go back to work from a conference or having read a book with check-box suggestions, such as the best times of the day to send a tweet, than it is to think about how we're going to build social capital in our online communities. Building relationships takes time, to say nothing of developing the skills for doing it, and, as discussed in

Chapter 3, the unspecified obligations, uncertain time horizons, and the very real risk of zero or unbalanced reciprocity can be a rather flat motivator (just ask your CFO). It's a tough bias to overcome, but it's crucial: we influence without power most effectively when we work on the social process of building relationships.

The second reason we resist the fact that leadership is social is because getting good at it is really hard. If I had a time machine, I'd find the point in time when someone invented the term 'soft skills' and punch them in the throat on behalf of anyone who has ever dedicated themselves to improving the relationship-building part of their professional game. These are very hard skills to develop, skills that require self-awareness and expose sensitive nerves like nothing else we can take on (explored no more meaningfully than by Dr. Brené Brown, as we'll see in a bit). Adding more videos to your social stream to try and increase clicks is the soft skill.

Leadership is a social exercise. It's a deceptively simple point, one that's reflected in just about all the leadership material a person can read (or not read, as Bayard might have it). But it's McCallum & O'Connell who lay it bare in a paper that synthesizes four studies of effective social capital leadership. Before diving into the thrust of their paper, they start by defining leadership as "a relational process between leader and followers [...] [L]eaders must [first] focus on their credibility and legitimacy with followers, then the development of a relationship via identification of followers' needs and motivations."[5]

Marketers, pay special attention. This is one of the stronger connections between marketing and leadership we can make. It's not just a Venn circle intersection between the two, it's a head-on collision with what you're trying to do with your brand. Especially in the social world, nothing could be more foundational: our customers, clients, and stakeholders want a brand that's credible, and will follow its lead when they feel they have a relationship with it. Branding is all about breaking down corporate walls and connecting in the ways customers want to be connected with, and demonstrating—not claiming—credibility.

Taking it a step further, McCallum & O'Connell flesh out their leadership definition with this gem: "leadership is based on the acuity of [a leader's] social perceptions and the structure of their social ties." Effective leaders not only develop social relationships well. They see social connections as bridges into other areas of value. Marketers often lazily boil down this area of their work to the banal notion of 'word of mouth.' If marketers could see it as leadership skills instead, they'd actually up their game to the most meaningful part of any professional marketer's job description.

What top-shelf marketers (like Kelly) are really doing is developing a fine-tuned sense of community-building, meeting their community's needs and motivations, identifying the ties in the networks that are most worth their time and effort, and interceding. Leadership best practices can help us understand the discipline of marketing in much more profound ways, especially in the realm of social acuity.

From this foundation McCallum & O'Connell devote some time to understand the difference between human capital (individual competencies) and social capital (relational competencies) so they can better tease out the differences when looking at leadership development. And then they get to the *how*. According to research, how do effective leaders build and exchange social capital? They answer this question with four areas that, according to research, are focused on by leaders with skills in building and using social capital. Three of them have nice lines-of-sight we can draw to what we think of (or, hopefully, by this point in the book, *used* to think of) as marketing communications in social constructs. According to McCallum & O'Connell, leaders adept at building and exchanging social capital:

1. Do not view leadership as rank and title, but as a position with responsibility to a diverse set of stakeholders.
2. Take a partnership approach with constituents, asking good questions of community members, and empowering them to work as partners.
3. Work as coaches in their community, sharing with constituents to build collective energy for creation and sharing.

Let's break these down.

First, leaders adept at building and exchanging social capital do not view leadership as rank and title, but a position with responsibility to a diverse set of stakeholders. This framework is reflected throughout the body of leadership development world but particularly in the area of servant leadership (we'll dive into that more when we look at the *Servant as Leader* work of Robert Greenleaf). From a marketing perspective, this is manifest in companies that enjoy success in their social networks by meeting their customers with an equal value exchange, and is why organizations are realizing returns from their social media investment when they use it for customer care.

A rather obvious lodestar for this is, once again, Zappos. The culture that Zappos was interested in sharing with the world was notoriously one with roles and respect rather than titles and power, something they pursued conceptually with activities like all employees entrusted with sharing the company brand on social media or the CEO not having an office, but also pursued structurally when, in 2013, they announced a 'holacracy' management system where roles—people with responsibilities—were put in place of managers, and democratic 'circles' work together to make decisions. The holacracy had mixed results but their approach to social media clearly reflects an ethos that values roles within a community of stakeholders rather than a system that valued managers over workers.[6] In other words, exactly the kind of egalitarian culture where social capital thrives and what McCallum & O'Connell found to be a marker of social-capital leadership.

For Zappos, it's simply a matter of engaging external customers as a part of their flat arrangement. Amy Gilmer, the more marketing-focused social media lead for Zappos, told me the difference between Zappos and her years of experience leading social media efforts for agencies and brands like Banana Republic and Facebook boiled down to a pretty simple concept. "The customer is truly at the root of everything we do," she said. "This is *their* space. We're just here to listen. Social media is a pretty unique place because the customer is in control. Everything we do is for them." Another Zappos executive put it this way: "We let our customers see our culture and decide if we are somebody they can relate with. It breaks down the barriers of consumer vs. company and becomes more about a consumer buying from a friend."[7] This recognition, particularly coming from a marketer like Gilmer, is profound. Those pulling the social media levers at Zappos understand who truly holds the power in social groups, and it actually sets them free to use the medium in ways their peers only read about in misguided case studies.

Zappos is legendary in the marketing world for their use of social media. It's easy to cite them as an outlier, an unhelpful data point in the horde of corporate environments that the rest of us occupy, like some kind of utopian dream where structures value people over rank and power. But there's no reason why a social media manager can't take an approach in their social communities that flattens if not the hierarchical relationship then the respect within them. As Mark B. Templeton said when he was CEO of Citrix: "You have to make sure you never confuse [...] respect and hierarchy, and thinking that low on hierarchy means low respect; high on the hierarchy means high respect [...] [H]ierarchy is a necessary evil [...] but it in no way has anything to do with respect that is owed an individual."[8]

Social communities require facilitation, at times moderation, and brands have a certain degree of power. Leaders of social groups recognize the need to act in that role as one of responsibility to the group, no more valuable than the others participating in it. In fact, the power and value is derived from the group itself. As we'll explore later, a leader must honor this dynamic in order to build social capital, and a social media manager doesn't need an internal holacracy in order to choose to lead this way in their day-to-day job. That's the real lesson of Zappos. And when you look at the Zappos social media approach anew through the leadership lens of building and exchanging social capital, do you think they're marketing shoes or leading people?

It's unsurprising that the Zappos CEO (rest in peace) who drove this innovative thinking went on to focus his efforts on community-building and urban renewal.[9]

The second way leaders build and use social capital according to McCallum & O'Donnell is by taking a partnership approach, asking good questions of community members, and empowering them to work as partners. This notion goes hand-in-hand with the first point, but takes it a step further. When leaders involve their constituents and act in partnership, they allow for agency. And as demonstrated again and again, when we feel we are a part of the decision-making process we're much more likely to act in a group setting toward action. In a way, a leader savvy in social capital creation is more a moderator with a catalyst bent.

In Chapter 3 we discussed the Ann Taylor LOFT *Legend of the Cargo Pant* example, where customers put themselves at the table with the social media managers by demanding that a certain pant demonstrate their brand promise of fashion for everyday working professionals.[10] That's working in partnership: honoring the concerns of the customer, listening, and acting in a way that embraces it. When Bandcamp, the social media platform and music streaming service, began hearing cries from their online community of customers and partnering musicians voicing their distaste for how little revenue artists receive from online streams, the platform launched Bandcamp Fridays, a day of the week where they waive their fees and cut of the sales in order to pass along more funds to their partnering artists. By demonstrating that it was alert to the issue of streaming revenues and acting in partnership with their constituents, Bandcamp realized fifteen times more sales on the first Friday of the program.[11]

The third way McCallum & O'Donnell found that leaders build and exchange social capital is that they work as coaches in their community, engaging with constituents to build collective energy for creation and sharing. To be clear, I'm not talking about some Knute Rockne, bull-headed driver of performance from a hierarchical position of fear and power. Quite the opposite, I'm referring to the kind of coach that finds and enables the best in someone by uncovering it in them. The kind of coach that's another good example of a dynamic we explored in Chapter 3: the output of social capital being the same as its input, its cause and its effect, "simultaneously its underlying conditions, indicators of presence, and chief benefits."[12] There is tremendous value to be gained from access to new intellectual capital, but social capital-savvy leaders know they have to offer it in order to receive it, that it's the work *and*, ultimately, the prize. In other words, good coaches are rewarded by others' success.

In the social media world we most often see this approach taken by caused-based organizations, probably because when an organization's center is shared with mission and profit it helps social media managers draw more direct and genuine connections between their goals and those of their members. By offering up their expertise and that of their community members at no cost, CareOne is the perfect example of this. Nichole Kelly put it this way to me: she and her team were "looking for opportunities for connection, not opportunities for conversion." The Livestrong Foundation's renowned online social community is also famous for providing brand-supported and community-generated coaching on everything from colonoscopies to cancer specialist recommendations. When it comes time to fundraise, social media managers are able to tap the online community to the tune of millions of dollars.[13]

It's clear from McCallum & O'Donnell's research that leaders interested in building and using social capital must find and dedicate themselves to a community-first orientation. This stands in sharp contrast to the all-too-common approach taken by marketing and public relations professionals, going about their business trying to wield power they don't have: considering online social communities as channels into which they broadcast controlled messages for conversions. Once again, participating and eventually leveraging the capital gained from these groups requires leadership skills, not marketing chops. The next chapter will uncover which of these leadership skills are most critical.

Listening to find hidden power and dreams

McCallum & O'Donnell uncover a difficult reality for leaders and social media managers alike: listening. In order to align values, build communities on the basis of shared goals and needs, and then meet the needs of the group in order to build reciprocity, a leader must develop the ability to listen. The marketing world spends a lot of time trumpeting the use of social media for listening purposes, but once again we tend to look at it through a marketing lens, not a leadership one. There's a gulf between listening to understand where a customer is in a buying cycle and listening to find aligned values and goals. Kelly agrees, telling me that "marketers really lack the skills to listen to the degree building community requires. You have to get past the tactics and understand human behavior and psychology."

Why do we as both leaders and as marketers continue to have a listening problem? Poor listening, trying to be better listeners, and the importance of listening has been drummed into our professional lives for decades and we insist on not being very good at it. And as we saw in Chapter 3, as marketers we're all too often tuned into the wrong frequency as well, 'listening' to metrics that are noise, distracting us from signals. Maybe we'd be better served flying from our marketing and business hives to better understand how the Aakash Mittals of the world listen to the musicians on a bandstand, weaving in and out of ideas together, focusing on what matters.

It's outside the scope of this book to tackle listening holistically but I've come to believe one thing for certain: marketers are poor listeners because our biases and agendas are in the way. When we listen to our customers, partners, and other stakeholders we're listening for *our* needs, rarely theirs. We may pay lip service to understanding the needs of the customer; you can find any number of willing consultants to help you identify and craft customer personas and journeys that look and sound sophisticated. But in the end, it's all in service to making a sale; moving someone through some kind of funnel, some kind of process. And that's OK: we all have livings to make and profits to realize. As marketers we have to "balance connection and conversion," as Nichole Kelly put it to me. Still, if the goal is to develop social capital to cash in on the kind of value derived from it, we have to take a different approach and not pretend that our current skillset, developed through a sales and marketing lens, is anything close to what listening as a leader looks like.

And the simplest place to turn to learn basic listening skills of this ilk, and the power to develop it, is in the coaching world. If you've ever had a decent professional coach, think about what they really do: They ask a lot of questions. Good, well formed, and intentional questions not only uncover values, needs, and goals but they allow those coached to find the path through challenges themselves. This is the essence of coaching: Give me agency. Let me own the process.

Strengthen my belief in myself. It's the most powerful, sustainable influencer there is.

If this were a traditional marketing book, we'd probably dive into the tools and techniques for listening in a digital world. Data-based and algorithmic sentiment tracking, approaches to aggregating *the what is* as opposed to uncovering *the what could be*. The tools that marketers use to look back in order to mitigate risk moving forward, as opposed to uncovering values that generate mutual possibilities. No. In order to build communities we need to fly from the hive, beyond even the qualitative paradigms that our marketing training has imbued in us. In order to build social capital, we need to expand and connect.

The kind of question-asking that expands and connects is well researched and documented in all kinds of books, papers, blogs, and podcasts, but it's well worth spending some time here exploring what kind of a question-asking frame we can use as it relates to building social capital. There are many fields we can buzz to in order to expand our question-asking knowledge and awareness, but one of my favorites is the colorful and delightful field of Fran Peavey.

Fran's *Strategic Questioning Manual* lives in a quirky online place of wikis and digital coop institutes that reflect her activist and freedom-seeking life.[14] You can always turn to a John Maxwell *Good Leaders Ask Good Questions* genus if that's your jam (we'll actually take a look at old-school thought leaders Kouzes & Posner's take on listening in a bit), but where's the fun in that? Personally I'd rather take some time to learn about question-asking from someone whose obituary includes these nuggets: "Fran performed as an Atomic Comic with Charlie Varon, and traveled abroad, sitting with a sign 'American willing to listen.' In India she [...] collaborated to form the Sankat Mochan Foundation in Varanasi, whose goal is to clean the Ganges River." Learn from a manual with an introduction titled "Strategic Questions Are Tools for Rebellion" and with a conclusion warning that "if you submit yourself to strategic questioning [...] you may uncover hidden power and dreams inside of you which may change your entire life. You may find yourself taking actions you did not expect, acting from a sense of power and commitment that you have denied for many years." Fran lays it on you. Please Google and explore her life and work after we skim a bit of it here.

One of Fran's foundational thoughts is framing the idea of questions in terms of leverage. Imagine your questions, she asks of us, as like opening a paint can: short lever questions will prise open the lid to allow you to see inside, get a sense of what's in there, make some basic decisions. Long lever questions on the other hand allow us to crack things wide open. Rip off the lid and let "a lot of the inert stuff out that's trapped inside a person's head." Long-lever questions, when built up to a strategic level, create a "new possibility for the creating of a synthesis, and increased motion and zest. Whereas before the person might have not known how to move, now that person has their own ideas of where to go and what to do."[15]

This is a marvelous idea and is exactly what good coaches do: find what already exists and act as an alchemist to mix up and make potent what was once inert. It's a powerful and, you could argue, the only true way to influence sustainable change. Critically, it follows that the coach/leader is as open to discovery as the coached/constituent. After all, why ask the question if you have all the answers? It's similar to how Carl Jung likened a doctor's influence over a patient to a chemical reaction in *Modern Man in Search of a Soul*. Both people—coach and coached, leader and constituent, doctor and patient—must be equally open to change. Jung in no uncertain terms found that we "can exert no influence" over others if we are not susceptible to influence ourselves. Shielding ourselves with "a smoke-screen of fatherly and professional authority" denies us information that allows us to uncover shared values.[16] And at the risk of sounding like Yoda, shared values lead to agency. Agency leads to action. Action leads to associability in groups.

Fundamentally, leading with questions is about removing the notion of hierarchy and thinking in terms of servitude among those you're leading/coaching to uncover needs and goals inherent in both of you. That synthesis is the work of the social capital-savvy leader, and questions are the way there. Questions bring reciprocity to a relationship, and uncover ways for individuals in relationships to discover their own agency, something a social capital-savvy leader is always interested in.

Peavey teaches us that for a leader looking to build social capital, asking good questions brings all kinds of value. It's the most effective way of creating change. In group settings, like online social media environments, strategic questioning creates discussions, and discussions can break gridlocks and move from sociability to associability. Even the most unsophisticated social media manager realizes the importance of engagement online, and using good questions to spark discussions might be the most effective approach. Good listening provides an opportunity to build a culture of empathy, and empathy connects, connection build trust, and trust leads to associability.

The next time a member of your social media community posts a comment or shares a post, don't just respond. Channel your inner Peavey and ask some questions.

McCallum & O'Donnell provide an excellent framework for exploring leadership techniques for building social capital, techniques found in the work of Greenleaf, Kouzes & Posner, Covey, and Brown.

Chapter 7

THE SECRET LIFE OF SOCIAL CAPITAL, PART TWO: A RUMBLE WITH FOUR LEADERSHIP ICONS

As social capital alchemists inspired by Peavey, we use our strategic questioning to move forward with "motion and zest," taking our own ideas of where to go and what to do, as she would put it. With the right questioning, we can confidently look the superabundance of leadership best practices Bill Silver warned us about in the eye, and start to identify the social capital best practices that now become hidden in plain sight.

We convene four leadership stalwarts and their keystone works for this discussion:

1. Robert Greenleaf's treatise *The Servant as Leader* (1970)
2. James Kouzes and Barry Posner's seminal *The Leadership Challenge* (1982)
3. Stephen Covey's *The Speed of Trust* (2006), and
4. Dr. Brené Brown's astounding *Dare to Lead* (2018).

Servant leadership is people-building: Robert Greenleaf and *The Servant as Leader* (1970)

The community-first orientation that's necessary for leaders to build social capital by way of McCallum & O'Donnell's research also leads us to an important body of work in the leadership milieu: if we want to help build social communities where we're in service to a diverse set of stakeholders, then we have to rethink what leading is in that kind of context. Communities that will ultimately deliver social capital not only demand that all involved contribute, but that power and hierarchy be dismantled. This is the pollen in the fields of servant leadership to which we are now drawn.

Servant leadership has had something of a resurgence lately. From my perspective this is due to the rise of Simon Sinek and his collection of works that orbit in and around the concept. He has worked with leadership stalwart Ken Blanchard on the topic as well, who in his later years has also decided to take up the trend.

Servant leadership does not require much defining. Leaders with a servant orientation look to serve first. The power of their influence comes from service: finding the strengths of others, identifying ways to help them thrive, and acting to empower them to achieve. The concept was born in 1970 from the mind of Robert Greenleaf in an essay titled "The Servant as Leader" and is a cornerstone of established leadership ideology.[1]

It's not without irony that Sinek and Blanchard fail to credit Greenleaf in their work on servant leadership, a concept requiring leaders to shed such trappings as authority. The irony meter flat out pegs with Blanchard because his riffing on the subject has at its center the life and example of Jesus, a moral figure who would certainly shun the practice of stealing even intellectual capital. Sinek and Blanchard, it seems, are taking advantage of a void in our collective memory about where the idea of servant leadership actually came from, living some kind of TED-talk Planck principle which promises that a new idea does "not triumph by convincing its opponents and making them see the light, but rather because its opponents eventually die and a new generation grows up that is familiar with it."[2]

Greenleaf is a wonderfully open and deeply thoughtful person, and it's a satisfying experience to read his work. He writes from his intuition, courageously admitting as much and accepting the risks such an approach involves. How well his intuition has served him, having founded a leadership practice that is still revered today! And there's plenty in Greenleaf's work that foretells social capital. He unhesitatingly declares that credibility, listening broadly, and building trust are a servant leader's primary causes, hallmarks shared with leaders interested in building social capital.

"Trust is at the root of it," he wrote about servant leadership. "Has the leader a really good information base (both hard data and sensitivity to feelings and needs of people) and a reputation for consistently good decisions that people respect? Can [they] defuse the anxiety of other people who want more certainty than exists in the situation?"

The language used in his essay may seem dated at times, especially its use of masculine pronouns and under-addressed issues of privilege. There's also a decision-making section that feels obsolete. But in all I find Greenleaf quite poetic, actually. A beautiful respite from the top ten lists and quotable Instagram memes of leadership works today, all of which fall notably short when trying to encapsulate the gray and messy humanity involved in trying to develop coach/coached, leader/led relationships. Unlike Sinek's propensity to lean on clever, uncontroversial phrase-twist aphorisms (don't hire skilled people and motivate them, hire already motivated people and inspire them; great leaders are willing to sacrifice the numbers to save the people, poor leaders sacrifice the people to save the numbers; leadership is not about being in charge, it's about caring for those you're in charge of, the value of a true leader is not measured by the work they do, but by the work they inspire others to do, etc.). Greenleaf, conversely, likes to "venture into controversy [...] freely." Since servant leadership is rooted in the social, it's complex stuff that doesn't fit into tidy and easily digestible marketing concepts. Both in style and substance, Greenleaf recalls Walt Whitman's "Song of Myself" more than some TED talk, as in this passage where he embraces the complexity of humanity and the messy notion of trying to find a place in it:

I believe in order, and I want creation out of chaos. My good society will have strong individualism amidst community. It will have elitism along with populism. I listen to the old and to the young and find myself baffled and heartened by both. Reason and intuition, each in its own way, both comfort and dismay me.

"My perceptual world is full of contradictions" Greenleaf freely admits. *Do I contradict myself? Very well, then, I contradict myself. (I am large. I contain multitudes.)*

When Sinek and others speak of servant leadership without a deep connection to the messy humanity of it, they ignore the fundamental notion that humans are wired to connect and build social groups, that what we need is encouragement and nourishment to believe in our innate nature and follow it, not some kind of paternalistic shield like a superhero taking the bullets, which is closer to what I see in Sinek's work on the subject. *Why Good Leaders Make You Feel Safe*—Sinek's TED talk with a servant leader label slapped on it—seems to advocate this. Taking the example of a parent, the "closest analogy [he] can give to what a great leader is," Sinek likens servant leadership to providing "opportunities, education, discipline [...] when necessary, all so that [those being led] can grow up and achieve more than we could for ourselves."[3]

Parents aren't at all servants, though (much as they may feel that way addressing the needs of demanding kids). More obviously, leaders' constituents aren't children. It's actually a fairly privileged perspective Sinek takes in supposing that a leader's definitions and sense of what kind of support (or protection) constituents need is what matters. Greenleaf had it right: servant leaders *listen* and allow people to tell us how we can support them, how we can allow them to grow and achieve.

Parents also possess and wield power very differently to a servant leader. As Greenleaf puts it, a servant's power is in "persuasion and example" in order to "create opportunity and alternatives so that the individual may choose and build autonomy." Yes, autonomy for children is the long game of parenting. But not the 'provide safety' end-all Sinek is talking about, at least to the degree he describes. Coercive power (often articulated through punishment) actually strengthens resistance. It doesn't create the kind of engagement Sinek seeks. All of this is something I think Sinek could have spotted had he paid more attention to Greenleaf, and perhaps Jung too. Remember Jung's thoughts: "a smoke-screen of fatherly and professional authority denies us information that allows us to uncover shared values."[4]

Sinek and Greenleaf diverge in other places, as when Sinek would have us accept the overly simplistic notion that leaders eat last when we know that leaders *know when* to eat last; sometimes a servant leader has to put their own oxygen mask on first to help others with theirs. Or Sinek's focus on a leader's vision with statements like "[t]heir leader's vision comes to life." It isn't the leader's vision that matters. It's the group's. Effective leaders interpret the group vision, and act as coach and catalyst to fulfill it. As Greenleaf puts it, as servant leaders we "meld [a group's vision] with our own leadings." (We've teed up the similar principle of *inspiring a shared vision* before, and we'll dive into it with Kouzes & Posner a little later.) And servant leaders don't give or get 'blood, sweat and tears' to or from anyone as Sinek likes to champion. Servant leaders, like those interested in building and exchanging social capital, hold positions of responsibility to a diverse set of stakeholders. In this sense it isn't about sacrificing, it's about contributing.

As I mentioned, servant leadership was a creative and intuitive pursuit for Greenleaf and it's clear now that his intuition was confirmed by Dr. Lieberman and many others, those who credit his work and those who don't. Greenleaf knew that we are wired to be in service to others. Building on the past is critical for all of us—but especially those who claim to take a servant leadership approach—because we're innately, deeply connected. As Faulkner wrote, the past is never dead. It's not even past. So my critiques of Sinek aren't just throwing shade. They point out flaws in his work that are fundamental to the very notion of servant leadership, and they function, I hope, as reminders to all of us who are building on what the concept means in today's world. Sinek isn't the only one posting trendy servant leadership memes on LinkedIn, after all.

Another area we can build on in Greenleaf's work as it relates to social capital is the tie between servant leadership and unknown returns. As we discussed in Chapter 3, building social capital means accepting unspecified obligations, uncertain time horizons, and a very real risk of zero or unbalanced reciprocity. Servant leaders operate in this world as well, full-on in the face of the rational actor theory. Servant leaders act with faith that their efforts will return results but there's no promise they ever will. Greenleaf acknowledges this dynamic: "This is part of the human dilemma," he writes. "One cannot know for sure. One must, after some study and experience, hypothesize—but leave the hypothesis under a shadow of doubt."

As uncomfortable as it may be to accept, servant leadership can very much be a subjective, Kierkegaardian leap of faith. Like servant leadership, building social capital (online or in person) requires operating under a shadow of doubt. As leaders in this arena (and managers of social media accounts), we need to come to terms with that.

The most powerful and direct way Greenleaf makes the case for social capital are his coined terms 'people-using' vs. 'people-building' institutions, the latter being "groups of people who, under the influence of the institution, grow taller and become healthier, stronger, more autonomous." This is essentially what we see in organizations rich in social capital as well as in online social groups, and I for one would like to see a resurgence of the term. It's a clear phrase, and buttons down the point especially when contrasted with his term 'people-using.' To Greenleaf, whereas people-using institutions are temporary, people-building organizations—those rich in social capital—are sustainable.

This sense of servant leadership and the assumption that such an orientation helps build community-first, diverse organizations in which leaders simply hold a position of responsibility makes it easy to see how Ann Taylor LOFT's view of customers and their relationship to them was what guided the social media managers to take and post photos of women employees in their office wearing the controversial pants. Or why Zappos redefined differentiating a company by sharing the affirming power of a business model that eschews rank and title. Why Bandcamp is so quick to give up revenue on Fridays to honor their artist partners. Or how CareOne and The Livestrong Foundation make money *as a result* of genuinely serving their stakeholders.

Whether the managers of these communities realize or can articulate it or not, their digitally-formed, social constructs were led by servants much more than they were managed by marketers, or at least led by the kind of talent Nichole Kelly likes to hire: the rare and brave marketers who've unlearned marketing.

Liberating visions and walking the talk: Kouzes & Posner's *The Leadership Challenge* (1982)

We're social beings and we want to connect with one another. It follows that a servant leader willing to be in service to this and to facilitate it can create social capital. We saw the social nature of leadership hidden in the intuitive work of Greenleaf, and we can find similar discoveries in the evidence-based work of other leadership fields. No pollen is a stronger attraction in this sense than Kouzes & Posner and their book *The Leadership Challenge*, which is where we buzz next.[5]

First published in 1982, *The Leadership Challenge* is such a staple for leadership development programs, undergraduate management classes, executive training seminars, and community-building workshops that it hardly needs an introduction. I first ran across *The Leadership Challenge* during my time at the business school, and it has been at the center of many leadership training and development engagements I've been a part of since. I've used it to guide my marketing practice through the years as well. It's top-qualified.

Over the years, Kouzes & Posner have accumulated thousands of case studies and millions of survey responses through their *Leadership Practices Inventory*. They use this data to determine both what leaders do when they're at their best and what characteristics constituents look for when they willingly choose to follow someone.

The book establishes the perspective of the constituent first, so we will too. Fascinatingly, the top four characteristics arising from Kouzes & Posner's research that have received at least 60 percent of the votes in their annual survey have hardly budged in 35 years. When it comes to willingly following someone, we look for a leader who's

- Honest
- Competent
- Inspiring, and
- Forward-looking.

They build their leadership model on this data because leaders respond to the needs of their constituents—a social exercise in reading and responding, listening and aligning. This is foundational to Kouzes & Posner: leaders respond to their constituents' needs, not the other way around, which is probably why they structure their book this way.

Breaking down two of these characteristics—honesty and inspiring —a marketer can not only find ways to improve the connection with customers in social constructs, but can find guidance for a helluva brand personality as well. So let's weave in and out of leadership, branding, and social media concepts as we investigate these two characteristics.

Honesty seems intuitive. It builds team cohesion and trust, and as we've seen in McCallum & O'Donnell as well as Greenleaf, credibility is essential in building an honest reputation. It's also helpful to remember that when we engage with someone who is dishonest, we're compromising our own integrity. This is at odds with Cialdini's influence principle of 'consistency' that we touched on in Chapter 2: we experience a cognitive dissonance when our actions don't reflect our beliefs. A leader (or brand) that isn't honest is asking their constituents to act against their wiring. Such leaders/brands stack the deck against themselves. Honesty is even more important in social constructs because of the unknown returns social groups represent. We disengage from a boss with a sign "My Door Is Always Open" hanging outside an office with a closed door, or from a brand when we're put on a terminal hold with the looping recorded message "We put our customers first," or from brands with social media managers who pay lip service to community-building while promoting products through their social accounts. We need a clear set of values to help identify what we're signing up for in social groups. It's one of the only clear assets we can count on when evaluating whether or not to get involved. Clarity of values—especially honesty—establishes this.

Inspiring should also be intuitive, especially to marketers. We seek to be connected to something larger than ourselves. Marketers in organizations from Starbucks to Granger to The Livestrong Foundation to CareOne spend most of their waking hours trying to find messages and tactics to connect their customers to something more significant than the transaction. It's at the root of what marketers do. Kouzes & Posner illustrate the power of *inspiring* by asking us to think about the opposite of it, which I find helpful in understanding how the dynamic works in marketing, especially within social groups. When you think of the opposite of inspiring you think of fear, and fear means our constituents feel unsafe. When we feel unsafe we don't share, and when we don't share we don't connect. Fear, as Kouzes & Posner point out, creates compliance, not commitment.

As we've seen, commitment to a social group is required in building social capital. First, commitment facilitates the sharing of values, beliefs, and norms upon which a leader can build a social construct. If no one is sharing, a leader/brand has no such building blocks. Then, later, these shared values create associability by putting everyone's beliefs in the game. Members of the group have their own sense of agency invested and engaged in the process. Giddyup.

Kouzes & Posner point out that the top four characteristics of leaders we willingly follow work together to create what communications experts call 'source credibility.' Leaders are evaluated based on three criteria as constituents decide whether the leader is believable: trustworthiness, expertise, and dynamism. In my opinion, the same thing happens when we evaluate brands. When Kouzes & Posner synthesize the characteristics of those leaders we willingly follow they, like Greenleaf before them, use the term *credibility*. This is their foundation of leadership, I think it's the foundation of branding, and it's clearly the foundation of creating social capital within groups.

To me the importance of credibility is yet another tie to Lieberman's work. When we put ourselves in the vulnerable position of starting a social relationship, we're guarded (armor, to use Dr. Brené Brown's wonderful term). We're protecting ourselves from the social pain that's processed in the brain the same way as physical pain. Credibility from a leader (or from a brand) is the first neurological test to pass before our wiring is willing to take the risk.

Kouzes & Posner don't deal with neurology, and they don't mention Lieberman. But I think their research has them arrive at their first law of leadership in a way that completely agrees with the science of social capital: if you don't believe the messenger, you won't believe the message. In social groups, authenticity is everything and bait-and-switches kill efforts to build social capital. Kouzes & Posner's research supports this important principle, demonstrated by data that shows when direct reports feel like their manager is credible, they (among other measurable outputs) feel 'significantly' more proud of their organization and will tell others about it. Take this outside the organization and you have the very purpose of most social media marketing efforts. A leader's reports in Kouzes & Posner's study are also more likely to see their own personal values as consistent with the organization's, which speaks to consistency and agency, key levers to influence in social constructs.

So what does credibility look like in a leadership (or branding) context? Kouzes & Posner have asked tens of thousands of people this question and the answers are always some iteration of the same simple concept: Walk the talk. Credible leaders do what they say, and say what they do. Their actions are consistent with their words. Words are important: We have to know where a leader or brand stands. But when deciding if a leader or brand is credible, we watch actions.

Social groups watch brands in much the same way. They know when Bandcamp says how much they value artists and when they're exploiting them, and when Ann Taylor LOFT says they care about the working professional while they turn to models more in line with a fashion runway than an office. We're hard-wired to spot the charlatan: if your social construct is working against this wiring, you're trying to outsmart evolution.

It's from this foundation that Kouzes & Posner build their leadership model, the five practices that research shows leaders employ when they're at their most effective. It's a model that is as simple as it is timeless:

**Model the Way | Inspire a Shared Vision | Challenge the Process |
Enable Others to Act | Encourage the Heart**

If you're with me so far, I hope you see how those practices could also
be the best practices of effective branding, as well as building and
using social capital in social groups. Let's break the first two down and
apply them to all three purposes.

Model the Way is the essential point of Kouzes & Posner's second
law of leadership. Find your values—your voice—then live them. Do
what you expect and want from others. Do you value a culture of
scrappy teams? Roll up your sleeves and be scrappy yourself. Want
honest customers to give you feedback so you have an advantage over
your competition? Be honest in your communications in ways like
publically owning mistakes.

Kouzes & Posner are emphatic in pointing out that it's the leader's
own voice that's critical. They've found that teams working for
someone who is clear about their leadership style score higher on all
kinds of team effectiveness dimensions, including 135 percent higher
in trust—that persistent term that follows social capital around like
gravity follows mass. Leading others begins with leading oneself,
they've found, a principle we've seen in McCallum & O'Donnell,
Greenleaf, and as we'll see in Covey and Dr. Brown. Credibility is
successfully built only when it's our own voice: when it's authentic
and genuine, when it's clear you're comfortable in your own skin.
Everyone has a bullshit meter, and it pegs when we're asked to connect
with someone who's asking us to change behavior, or act in alignment
with a group, when they themselves aren't so willing. So as leaders we
need to get our Self together before we can lead others. Comfortable
and confident in who we are, true and clear about our style, strengths,
and weaknesses.

Shout out to Bill Silver here: His leadership model presentation
those many years ago represented my first reckoning of the importance
of self-awareness in influence and leadership effectiveness. I credit him
with sparking the connection between self-awareness and brand strategy, too.

As marketers, can you see the connection? Brand strategy is not a nice-to-have. We need to get our brand strategy squared away from the jump so that everyone involved in managing it is confident about how to go finding and engaging the people in the marketplace who'll care. Kouzes & Posner put it this way: intrinsic cohesion results in external alignment. That's a leadership notion, but they may as well have been talking about brand strategy and integrated marketing. It's also a social capital gold nugget because as we've explored, external alignment begets associability. People are significantly more engaged when they don't have to bend their values to match their actions. It's the very mechanics of social group action. Clarity in values and leadership style creates an opted-in consistency in beliefs and action among group members.

The way Kouzes & Posner put it, leadership is about forging unity, not forcing it, and nothing could be truer when building social capital. They have a saying: "You cannot mandate unity," and it's the same as Cohen & Prusak's notion we saw in Chapter 2: Communities cannot be commanded or managed into existence.

Cutting to the chase, Kouzes & Posner say that either you lead by example or you don't lead. And you do it every day, all the time. It's the million little things, unplanned "critical incidents" that matter. To allude to Emerson, the volume of all our little actions is so loud that people can't hear what we're saying. We know this to be true in social media marketing efforts since we first decided to use social media for commercial purposes. It's the drip-drip-drip of consistent and socially acute actions that eventually returns value, just like Zappos illustrates and as CareOne's social team realized. "Building trust online is actually easier than people think," Kelly told me. "You show up, be consistent, and community follows." This gem certainly has to be the most incredibly simple equation available to us in the sea of social sophistication, particularly compared to the machinations and contortions social media marketers put themselves through when trying to decide how much of what kind of content to 'broadcast' to their social 'channels.'

All of these trust-building actions must be in service to some kind of vision, of course. Otherwise we're wanderers without a place to go and we disengage. Which is why *Inspire a Shared Vision* is a best prac-

tice for effective leaders. On its face, *Inspire a Shared Vision* seems intuitive as well. As Kelly told me, "Communities need a movement.
Something to rally around, something to believe in." But to really feel
the weight of Kouzes & Posner's phrase, flip it to see what effective
leaders are *not* doing. At the risk of Sinekizing things, it's not *share an
inspired vision*, it's *inspire a shared vision*. This is a critical distinction for
the purposes of building and using social capital.

Kouzes & Posner break apart this practice into two functions: *imag-
ining the possibilities* and *finding a common purpose*. Much of this section
in their book focuses on the first part of this practice, and there's plenty
to learn from it (like the fact that constituents who rate their leaders in
the top 10 percent for providing clarity about the future are thirteen
times more likely to also rate them as effective). It's the *finding a
common purpose* part I want to emphasize for our social capital-focused
intentions.

Contrary to common belief, it isn't necessary for leaders to be the
sole visionaries. In fact, it's more important that everyone's involved.
It's a *shared* vision leaders must create, not create and sell a personal
view of things. Again, we're motivated by agency and consistency
between our beliefs and actions. When we have ownership of the
vision, we're more likely to work toward it, especially in social
constructs.

That's not to say a leader's input isn't required. In fact, it's integral.
Kouzes & Posner lay out the ways by which effective leaders play a
central role in the shared-visioning process, and it's extremely helpful
for leaders interested in building social capital.

First, serious self-reflection is required before accepting the responsibility of inspiring a shared vision. It's the same theme as before: we
can't find our authentic voice in and around group passions and goals
without a clear sense of Self. Leaders must get their Self together (like
brands must get their strategy together) before even thinking about
what inspiring others, let alone actually doing it.

Kouzes & Posner then deal with the importance of listening. (If
Fran Peavey was too Kathmandu for you, Kouzes & Posner will give
you a more Brooks Brothers insight into listening: their message is the
same, just more pressed and with a bit of starch. And tucked in.)

Leaders need to listen in order to uncover a shared vision, but listening isn't just about getting the facts. Good listening also provides an opportunity to build a culture of empathy. Empathy connects, connections build trust, trust leads to associability.

Kouzes & Posner build on listening to articulate an idea they describe as *make it a cause for commitment*: A synthesizing of several themes their research has uncovered regarding what keeps an employee committed to an organization. Much of this is corporate culture stuff, be we can cherry-pick a few that apply nicely to social capital development. The parallels between building associability in groups and building a corporate culture with loyal employees are strongest among these ideas:

- Integrity: Pursuing values and goals congruent with our own (consistency)
- Purpose: Making a difference in the lives of others (servitude)
- Belonging: Engaging in close personal relationships (satisfying our social wiring)
- Autonomy: Determining the course of our lives (agency)
- Significance: Feeling trusted and validated (also satisfying our social wiring by way of safety).

There's a clear theme here. People commit to causes, not plans. This nice aphorism is Kouzes & Posner's version of *start with why*, coined a full three decades or so before Sinek's TED talk-generated boom. Kouzes & Posner had done the *start with why* work in 1982, and even have the data (data that's missing from Sinek). In Kouzes & Posner's surveys over the years, 90 percent of respondents who say their company has a strong sense of purpose also say it has performed well financially over the year in which they took the survey, and a similar percentage also say their company has a history of strong financial performance. This is in contrast to those who say their organization does not have a strong sense of purpose: two-thirds report that their organization did well financially in the last year or has done well historically. (Kouzes & Posner throw a nice mention Sinek's way in an updated version of *The Leadership Challenge*, but I can find no mention of Kouzes & Posner in Sinek's work.)

Kouzes & Posner take the importance of committing to purpose and spend a significant portion of *The Leadership Challenge* dealing with what the authors call *enlisting others*, essentially appealing to common ideals with a healthy dose of energized visioning. People want to connect to something larger than themselves, larger than the transactional nature of work. Something that will change lives—including and maybe especially their own—or change the world. But critically, these visions must be shared. The key takeaway we can apply to effective social capital-building leadership is this: "liberate the vision that's already stirring in constituents."

This is reminiscent of Peavey and Jung: leaders act as an alchemist to mix up and make potent what was once inert. It's stirring language to apply to building social capital online, reframing how we think of connecting to constituents in these spheres. Instead of selling or even offering customer service through a marketing channel, it makes much more sense to imagine The Livestrong Foundation's social media managers' liberating visions of cancer-free living, Ann Taylor LOFT's liberating customers from the transactional into the relational, and Bandcamp's liberating artists from commodity into community.

"Building community is the future of marketing," Kelly told me. As a marketer I find this notion appealingly liberating.

The Confidence to Connect: Stephen M. R. Covey's *The Speed of Trust* (2006)

When it comes to searching for social capital-building topics in leadership development books, there's no more obvious place than Stephen M. R. Covey's *The Speed of Trust*, where we'll quickly buzz to next.[6] Trust, as we've seen, is so inexorably linked to social capital that it becomes necessary for its creation and as one of its primary sources of value. An input and an output. It would seem that Covey certainly agrees with the value part of it, writing an entire book on this single concept that, he says, changes everything in organizations.

Covey's idea of trust and its value is simple enough: trust is confidence, lack of trust is suspicion. When trust levels increase in an organization, speed in all kinds of areas in an organization goes up with it, while costs go down. Claiming that trust "is the key leadership competency of the new global economy," Covey goes so far as to invent some interesting cost/dividend formulas applied to various levels of trust in organizations in order to measure their value which, in my reading, is social capital even though he never mentions it as such.

There's a chicken and egg dynamic with building trust, something we've already seen when exploring unknown returns from social groups, and as we'll see a little later when we look at Dr. Brené Brown. Realizing the value of trust (social capital) requires trust itself. As we've explored already, there's risk in joining social groups because they work against our rational actor wiring. Trust, then, is critical in establishing and growing associability in such settings. We've even touched a bit on how trust is built, particularly through Kouzes & Posner and Greenleaf. Covey's advice on building trust aligns well with these and other leadership models, and his work is interesting because it's a lens sharply focused on this important leadership dimension.

Covey sees trust as a function of two demonstrable components: character and competence: "Character includes your integrity, your motive, your intent with people. Competence includes your capabilities, your skills, your results, your track record. And both are vital." And both, as we've already seen, are also vital to building social capital.

You could call this credibility, as Greenleaf and Kouzes & Posner do. Covey further develops the notion by crafting a model, typical of many leadership development processes, that builds in stages: Self → Team → Organization → Market (what other models refer to as community) → Society. We saw a bit of this in Kouzes & Posner's work with their position that an effective leader first has to get their Self together in order to establish credibility through authenticity, and we touched on it as a brand strategy must-have as well. Covey underlines the notion that leaders/brands have to find an authentic and confident voice before accepting the responsibility of leading others.

The next steps in Covey's model are to build trust among teams we lead, organizations we work with, the market or community we're a part of, and then finally the society to which we have responsibilities. Each builds on the other and a leader (or brand, I argue) can't skip steps.

Back to the Self: like Greenleaf and Kouzes & Posner before him, Covey recognizes the need for a foundation of credibility, that critical first element for constituents as they decide to follow a person (or brand, or join a social group). He outlines four 'cores' to credibility that could serve as a template for building online communities as well:

1. **Integrity — do you do what you say?** This principle is so critical to leadership that, as we've seen, it's expanded in detail and considered a core practice of leadership with Kouzes & Posner's *Model the Way*. And those in social groups demand it in order to participate in a value exchange. Show up and do the work, as Nichole Kelly told us.

2. **Intent — do you have a hidden agenda?** Bait-and-switches kill social capital, which is why marketing in social communities is such a flawed idea from the start. Like the separated social media functions in Zappos, McKenzie Eakin's Xbox team were separated from the marketing and sales team, a structural reality that also removed them from the need to market and promote. It allowed The Elite Tweet Fleet to focus on "The fun bits of their jobs, what we put out into the universe to build the community" as she expressed it to me.

3. **Capabilities — are you relevant?** Clarifying the focused purpose of a social group allows potential members to decide if they wish to take the risk and join. Newcomers to social communities first consume value as they feel out the situation, slowly building an obligation to return the value they're consuming. In such early settings, "knowledge is constantly being regenerated and re-contextualized in order to maintain its relevance to the community" as the study that looked at P3 communities put it.[7]

4. **Results — what's your track record?** Constituents have the
   power in leadership relationships. We can simply stop
   following someone if they, say, bait-and-switch or
   demonstrate incompetence. This is true in social
   communities as well. Building them takes time and happens
   in stages because members of social constructs demand
   consistency. As the P3 community study showed, when
   following or engaging in social groups the "observed
   stability in the structure of [the] social capital" matters.[8]

From there Covey explores the importance of consistency as key to
building relationship trust, which should ring intuitively true to even
the most luddite of social media managers. Realizing value from social
media takes time. Drip-drip-drip, long-term investments in demonstrating behavior worthy of trust. Social media has never been a punctual tool, and as we saw from the WARC research, it actually risks
damaging long-term organizational value when used as such.

From there we come to Covey's list of thirteen behaviors that, he
says, must be consistent in developing relationship trust. They read
like a listicle from some blog post about effective social media
marketing:

1. Talk straight
2. Show respect
3. Be transparent
4. Right wrongs
5. Show loyalty
6. Deliver results
7. Get better
8. Confront reality
9. State expectations
10. Be accountable
11. Listen first
12. Meet commitments
13. Extend trust.

Covey then moves into organizational trust, and one of the more interesting parts of this section is his exploration of symbols. Symbols powerfully "communicate underlying paradigms to everyone in the organization"[9] and play a significant role in building organizational trust. A CEO who gets the best parking spot sends completely different signals than, say, Tony Hsieh's no office policy. Research shows that symbols play a vital role in building social capital as well. The paper "Social Capital, Intellectual Capital, and the Organizational Advantage" refers to them as the "cognitive cluster" of social capital formation.[10] The study "Social Capital Production in a Virtual P3 Community" refers to them as rituals and traditions.[11] I call them cognitive bonds, and we'll touch on them more in Chapter 7.

Covey also addresses the importance of aligned structures and systems when building organizational trust, using an example of an organization's internally-focused return policy mismatched with a promise of putting the customer first. We know this to be true when building social capital as well. When social groups have alignment with an organization's other groups, more value is generated because each group has access to the value of the other. A fairly straightforward concept, convolutedly referred to as a "multilevel optimal configuration model" in social sciences.[12]

Covey is swimming at the deep end of the social media pool. His concepts are so strongly tied to social capital concepts that I have a hard time reading them without wondering why he doesn't make the connection. The only time 'social capital' is so much as mentioned in *The Speed of Trust* is in the notes when referencing a book about it. This strikes me even more dramatically when he writes about the dividends (and taxes) that trust (or lack thereof) create in organizations, laying bare the *capital* that trust generates. It's right there, in financial terms, ready for the connection. Many of his dividends have been studied by social media scholars as well, albeit termed differently. Drawing on four different social capital studies, McCallum & O'Donnell outline five positive impacts that map very closely to Covey's 'dividends': reduced transaction costs; knowledge creation and sharing; speed of action (or what they call "coherent action flows from organizational stability and shared understanding"); reduced turnover; knowledge retention (due to less turnover); and above-average financial returns by balancing cooperation with competition.[13] Compare that list to a few items from Covey's dividends: enhanced innovation through knowledge-sharing; stronger collaboration with external partners (as well as internal employees); and speed-to-value through more effective execution of strategy.

Covey also cites a few studies that link shareholder value to high-trust organizations in his discussion of trust dividends. These conclusions also agree with similar studies in the social capital world. One Organizational Sciences paper, "What Do Firms Do? Coordination, Identity and Learning," suggests that organizations are social entities in the first place, operating as nothing less than "a social community specializing in the speed and efficiency in the creation and transfer of knowledge."[14] It stands to reason, the authors argue, that trust, which generates social capital, can create a significant competitive advantage. This is the entire point of Janine Nahapiet and Sumantra Ghoshal's paper "Social Capital, Intellectual Capital, and the Organizational Advantage." An organization "dense" in social capital, they find, "facilitates the creation and exchange of knowledge," establishing the most important of competitive advantages.[15]

Covey is flat-out talking about social capital in *Speed to Trust*. As one last example, consider this passage from the Societal Trust section and see if you can spot any difference between his notion of trust and the notion of social capital in communities:

The great bulk of contribution that is woven through the fabric of society is made by individuals contributing in communities throughout the world. Thousands of doctors and nurses donate their time and means to perform medical surgeries [...] Many from all walks of life donate money, time, and other resources to help victims of disasters [...] In local communities, people volunteer their time and energy.[16]

Trust and social capital are inextricably linked. Between individuals, teams, larger communities, and yes, online social groups.

Drop the Armor: Dr. Brené Brown's *Dare to Lead* (2018)

Building trust is hard. It requires us to ignore the warning flares our hard-wiring sends up to protect us from feeling the pain of social disconnection. In other words, it requires us to be vulnerable. "The emotion that we experience during times of uncertainty, risk, and emotional exposure" is the first mountain to climb in the journey toward trust.[17] And there's simply no better person to help us think about vulnerability and how dealing with it can transform how we lead and, it turns out, build social capital, than Dr. Brené Brown.

If you agree that leadership is social, then you could argue that Dr. Brown's book *Daring to Lead* is at the heart of all leadership, full stop. In fact, I find the very premise of the book to add exclamation-point emoji-reactions to my beliefs regarding social media marketing. First of all, marketers need to find the courage to lead social groups instead of marketing to them. Second, a servant leadership approach to influence and change can only nebulously promise an ROI, so we're asking constituents and customers to muster courage to take that leap of faith. Third, it also takes courage to challenge the status quo in our organizations and with our clients to change the social media marketing mindset. Lastly, it takes more than a little bit of vulnerability on our part, as professionals but also on the part of our brands, to come to terms with the fact that we've been doing it wrong for quite a while.

In terms of leading in social media settings, marketers could do worse than signing on to Dr. Brown's goal of filling the online world with leaders who take "responsibility for finding the potential in people and processes, and who [have] the courage to develop that potential." I probably couldn't have asked Dr. Brown to write anything more perfectly in line with social capital development. She weaves related notions throughout her book, insisting that leadership is really about taking responsibility within a group of diverse stakeholders—a servant-as-leader, double-underline principle we've explored in McCallum & O'Donnell and Greenleaf.

Like the thought leaders we've examined so far, I find much of Dr. Brown's work full of parallels to social capital-focused leadership, social media community building, and branding best practices. Let's once again weave in and out of and, as she puts it, rumble with a few of them.

Leadership is clearly a social exercise for Dr. Brown. I brought this up in the introduction to this book by quoting a director at the London School of Economics who Dr. Brown uses to open one of her chapters: "Once work was about muscle. Now it's about brains. Tomorrow it will be about the heart." People are emotional beings, "like it or not" she says. Leadership is about connecting as a human to a human.

At the foundation of Dr. Brown's work is shame, tapping into empathy and vulnerability to lead ourselves and others through and out of it, and living "wholehearted" lives. To Dr. Brown, the key to wholehearted living, thriving relationships, and sustainably leading others is to recognize that shame is an incredibly powerful "master emotion" that drives us to erect armor and protection around our emotions, which in turn prevents us making meaningful, trust-building connections. Shame makes us feel like we're not worthy of connection, belonging, and love, and so we try to protect ourselves because, as Dr. Lieberman discovered, we experience loss of connection and belonging just like we feel physical pain.

What does this all mean for social media marketers? Everything, in my opinion. Some think that interacting online is actually armor. That we can put on some masks, raise our shields, and be whoever we want to be in online social settings. But we know the opposite is also true: these social platforms can cause real harm by way of cyberbullying and shaming, leading to all kinds of in-real-life emotional damage.

Making connections, building trust, and ultimately leading social groups online requires vulnerability. It requires us to expose our brands as a human, unpolished, fallible side to the corporate armor we as marketers have been conditioned to build. A brand is essentially a neutral third space where a human can come to interact with a non-human thing. If that third space is a corporate wall unwilling to admit mistakes, human customers will treat it as such. If it's the kind of space that apologizes to customers and posts photos of all the different women—and their body types—in the office wearing a questionable pant, connections are made. If the neutral third space is an inflexible, message-controlled void instead of one that doesn't censor and sometimes even uses the kind of language that frustrated Xbox gamers use, trust is built. If the neutral third space is offering coupons and other baits to encourage a financial transaction instead of one that meets customers where they are in a democratic arrangement to solve mutual problems, associability occurs.

Armor also prevents us from hearing our customers. If we want customers to share their needs and wants in order to help us build marketing strategies that meet those needs and wants, *especially in social groups*, we have to Model the Way. Legacy corporate and branding models build armor, social groups require vulnerability.

Dr. Brown finds that power and exerting the kind of power leaders are accustomed to leveraging actually triggers armor, and this ties into much of what we've talked about in this book as well. A servant leader, you'll recall, interested in building social capital sees themselves not in a position of power, but as someone with a position of responsibility within a diverse set of stakeholders. "When someone holds power over us," Dr. Brown writes, "the human spirit's instinct is to rise, resist, and rebel." Precisely the opposite of what we seek from our online social groups. (Importantly, overly positive, gilded perfection erodes trust, too. We'll see how Dr. Brown touches on that a bit later.)

For alternatives to what she calls a 'Power Over' approach, Dr. Brown cites a publication by Just Associates, a global interdisciplinary network of activists, organizers, educators, and scholars called *Making Change Happen: Power*.[18] The work offers three other power frameworks that are helpful in understanding what it means to hold a position of responsibility in social groups. Instead of Power Over, leaders in social constructs can think in terms of Power With—finding and using common ground and interests to multiply the collective value; Power To—giving agency and inspiring a sense of individually making a difference; and Power Within—a grounded respect for others with a foundation of self-worth. All three of these frameworks harmonize with Greenleaf and Kouzes & Posner: seek to craft people-building social groups, not people-using ones. In the end, if you want to build social groups that drive value, ego and Power Over need to be left at the door.

This is courageous work, 'courageous' being a word Dr. Brown has so wonderfully grasped and now owns as a way to recognize that opening ourselves up for the kinds of connections we desire requires some serious chutzpah, some daring, a double-middle-finger to the person who coined the term 'soft skills.' She articulates ten behaviors that stand in the way of organizations finding this kind of courage, three of which are particularly helpful toward understanding how to build social capital.

Avoiding tough conversations. How vulnerable and honest are you willing to be in your social communities? Can you face the criticism and listen? McKenzie Eakin told me she built her Xbox community by staying humble, recognizing that it was a new space for her support team to be in, and focusing on listening to the community for much of the team's development. She said it took a thousand little things, like letting the language fly and learning not to be defined by the trolls, but she said most everything was welcomed on the table.

This requires some skill in cutting out the noise. We can learn two things from Dr. Brown with respect to what and who is bringing constructive but tough conversations and who's not. First, if the person giving the criticism is "not in the arena getting [their] ass kicked on occasion," as she so adeptly puts it, "[don't be] interested in or open to [the] feedback."[19] Those not participating in the arrangement of reciprocity need not take your time, but more importantly, they actually erode the social capital built by those who are in the arena if you give it to them. Trolls are shouting from the arena's cheap seats, as Dr. Brown puts it. Find ways to ignore them and cut them out. I used to believe that censoring online comments exaggerated problems, that it dumped fuel on the fire. I've come to understand that it's more nuanced than that. If negative comments come from community members in the arena, then that adage holds true. But if they're not, cut that junk out and serve your community. Learning to understand the difference, of course, is the devil in the details (or perhaps better put, the troll in the tactics) and is something we'll explore a bit more in the next chapter.

Secondly, Dr. Brown offers some solid advice on differentiating between honoring emotions while drawing boundaries around harmful expressions of them, advice that practically reads as a *How to*

Deal with Online Trolls policy. To handpick one of those boundaries, consider cynicism and sarcasm. These are "first cousins who hang out in the cheap seats" and quickly become systemic. If you're hearing or using sarcasm and cynicism in your social communications, cut them out. Combat them by staying clear and kind, practicing the courage to say what you mean and mean what you say.

Opting out of diversity and inclusion conversations for fear of saying something wrong or being wrong. I gave a talk about Kouzes & Posner's five leadership practices at a symposium once, and I received a comment during the Q&A that completely changed my orientation about their *Challenge the Process* practice. "Challenge the Process comes from a place of privilege," the commenter courageously told me and the ballroom of colleagues. "It's important to recognize that people of color, especially when we're the only person of color in the room, are often accused of having agendas that white people don't. We aren't encouraged or rewarded for challenging processes because processes are built to support and protect those in positions of power." It was a potent and influential moment for me. To those of us in positions of relative privilege and relative power, being uncomfortable—not just about the terminology related to DEI (diversity, equity, and inclusion), but about how the values of innovation and status quo-challenging need to apply to *everyone*—is a requirement of the first order. The discomfort generated when confronted by DEI blind spots, missteps, misalignments, or outright willing ignorance is nothing compared to the discomfort of feeling disconnected from social groups (physical pain, remember). The least we can do is accept and admit when we're wrong, and listen. Connections and trust depend on it.

Promoting aspirational values as measurable and real. Speaking of DEI, this behavior is often associated and clearly exemplified with fledgling DEI efforts, but occur with a variety of other values leaders of organizations put forth (and put forth in online social communities, too). Are you *Modeling the Way*, as Kouzes & Posner put it, with the values you put into words? If a value is aspirational, are you willing to say you're working on it? Think about what you hope to achieve in your social media communities and make it real and measurable.

From there Dr. Brown dives into a set of courage-building skills.

Courage and vulnerability go hand in hand to Dr. Brown, and the four skillsets for courage-building go hand-in-hand with building social capital as well. She dedicates entire chapters to them, so glossing over them will not do them justice and I risk creating "2 + 2 = 57" conclusions that Dr. Brown herself laments happens with her work all the time. So please: read (or don't-read with intention and care) the book.

As it relates to developing the leadership skills necessary for building social capital, here are a few of my key takeaways from Dr. Brown's four sections on the skillsets required to activate courage for connections, reinterpreted though they may be.

1. Rumble with vulnerability. Vulnerability, the path toward connection and trust, requires some difficult, uncomfortable work. To Dr. Brown, if you're facing "the suck of vulnerability," then you get what it will take to work with it. And critically, you can't do it alone. After all, what kind of trust can you learn to build by yourself? From a brand perspective, trying to build trust and associability online doesn't come easy and it will run against every fiber of a marketer's branding-and-messaging, perfect-Zoom-background-rating impulses and training.

Dr. Brown makes one thing abundantly clear in *Dare to Lead*: the incessant need to connect with people, and our hard-wiring that erects armor to vainly try and protect ourselves from disconnection, is innately human. She obviously agrees with Dr. Lieberman: once we feel a threat to our emotions, it's in our human wiring to go into "lockdown, [unable to] really hear or process anything that's being said because we've been hijacked by the limbic system and we're in emotional survival mode."

I've been a professional-level armor builder throughout my life. Personally and professionally. My wife has wasted more time trying to pierce my armor to get to my emotions than should be asked of anyone. I've had team members do the same thing in my marketing firm. My unwillingness to show some vulnerability around stuff my ego stubbornly insists that I should know has resulted in hours of extra work and unnecessarily elevated levels of frustration (Joey, I'm hat-tipping to you). I work on this all the time, and like so many others who've been impacted by Dr. Brown's work, I'm so grateful for the term "rumble": trying to drop the armor is not a sanitized process. It certainly isn't a state of being. It can really suck. You use whatever weapon you can find in the alley at the time. You get dirty. You can come out of it feeling like your ass was kicked even if you made some progress, wondering if it was even worth it.

And sometimes you get called into the rumble whether you want to go or not. Neither you (nor your brand) can choose shame and vulnerability, or the moment they'll make their appearance. And here's a key for organizations or personal branding consultants that are using polished brands and messaging frameworks as armor to shield the imperfect humanity behind them: vulnerability connects us, it doesn't separate us. Dr. Brown's research shows that to shed the armor and find ways of living into our whole selves requires social connection. We can't go through it alone because we're wired to be together. It's a binder. So if you want to build social communities that deliver social capital, the armor has to come down.

And by the way, if you aren't owning your brand's story, pimples and un-ironed and misspelled and dirty-laundry-on-the-table-behind-you as it is, someone else will. And is. In a way, you either choose vulnerability or it will choose you.

Vulnerability doesn't just build trust. Vulnerability is required *before* trust. Realizing the kind of value that Covey talks about, the kind of value social capital can bring an organization, follows vulnerability. Which can be really bad news for people like me, armored up as we are. Trust is built upon vulnerability, in small and consistent "trust-earning behaviors [...] Not through heroic deeds, or even highly visible actions, but through paying attention, listening, and gestures of genuine care and connection." A drip-drip-drip approach in a democratized structure where leaders are servants attending to the needs of their constituents. McKenzie Eakin admitting she doesn't have a Twitter account. Zappos staying true to their corporate culture even with a thick-headed stranger writing a book. Nichole Kelly turning the shame of debt into something to admire.

Like many other social capital studies we've seen, Dr. Brown also takes time to point out that these actions can't be contrived. Leaders (and I argue brands) can't say their doors are always open while failing to provide the emotional safety people need in order to share. Remember, bait-and-switches kill social capital:

Not only is fake vulnerability ineffective—but it breeds distrust. There's no faster way to piss off people than to try to manipulate them with vulnerability. Vulnerability is not a personal marketing tool. It's not an oversharing strategy. Rumbling with vulnerability is about leaning into rather than walking away from the situations that make us feel uncertain, at risk, or emotionally exposed.[20]

Unsurprisingly, Dr. Brown's research, like Covey's, has found that empathy is critical for developing trust. Dr. Brown lays out four ways to practice empathy as a leader, two of which I'd like to highlight as particularly salient for building social capital, in person or online:

1. **See the world as others see it.** Learn perspective-taking or find someone on your team who can. Like McKenzie Eakin at Xbox, hire people who've been there, who can bring diverse perspectives to the table. More importantly, be prepared to receive it. I think equity and inclusion practices help tremendously with this. Learn DEI best practices and let them transcend into the rest of your organization.

2. **Leave judgement at the door.** This is one of those things that is easy to say, but with respect to which it's much harder to pinpoint actionable tactics to bring about real change. Dr. Brown suggests starting here: judgment comes from a lack of self-confidence. We don't judge when we feel confident, and I think this is true for brands, too. Building a brand strategy that can connect and build trust starts with what you do well *today*. The look-yourself-in-the-mirror kind of assessment that everyone involved in advocating for the brand will feel completely comfortable with. Once again, get your Self (and brand strategy) square.

The kind of confidence required of a leader (and brand) to rumble effectively with vulnerability ties into another bit of social capital-building lesson we can glean from Dr. Brown: confidence generates curiosity. Curiosity, of course, leads to excellence derived from sustained curiosity and learning. But it also builds trust. As leaders (and brands) we can thrive by learning what our constituents value and need so we can build visions and direct our servitude accordingly. But only if we're willing to rumble with some vulnerability and build what Dr. Brown calls grounded confidence.

This section in *Dare to Lead* resonates with me deeply. I hate to admit it, but I look back on my life and wonder what I could have learned from the incredible (and incredibly patient) people in my life had I dropped the self-conscious ego and asked more questions. I work on it to this day. All compassion to my wife, once again, who has twenty-plus years of countless pride-sucking moments where I've come to conclusions she's tried in vain to illuminate for me. And when I'm in a position where my ego isn't playing a role—like a branding engagement where I'm not expected to be the expert as I perform the early research—I see startling differences as I uncover judgement-free, valuable insights.

Like Greenleaf, Kouzes & Posner, and Covey before her, Dr. Brown recognizes that self-awareness and self-love matter. Who we are is how we lead. Unless we rumble with our fears, superpowers, knee-shaking insecurities, kick-ass skills, and blind spots, we can't be vulnerable with others in order to connect and build trust. This is a strong lesson for building brands that connect and build social capital as well: a brand strategy with core and honest *What We Do Well and What We Don't Do Well* components becomes all the more important.

As we touched on above, vulnerability necessarily comes with boundaries, though. Who we listen to, what we take in as advice, and how we honor emotions while not tolerating the harmful expressions of those emotions are like boxing gloves when rumbling with vulnerability. "Vulnerability minus boundaries," Dr. Brown writes, "is not vulnerability. It's confession, manipulation, desperation [...] disclosure or emotional purging." Back to the notion of understanding our roles and responsibilities as a servant leader, leaders adept at building and using social capital never forget the importance of credibility and clarity of intention.

Clear is kind, to Dr. Brown, and unclear is unkind. We could do worse than adopting that as our one and only management mantra.

Leaders in service to communities of diverse stakeholders recognize that we build armor around organizational cultures, not just around ourselves. And this prevents meaningful connectivity to build trust and social capital. To Dr. Brown, this is hard and messy work that seeks to integrate thinking, feeling, *and* behavior (Dr. Brown "loves" the "Latin root of the word integrate: *integrare*, "to make whole"). There are clear parallels to building online communities here. Repurposing Dr. Brown's words, ask yourself if you're "keeping [your online social communities] easy and comfortable instead of embracing the necessary tough and awkward conversations [and if you] value all-knowing over always learning and staying curious." The path to social capital flows through the courage of organizational vulnerability.

For Dr. Brown this courage extends into three other areas:

2. Living into values. Values-based leadership, an important leadership theory in and of itself, is at the heart of this concept. If we're anchored by values, they'll serve as a pivot point during the hard times. They'll allow us to face the tough and uncomfortable conversation head-on because we're sure in our footing, and they make acting on values—that ever-present leadership principle that dictates we must walk the talk—a nonnegotiable factor. From a branding perspective, this is why my firm includes 'Values' as a dimension in the brand strategies we develop for clients. What are the nonnegotiables, the lines we won't cross, in order to move our efforts forward?

3. Braving trust. "No trust, no connection." Dr. Brown is unequivocal. Her section on trust is an excellent accompaniment to Covey (in fact she credits Covey as one of the thought leaders who influences her own leadership style) and it has a seven-behavior construct (BRAVING) for building it: Boundaries, Reliability, Accountability, Vault, Integrity, Nonjudgement, and Generosity. A powerful list for social capital-savvy leaders, and you could do worse in writing a social media best-practices manifesto for your organization.

4. Learning to rise. Dr. Brown writes that we all have to learn to land before we learn to jump. It allows us to write the ending to our stories, as she puts it. She details some excellent ways to develop this buoyancy (a term Daniel Pink coined in his book *To Sell Is Human*), including several ways we "offload" emotions instead of dealing with hurt.[21] There's a great nugget in this section for building brands online, and how critical it is to articulate a brand's fallacy in these spaces: "We don't trust people who don't struggle," Dr. Brown writes, "who don't have bad days or hard times. We also don't develop connection with people we don't find relatable. When light and dark are not integrated, overly sweet and accommodating can feel foreboding, as though under all that niceness is a ticking bomb." Your perfect-at-all-times brand is very likely disconnecting people in your social communities. Admitting that a pant might not look good on the body types of all working professionals, and then posting pictures of it—raw and up for discussion—is what connects.

Leonard Cohen reminds us that there's a crack in everything. That's how the light gets in.

One last thought offered by Dr. Brown that I find interesting as we tie her work into online social groups:

The irony across all self-protection is that at the same time as we're worrying about machine learning and artificial intelligence taking jobs and dehumanizing work, we're intentionally or unintentionally creating cultures that, instead of leveraging the unique gifts of the human heart like vulnerability, empathy, and emotional literacy, are trying to lock those gifts away.[22]

Once again: when it comes to realizing value from our online social groups, it isn't the technical capital that matters. It's the social capital. By working with online social groups too narrowly within traditional marketing and technology frameworks, we're locking away the gifts they can provide. Dr. Brown's call for courageous actions to dismantle armor has been life-changing for many people, and why her researched-based thought leadership in this space is so transcendental. We can learn as much about social capital and connecting with constituents in online social communities as we can about ourselves and our leadership effectiveness from the courage of Dr. Brené Brown.

━━━

Just as Dr. Brown can spot someone who doesn't get vulnerability until they embrace the suck of it, I see warning flags of a person's leadership acumen when they post simple aphorisms and memes about it. Leadership is complex because people are complex. It's difficult work because fundamentally we resist being led. Embracing leadership is about recognizing the degree of concept-juggling required of leaders, that you're bound to drop more than a few balls along the way, and that it takes continual learning, studying, and reminders. It never ends. Leadership is a rumble itself.

It seems that too few of us are willing to drop the ego and titles we see as associated with leadership. When someone is attracted to leadership because of the rank or some kind of perceived prestige, they're in for a rough ride. Whether old-school, rank-and-title, Power Over leaders want to admit it or not, the kind of leadership I'm advocating in this book is empowering: anyone can exercise it anywhere within an organization. I've always been wary of military examples in leadership books for this reason. Very few of us operate in a military context with (a) a critical, elevated mission like saving lives and national defense at our organization's core, and (b) unless they're conscripts those operating in the military have willingly signed up for the hierarchical system it demands. In such a context it makes sense to follow orders and tamp down agency in favor of chains of command. In the rest of the world, people are simply not motivated that way, won't recognize titles over earned experience, and leaders will find themselves in organizations that don't give them a power position anyway, no matter how much they desire it. I recognize there's nuance here. Military teams work on concepts like agency within their hierarchical system to increase team effectiveness. But when things go south, they always have the hierarchy to fall back on.

In most contexts leadership is a social exercise. If we're interested in developing social capital-building in our leadership skillset, the lessons from research and thought leadership abound. But it also means we have to work for it. And if leaders resist it, it would seem that marketers are guerilla warrior-level resistors. We marketers prefer lists, simple books, memorize-and-pass-test-oriented certifications, and check-box concepts that feed into our tactical leanings. No matter how many times thought leaders in the marketing space unveil supposed breakthrough concepts—concepts that invariably have been covered in the leadership discipline's opus—like tribes, trust agents, thank-you economies, or groundswells, marketers are insistent that it be easily digestible. It's long overdue that we embrace the mess that is people and our socially-wired brains. Acknowledge that we're trying to influence people, not market segments, who have the power in the relationship. It's time to see our world of work as Greenleaf does, as a "perceptual world [...] full of contradictions."

Leading social groups also means honoring the integrity of the discipline. Integrity, as Dr. Brown puts it, means "choosing courage over comfort [...] choosing what's right over what's fun, fast, or easy; and it's practicing your values, not just professing them."

Dr. Brown also writes about how we use numbing techniques to avoid the hard work of rumbling with vulnerability—"food, work, social media, shopping, television, video games, porn, booze." I'd argue that marketers numb ourselves with ideas that ease our minds into a tactical malaise (probably amplified with bad data) to avoid dealing with the tough stuff that the work of building and using social capital actually requires. It's too bad. We're shying away from the work required to make ourselves leaders, something entirely more sustainable and valuable.

With this as a backdrop, here are some thoughts to summarize our journey away from the marketing hive in this chapter, a few common themes to take away from our dissection. When it comes to shifting our thinking from marketer to leader, away from converting and toward building social capital, a few areas of focus emerge:

Embrace the complexity. Acknowledge the sophistication. You're performing sophisticated work as a marketer/leader, and just because someone can more easily get you to click on a blog post link when it's easily digestible doesn't change that.

You're interacting with people, not segments. And unlike segments, people are made of emotions. Marketers have known this to be true since the beginning of time, and have manipulated it for short-term sales lifts for just as long. But asking groups to trust one another and generate social capital takes more than temporary appeals to surface sentimentality. Look to experts like Dr. Brené Brown who have the research and data for help, and avoid easy-out marketing-speak.

Get your Self/brand together first. Authenticity is a word bandied about without much nuance these days. But in order to successfully build trust and ultimately social capital, leaders and brands need first to build credibility. Credibility starts and ends with how sure we are in our values, our voice, and the energy we bring to an engagement. We need assuredness in our values to lead through crises, we need to control our story when (not if) we fail, and if we want our constituents to bring their whole selves to our social groups then we need to model it. This passage from *Dare to Lead* quoting Maya Angelou says it best: "I don't trust people who don't love themselves and tell me, 'I love you.' There is an African saying which is: Be careful when a naked person offers you a shirt.'"

Credibility follows Self, and it matters. Credibility is built with genuineness, so once your Self/brand is on a solid footing—once you're reasonably comfortable with your values, direction, strengths, and purpose—act in accordance with them. Say what you'll do, but more importantly do what you say. Remember Emerson: Your actions speak so loudly, we can't hear what you're saying.

Orient around service to a community. Members of social groups are every bit as powerful and important as the person trying to lead them to associability. Start with that orientation.

Be ready for and OK with uncertainty. Members join social groups with little to no guarantee of return. Now that you're a servant to these groups, you need to be alright with that arrangement, too. That's the way of reciprocity.

Get ready for the long haul. Trust is built in stages, over time, and with small opportunistic moments. Rarely does this happen overnight. Dr. Brown talks about conceptual 'trust jars' into which we put marbles for every little action that builds trust, and we take them out when we erode it. It'll take a while to fill the jar.

Ask questions: Coach and learn. Asking and answering questions is not just a path to empowering agency (the most powerful motivator there is), but also a path to learning and understanding the values and needs of the group you're serving. And oh and by the way, if you're really willing to listen it might just humble you a little bit, and help you with your servant leadership orientation, too.

People-build, don't people-use. As a marketer, shed your segments, audiences, and channels thinking and your conversion and funnel training. Social capital comes from reciprocity and, as Greenleaf says, helping each other grow "taller and become healthier, stronger, more autonomous." You'll recall what Nichole Kelly told me of her approach to building her million-member social community: hold "space for whatever they need from you. You provide encouragement, you answer questions, and sometimes you're just a person to listen and witness and say 'I see you, I hear you, I understand, I connect.' These things don't have anything to do with funnel-driven converting, a decidedly people-using pursuit.

That's a heavy dose of leadership principles necessary for building social capital. Now that we have a solid foundation for our approach, let's check out some mechanics of building the kind of social communities that deliver social capital.

Chapter 8
STRUCTURAL BONDS: THE NEW AREA OF FOCUS FOR SOCIAL MEDIA MANAGERS

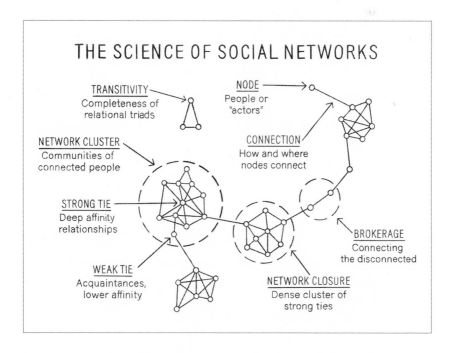

THE SCIENCE OF SOCIAL NETWORKS

TRANSITIVITY
Completeness of
relational triads

NODE
People or
"actors"

NETWORK CLUSTER
Communities of
connected people

CONNECTION
How and where
nodes connect

STRONG TIE
Deep affinity
relationships

BROKERAGE
Connecting
the disconnected

WEAK TIE
Acquaintances,
lower affinity

NETWORK CLOSURE
Dense cluster of
strong ties

From the jump I've discussed three bonds that leaders interested in building and using social capital concern themselves with. This notion comes from an *Academy of Management Review* paper titled "Social Capital, Intellectual Capital, and the Organizational Advantage" in which Janine Nahapiet and Sumantra Ghoshal identify three "clusters" that leaders interested in developing social capital concern themselves with: cognitive (shared representations, interpretations, and systems of meaning), relational (the relationships and trust built between people in networks), and structural (the impersonal configuration and linkages of nodes in networks).[1]

You'll recall that we foreshadowed this in the introduction when examining how Erik Proulx built his ad agency community. He kept the network focused on ad agency pros which facilitated the use of terms, phrases, projects, and situations unique to the cognitive construct of the industry (cognitive bonds). His community was nationally built, finding and connecting diverse groups with similar interests, and he intentionally interceded in it to find influencers who connected him to professional filmmakers and airline CMOs (structural bonds). And his willingness to be brave and vulnerable by sharing his own story of being laid off and transitioning into a different life pursuit built trust and resulted in more connectivity and sharing from the community (relational bonds).

Here's the good news: you've got two of these down. First, marketing people already know how to work cognitive bonds. We're trained to use the power of stories, symbols, and language to influence others and we do it all the time and in our sleep. We make nostalgic commercials of 1990s hip-hop groups serving ice cream with all the trappings from our customers' memories of that time. We use the power of cognitive bonds in our logos and wordmarks on shirts, characters in video games, icons for Olympic wayfinding, and mascots at universities. We invent words and amalgamate them for names and slogans that stick and actually define an entire brand promise with just a sound. We create new names for products and movements that are so unique and bonding they come to represent the actual product or movement itself.

Marketing communications professionals live in the world of cognitive bonds. It's simply a matter of intentionally building and using these skills when communicating in social groups.

Second, you learned about relational bonds in Chapter 7. Community. Trust. Servant orientation. Leading by example. Credibility. Consistency. Shared visions. Vulnerability. *Humans.*

Congratulations: Two down.

The structures of networks, on the other hand, is largely a new frontier for marketers but they matter very much to leaders. The nodes of a network, how they're related, how connected they are, to what degree they have bridges between other networks, how diverse their connections are, and their density (or lack of density) all play a role in how a network functions and a leader's role in facilitating action in it. The dimensions of a network's interpersonal ties have an impact on how a leader manages a group and the social capital they extract from it. Ties can have the same position in a network and share similar connections but have long or short histories of interaction, different levels of respect, and have built different levels of trust. A dense network disconnected from other networks is terrific for centralized decision-making but terrible for generating new ideas. If someone in your network has a connection to a competitor's network, that can mean an opportunity to gain privileged information or a threat to lose it. Many scholars believe that social capital is inextricably linked to network structures. One study goes so far as to define social capital as "opportunity structure created by social relationships."[2]

If you agree that building social capital in online groups is a function of leadership more than marketing, then it follows that social media managers would be well served to pay attention to the structures of their online social networks, too. This isn't much talked about in social media marketing circles, except in the area of influencer marketing, which we rumble with in a bit. But we know that leaders interested in building and using social capital concern themselves with the structure of their networks and manage them intentionally.

An odd and rather harrowing example of this comes from a *Leadership Quarterly* paper titled "The Ties that Lead: A Social Network Approach to Leadership."[3] A company had fallen under siege to a low-level manager who took it upon himself to build a systematic process of hiring friends and family over a 30-year period, essentially building a network of influence in the company for his own gain without senior-level leadership ever knowing. He was able to drive wedges between his network and the influence of leadership to such a degree that the founder and CEO had lost complete control. The situation spiraled to a state of bomb threats and shootings.

The basic lesson? If you don't figure out the structural mechanics of your network, someone else will. The authors of the paper identify a gap in leadership skills among working professionals in the area of "network relations that connect people, and to actively manage these network relations." Those who have an understanding can intercede in "network structures and the exercise of social influence" outside of an organization's hierarchy.

When it comes to understanding the structure of networks, a few helpful places to turn are *Connected* by Nicholas Christakis and James H. Fowler, the University of Chicago scholar Robert Burt, and the Stanford scholar Mark Granovetter.[4] The depth to which *Connected* goes in trying to understand how our social groups influence and move us is breathtaking and, in my opinion, the kind of material social media managers should be spending more of their time on. It examines how social networks influence our behavior and life practices like happiness, finding love, smoking, and loneliness if those in our network practice them. Burt and Granovetter, meanwhile, have established foundational principles for how the structures of networks operate and generate value. They are omnipresent sources and experts in studies that deal with the role structure play in generating value and creating competitive advantage in social networks (including in *Connected*).

Collectively, these works remind us that social networks do not, as we mentioned in the introduction, "extend outward in straight lines like spokes on a wheel. Instead, these paths double back on themselves and spiral around like a tangled pile of spaghetti, weaving in and out of other paths that rarely ever leave the plate."[5] Once you dip your tiniest toe into the scientific waters of structural networks, it's clear that marketers' practice of applying segmentation and channel thinking to social network structures is rather absurd.

There are many kinds of social networks that behave in entirely different ways with different rules and norms. The dynamics that control the spread of sexual activity among high schoolers, or the forces behind bank runs, or the flow of cash exchanges operate very differently from one another. As we become more sophisticated in our understanding of our own unique social networks, it becomes necessary for us to adjust the way we build and curate them in response to their unique rhythms.

Like that first crack of a shell as a chicken is hatching, I think the influencer marketing movement is an unfledged indication that marketers, somewhere deep down, recognize that it takes more to move social groups to action than blasting promotions in a channel-thinking way. However, influencer marketing is at the same time a movement that mirrors marketers' penchant for applying traditional marketing approaches to social media. Largely thought of in terms of promotions, influencer marketing typically involves a marketer finding a channel and hiring a celebrity spokesperson to influence within it. Despite clearly having its roots in traditional marketing soil, influencer marketing at least has taken a step in the right direction toward a deeper understanding of social networks by recognizing that different nodes in networks behave differently. As the practice matures it will be interesting to see if we take the next step in recognizing how truly sophisticated social network structures are.

As it is, influencer marketing is still in its infancy and we're seeing the results typical of a movement that's still figuring out the rules of the game. A 2018 Association of National Advertisers study found that while 75 percent of companies in their survey currently practice influencer marketing, and 43 percent are planning to increase their spending on it in the next 12 months, only 36 percent think it's effective, and a full 19 percent said it was ineffective.[6]

Like marketing data in general, it's hard to get to the bottom of influencer marketing. The data behind social media influencers and influencer campaigns often mixes traditional spokespeople with all kinds of amalgamations of online and social media influencers, another sign that when it comes to social media influencing we're stuck in a legacy-marketing mindset. One report promisingly claims that half of US consumers have purchased something due to an influencer recommendation, and that 44 percent of us trust influencers.[7] But when you drill down, this data rests on the apparent inability of market researchers to separate brand affinity from followership we looked at in Chapter 3. Take a look at who these survey respondents put in their top ten list of influencers: Michelle Obama, Beyoncé, LeBron James, The Rock, and Serena Williams. I'd love to be in the room when someone insolently asks First Lady Michelle Obama how she went about building her social media influencer following.

Curiously, the same report found 33 percent of people think there's "a future" for AI influencers like Lil Miquela. Lil Miquela is a computer-generated avatar, programmed and developed specifically to behave like a social media influencer. "Puppeteered" by Brud, a "transmedia studio that creates digital character-driven story worlds," she promotes well-known fashions while complaining about her allergies and the weather.[8] Lil Miquela's acceptance by a third of the consumers in the study indicates that the arrangement we make with so-called social media influencers is decidedly transactional. We know what we're signing up for when we follow Kim Kardashian. This is not, of course, at all the same as social capital-based influencing. It's advertising, which is an entirely different discipline for those of us trying to build and use social capital, to say nothing of the budget required to afford someone like Ms. Kardashian (or build a digital version of her).

A more typical example of influencer marketing, and a more helpful one as we consider its place in the leadership pursuit of building and using social capital, is the influencer campaign #EarthOvershootDay that the German-based MESH Collective2 produced in cooperation with the World Wide Fund for Nature (WWF). They used influencers who started and built their reputations on YouTube to deliver messages of environmental sustainability and climate change, intended to reach and influence 12–19-year-old Germans.

According to the campaign's directors, this demographic is likely to regard their environmental actions as having little impact, and too much action can negatively label someone a "tree hugger." Cognitive biases kick in, and a strong indifference toward the topic of environmental sustainability has been built among them. Many in this demographic even view climate change as an issue happening on another continent. Someone else's problem.

Wading into the YouTube waters, especially with regard to environmental issues, is tricky. As one researcher put it, it's an "El Dorado for conspiracy theorists."[9] As a marketer you can take that to mean that there's a low trust factor on the platform and you have a lot of noise to cut through, or you can decide that the social media platform can be influential in your favor, as evidenced by the amount of misinformation that so easily spreads and influences there. The scientific community has not been terribly active on the platform, understandably turned off by the charlatans and cranks, which probably contributes to the problem. But given that 42 percent of 14–29-year-old Germans use the platform frequently or very frequently, MESH and WWF decided to give it a try for delivering #EarthOvershootDay video campaigns using social media influencers. Scientists would wait in the wings, eager to have a dialog in the comments section.

The campaign faced several challenges, not least simplifying scientific language for young people while maintaining authenticity. You'll recall the inexorable role authenticity plays in building social capital, and as any of us who've tried to market to young people with social capital know, it's a razor-thin line to walk when it comes to moving them off biases and toward action. Simplify too much, and you're talking down to them. Use jargon even a half hour out of fashion and you're the dad in white socks and sandals yelling "don't do drugs!" Establishing proximity to the target audience (as we like to call it marketing circles) in this setting isn't easy. Influencers can help—have the message come from someone viewed as more in touch with the demographic instead of a lab-coat scientist—but if the message doesn't come from an authentic voice, in other words something the influencer truly cares about and seems to be in line with their values, it can backfire.

Remember Kouzes & Posner, Covey, and Dr. Brown: leaders building social capital have to establish credibility and model the way. This is the sticky part of influencer campaigns, no different from celebrity endorsements but magnified in social settings. Also, an emerging challenge when working in the influencer world is the lack of guidelines and policies regarding the influencer's need to disclose their financial arrangements with brands. Mindful that bait-and-switches kill social capital formation, influencers face this issue when trying to influence their followers within a paid brand relationship.[10]

Influencer data is confusing especially among young people who, I think, confuse trusting social media influencers with wanting to be them. One report finds 50 percent of millennials (this is the study's demographic, I'm not trying to say "young people" with a lazy proxy) trust social media influencers while finding 86 percent of them want to *be* social media influencers.[11] I'm not sure how to tease out the desire among these millennials for social media influencing to work so that they can satisfy the biases built around their desire to do it. Nor am I certain of what to make of nearly 90 percent of millennials wanting to be a part of something that half of them distrust. One thing is certain. The curtain has been pulled back on the practice of influencer marketing among generations who've grown up with social media platforms at their disposal. This is another challenge, this dual-reality, that marketers who are producing influencer campaigns aimed at younger generations have to negotiate. The audience knows exactly what MESH and WWF are up to.

The #EarthOvershootDay campaign producers decided to walk this tightrope with influencers that fit the marketing-centric, celebrity spokesperson model. It's different from a model the social sciences suggest is necessary for influencing, one that dictates influencers be three degrees away from those they're influencing. We'll take a look at that principle later, but the influencers they chose at least built their followings in social media spheres, as opposed to cross-over stars that generate followings on social media because of other accomplishments (like Michelle Obama... I may never get past that).

#EarthOvershootDay used NiksDa, a social media enthusiast with popularity in the gaming and electronic music space; Typisch Sissi, another social media buff with a "shopping addition"; and Dylan White, a fashion, lifestyle, and travel-based social media power user. They made a series of videos extolling the virtues of sustainable living: NiksDa on a date discussing the environmental impact of meat consumption; Typisch Sissi in her typical at-home setting discussing responsibly-sourced fashion; and Dylan White travelling to Croatia to discuss the plastic waste problem. It was a very marketing-centric approach. Keep each influencer in their comfort zone as much as possible with content as close to their authentic interests as possible, while creating content that they and their audience would expect. Then *bam*—slip in some messaging about environmental sustainability.

An evaluation of the campaign conducted by professors from the Karlsruhe Institute of Technology found, conclusively, that the campaign's goal of "a dialogue between scientists, YouTubers and young people [...] could not be realized." Comments were generally positive, but no kind of marker toward associability could be found. No dialog with scientists (a stated goal) occurred, or any dialog at all for that matter. "Direct communication between scientists and young people via YouTube comments did not take place [...] Discussions in the comments could generally only be found for one of the videos."

The news wasn't good for long-term value either. It "concluded that solitary videos on science and environmental topics within the channels of influencers, as was the case with the #EarthOvershootDay campaign, are not sufficient to reach the target group lastingly." The scientists and the foundation that funded #EarthOvershootDay realized what we've seen over and over again: you may as well hand out hundred dollar bills to customers before running punctual campaigns on social channels.

Influencer marketing confirms that networks have structures by acknowledging that different nodes play different roles. And, again, social capital relies on a leader's ability to recognize the structure of the social group they're working with and the nature of the ties within them in order to build social capital. Networks are inextricably linked to a leader's pursuit of building and using social capital, and as marketers it feels like we're not even in the ballpark when it comes to identifying structural differences and curating them accordingly. We know where the stadium is, and some of us have parked our cars. But the rules are vastly more complex than the skills our marketing training has provided us. Developing the kind of social capital realized by CareOne and Zappos takes very different approaches and tactics than that of typical influencer marketing campaigns because the rules of social networks are very different from the rules of celebrity endorsements.

It follows that if networks indeed have rules regarding their structure, then it's important to better understand them in order to build and curate community in order to facilitate action in social groups. Christakis & Fowler lay out a few such rules that I find helpful for social media managers and leaders alike. It's the type of foundation that influencer and social media marketing fails to build and use but leaders savvy in the discipline of social capital understand. Based on Christakis & Fowler's work, and with an additional principle from Burt and Granovetter, I've created a framework of five structural rules that can give leaders interested in building social capital a better understanding of the structural bonds of their networks. This is something we don't spend a lot of time with as marketers, but in my opinion it anticipates the coming evolution in a leader's ability to lead social groups effectively, including those online.

Rule One: We Like to Control Our Networks
Rule Two: Our Networks Shape Us
Rule Three: Networks Have a Mind of Their Own
Rule Four: We're Connected by Six Degrees, but Influenced by Three
Rule Five: Weak Ties Matter

Rule One: We Like to Control Our Networks. We choose our interests and the people we surround ourselves with. Birds of a feather flock together, and we choose these flocks in two ways: how many friends we want, and how dense we want the structures (to illustrate, do you throw a party and invite all circles of friends or just your work colleagues?). In fact, social scientist Nan Lin in *Social Capital: A Theory of Social Structure and Action* calls sociology itself the study of social choices: "choice behaviors in the context of structural opportunities and constraints."[12] This isn't the best news for organizations building social groups online. You have to find people interested in what you're organizing around, in itself a fairly obvious challenge, but you're also asking someone to opt in to a structure over which they have no perceived control. It makes the leap of faith in joining social groups we discussed in Chapter 4 all the more significant, and building trust through authenticity and consistency all the more important.

Why is it important for us to shape our network? Why are we predisposed to shaping it ourselves? Because…

Rule Two: Our Networks Shape Us. Some of the more fascinating findings in *Connected* are how various social contagions spread through networks like physical contagions do (hello, coronavirus). Contraception use, healthy eating habits, and marriage rates are all spread through our social networks, and we continually make adjustments according to what we wish to get out of them. For instance, imagine a friend you know who seems to know everyone, and one who keeps to themselves. "Ask yourself," Christakis & Fowler challenge us, "which person you would rather be if a hot piece of gossip were spreading. Now ask yourself which person you would rather be if a deadly germ were spreading." We innately like to have some control over our networks because we know they shape us.

Despite our desire to control social groups because we know they shape us, it's important to remember that the world of social capital is human, complex, and can seem contradictory. So we have to somehow get comfortable with the idea that…

Rule Three: Networks Have a Mind of Their Own. Like a murmuration of starlings, a wave in a soccer stadium, or a school of fish, social groups take on a life and rules of their own, manifesting "a kind of collective intelligence" (as when the murmuration flees predators), with a volition that cannot be attributed to a point of central control. Social groups have "emergent properties," which means the group makes the rules as the group evolves.

These first three rules impact how we build social capital in online groups in several ways. Because actors in a social group have a hardwired sense to control it, and the group will have its own rules that emerge and change, social media managers must be exceedingly sensitive and flexible, able to listen and understand the groups' emergent properties, and be willing to move away from initial goals and ideas. The CLT social team at Zappos made it clear that social media is their customers' domain. They're just there to add value by adapting to serve the needs and priorities of the group even as they shift over time. And the CLT continually informs the more marketing-centric group about what's resonating, what's not, and what they're hearing as the most pressing concerns in Zappos' social media milieu.

When hiring someone with these sensibilities, the stronger candidate would look more like a jazz musician than an inbound marketing expert. And it's why we need to amp up our distrust of one-size-fits-all, numbingly (to harken back to Dr. Brown) comfortable lists and 300-word blog posts when seeking help in facilitating social group value. When you start diving into the mechanics of social groups, it becomes abundantly clear that it's a highly contextualized arrangement.

I work with a client in the school safety space. They develop protocols for first responders and school administrators to use when reacting to crises. Through this partnership with law enforcement, they've developed a principle: the environment dictates tactics. You can and should plan for a crisis, but the context and situation will dictate how it's executed. You have to read and respond.

Borrowing from this concept, social groups are contextual so your tactics will vary. Yet another reason to be skeptical of one-size-fits all social media recommendations.

Generally speaking, building the scaffolding of social groups can't happen in meaningful ways with typical, marketing-focused follower campaigns because they (a) are contrived, have low affinity (and end up attracting a lot of bots) and so tend to not last, and (b) can damage long-term value for brands (the WARC report taught us that). Interceding in social networks to facilitate social capital requires a hands-on approach: mining CRM systems for social media accounts of customers and clients, engaging with them, tracking who among them is engaging with you, and communicating directly with them in different ways than you do with the larger group. McKenzie Eakin told me that Xbox's Elite Tweet Fleet (that name never gets old) knew their most engaged followers by name and sometimes met them in person. "It felt like we knew them personally," she told me. And they often did: "We'd meet some of them at gaming conventions where we were asked to speak on panels. [Meeting users] was one of my favorite parts of my job." Nichole Kelly built her CareOne online community and convinced previously anonymous posters to overcome their shame of debt and to publicly post advice by "meeting community members where they were," identifying the most insightful posters and reaching out to them individually and directly.

This type of approach is necessary not just because social media managers need to be in tune to the rhythm of their organic communities. It's also important because...

Rule Four: We're Connected by Six Degrees, but Influenced by Three. Christakis & Fowler point to several studies that support the six degrees of separation axiom. You are indeed six email-forwards away from a random policeman in Thailand. Or Kevin Bacon. The world is fairly small, and building the social apparatus by way of connections in order to achieve sociability online is a doable proposition. But we're *influenced* by three degrees: our friends' friends' friends have sway over our behavior. Which is at the same time an amazing finding in *Connected* and rather disheartening for those wanting to build value within online social groups. On the one hand, how incredible it is that behavior spreads in our social groups the same way viruses do. It puts entirely new heft to the idea of *we are who we surround ourselves with,* and should motivate all of us to intentionally surround ourselves with people who'll help us realize our best selves.

On the other hand, it puts a daunting issue in front of social media managers trying to achieve associability online. First of all, as Dr. Lieberman also discovered, Christakis & Fowler found that when it comes to our innate desire to connect with others, the three-degree rule may be evolutionary. We appear to have evolved in small groups with no one more than four degrees away from us. Social media managers are working against nature when building online social groups. They have somehow to manufacture relationships that feel at least three degrees away, or try to outsmart millions of years of evolution. As Christakis & Fowler write:

The Three Degrees Rule applies to a broad range of attitudes, feelings, and behaviors, and it applies to the spread of phenomena as diverse as political views, weight gain, and happiness. Other scholars have documented that among networks of inventors, innovative ideas seem to diffuse to three degrees, so that an inventor's creativity influences his colleagues, his colleagues' colleagues, and his colleagues' colleagues' colleagues. And word-of-mouth recommendations for everyday concerns (like how to find a good piano teacher or how to find a home for a pet) tend to spread three degrees too.[13]

In addition to the evolutionary reasons for this rule, there's also "decay in the fidelity" of influence in social groups. Networking nodes in social networks are unstable. We all drop out or become less engaged in networks as other interests pull us away. Your online social group's fidelity, you could argue, is compromised from the jump because it's digital (Christakis & Fowler find convincing evidence that physical distance impacts influence in networks) and wasn't created by the people in them (see Rules One and Two). Leading an online social group requires attention and care, constantly curating and understanding when engaged and influential nodes drop off. I call these *acts of curation*. In order to realize the value of social capital, acts of curation require much more care than the simple marketing tactics organizations typically deploy. Curators of social groups like McKenzie Eakin and Nichole Kelly know they have to be hands-on.

Tactically this can look like many things and, again, should be driven by the context. But to help illustrate the point, a brand can reward the nodes in the network that are displaying the kind of actions it wants to see with public kudos. Or perhaps you're looking for more idea-sharing in your social networks but your network is too dense and lacks bridges to other networks. Reach out to actively engaged members of your community for help in bringing others into the fold. Maybe you're seeing a hierarchy unfold, one that closes off newcomers and is disengaging community members. Model the way by stepping up your own actions and how you appear in the group as one of a servant leader, while reaching out to others for help with supporting the newcomers. Or again, mine your CRM system for your brand ambassadors and actively bring them into the fold by following their and their corporate accounts, and by celebrating in their wins whether they have anything to do with your brand or not.

Rule Five (and this is a biggie): Weak Ties Matter. Many social media marketers understand intuitively that influence happens in varying degrees between nodes in networks. The #EarthOvershootDay influencer campaign and others like it illustrate this. By finding and using so-called *bridge nodes* with influence in young people's social network, climate change scientists tried to intercede and insert their messages into networks they were not so fully engaged with. Social capital scholars and leaders who practice the building of it understand that different kinds of value can be created by encouraging the development of various connections. This adds another layer of sophistication underestimated by social media marketers.

Social networks made up of so-called *strong ties*—defined by the amount of shared connections among them, or *transitivity* as we introduced in Chapter 3—tend to exhibit such characteristics as emotional intensity and high levels of intimate sharing. They generate the kind of social capital we intuitively imagine when we go about trying to build strong teams: intimate networking clusters made of strong ties that create value through increased cooperation and collaboration, generating their social capital because they're more proactive and require less supervision and management. When trust levels are high, value through efficient teamwork follows.[14] Erik Proulx's network of willing and self-directed filmmakers is a good example of this type of network outside of an organizational setting. Peer-to-peer support groups like the P3 case study we examined in Chapter 3 are examples of tight clusters exchanging this type of social capital online.

Strong ties have their drawbacks though. They're more homogeneous (you'll remember the *birds of a feather flock together* principle). They can discriminate and strengthen the status quo: the *good ol' boys network* syndrome or the creation of so-called "assistance clubs."[15] Tight-knit networks can push back against diversity and equity efforts and create the kind of excuses you hear from organizations that can't seem to hire diverse talent, the kind that throw up their hands in response to being questioned about their lack thereof and say "we couldn't find anyone qualified from diverse backgrounds. Where's the talent?" I find this kind of myopic understanding of social networks deplorable, by the way. The science behind strong and weak ties has been in the mainstream for decades, and organizations who still claim a lack of diversity in their pipeline while not actively seeking ways to find and build bridges by way of weak ties leave me with one conclusion: they're willingly—comfortably numbed, no doubt—maintaining their status quo. They're simply affirming that closed networks benefit the privileged (themselves). Nan Lin's writing comes right out and lays it bare: "for the privileged class, it would be better to have a closed network so that resources can be preserved and reproduced."[16] Could there be a more clear and literal example of systemic discrimination?

Moreover, we've been talking about (and assuming) positive connections in this entire book, but ties in our social networks are certainly negative as well. When strong negative ties exist in social groups, more "psychological strain" is generated, eroding value.[17]

Setting aside negative network ties, let's go back to the notion of *transitivity*. When social scientists look at ties in networks they evaluate the degree to which those ties overlap their connections. When a triangle relationship occurs—Aaron knows Gina, Gina knows Vanessa, Vanessa also knows Aaron—it's said to be transitive. The higher transitivity, the stronger the tie. The lower the transitivity, the weaker the tie.

'Weak' in the social sciences terminology anyway. Because what we know is that so-called weaker ties aren't weak at all when it comes to generating value. A fascinating study published by Brian Uzzi and Jarrett Spiro (and featured by Jonah Lehrer in his book *Imagine: How Creativity Works*) called *Collaboration and Creativity: The Small World Problem* looked at the networks of Broadway musical companies from 1945 to 1989 and illuminates the value of weak ties.[18] Musical production is a highly collaborative industry. Choreographers, librettists, directors, producers, musical directors, and creative directors all come together to lend their particular area of expertise to a given project. And while there are fairly well established conventions that draw audiences to seats, it's necessary to contribute some new way of creatively expressing the conventions in order for a musical to find commercial success.

The teams involved in musical productions during the time period of the study were fairly easy to identify as credits for musicals are publicly published. From there the study's authors mapped the crossovers between networks of the musical production companies and found the structural makeup of these networks had significant effects on the success of each show. The tighter, more transitive, more homogenous the company, the lower "the ability of creative artists to develop successful shows." The more the principal creative forces interacted with other companies, the weaker their ties, the more innovative the ideas and the more risk-tolerant each production was. The effect transmitted value beyond each production company as well, because it was contagious. This adds value to the global network, or industry in this case: The more artists saw creative sparks fly (and the dollars from ticket sales flow) within internetwork production companies, the more they wanted to follow the model. Also, the more intercompany collaboration occurred, "trust and reciprocity [rolled over] to common third-party ties, increasing the likelihood that risks of collaboration or creativity are spread among friends of friends." The practice of diverse networks snowballs, builds momentum, and helps entire industries rise.

The dynamic becomes a kind of industry itself. As Burt puts it: "it is creativity as an import-export business. An idea mundane in one group can be a valuable insight in another [...] [P]eople often make the mistake of thinking that they create value when they have an idea born of sophisticated analysis. That is not true. An idea is as valuable as an audience is willing to credit it with being."[19]

Networks with weak ties find homes for good ideas, creating value across larger communities. Through this lens you could argue that building diversity and equity in the network groups we have influence over is a moral decision. Not just one of recognizing the dignity of the people we choose to be or not be a part of our organizations, but strong-tie networks deny our broader community and world an opportunity to participate in the idea import-export business. DEI deniers may be preventing a place for an idea to find a home and thrive. In this way, DEI efforts in organizations have moral implications much wider spread than simply the beliefs of those prioritizing them in a single organization. Like not wearing a mask in the middle of a pandemic, your decision isn't just affecting you and your organization.

Uzzi & Spiro uncover another important finding: strong and weak ties bring value to our social networks. But taken to an extreme can have negative effects. They call it *parabolic*: "past a certain threshold, these same processes can create liabilities." For those of us actually tasked with building and curating social groups, I think it's more helpful to think about this concept as balance. Achieving a network "richly distributed in a structure between [the] extremes" should be the goal of social network managers.

Anyone who has mentored or coached will recognize that a person needs to build a tight, trusted network of allies and supporters to build confidence, but balanced by connections outside that cluster for more critical feedback that a close friend might not see or be willing to offer. These "small world network structures" as they're called in the social sciences generate value of trust and information-sharing balanced with perspectives from other domains.

So weak ties have tremendous value and in ways very different from strong ones in tight clusters. They're Malcolm Gladwell's *Connectors* in his *Law of the Few*.[20] Before Gladwell they're what motivated Granovetter to generate a famously oxymoronic title for his breakthrough paper "The Strength of Weak Ties."[21] This study is probably best known for the finding that we are more likely to be referred to jobs through weaker ties than stronger ones. Weaker ties move in circles different from our own and so have access to other networks and information that generate a different kind of value than is exchanged in close-knit social groups. Granovetter found that this dynamic of weak ties results in a full 85 percent of us finding jobs through people we see occasionally (more than once a year but less than twice a week) or rarely (once a year or less). Usually the tie responsible for helping with our new job isn't very strong to begin with and is only 'marginally' within our current network in the first place. Some random college friend, or that coworker you spotted $10 to and haven't seen in years, someone you "never" see anymore in a "nonwork context" and will "by chance" run into, someone whose "very existence [you] have forgotten," is probably going to help you find your next job.

Your kindergarten teacher was right. Don't burn bridges.

This is hardly novel and probably confirms an intuition or two you have about social networks. Study after study and real-world network after real-world network has demonstrated the value of maintaining bridges between tight clusters in our networks. Business leaders who are known for their access to seemingly disparate fields. Scientists publish more breakthrough papers when they're connected across domains. Higher success factors with mergers and acquisitions. Bridges between photographers and wedding planners. Management techniques that pull a developer out of their department for a week to better understand the sales side of the business. Jazz musicians who flourish by learning new influences outside their gig circles.

As the field of DEI unfolds into a mainstream business discipline taking its rightful place alongside management pillars like accounting and finance, the value of diversity—building a talent pool with a multitude of bridges into a multitude of network clusters, or talent that provide *brokerage* between groups—is to my mind uncontroversial at this point. More diverse companies are better able to attract top talent, to improve their customer orientation, employee satisfaction and decision-making, and to secure their license to operate.[22] Organizations with inclusive cultures—the organizational component necessary to welcome and capture the value of diverse talent—are six times more likely to be innovative, six times more likely to anticipate change and respond effectively, and twice as likely to meet or exceed financial targets.[23] Companies with inclusive environments have been found to have operating profits almost three times higher than those that don't.[24] This is supported, in fact predicted, by social networking science and the notion of weak ties, brokerage, bridges, and structural holes.

This is the science behind DEI that those pushing against it conveniently (and ironically) ignore. To invoke the dismissive and glib 'cancel culture' in order to malign a brand for taking steps to widen their circle and welcome more nodes into their network is to simply expose one's illiteracy of social capital. By, say, removing an outdated product from a shelf, changing an offensive logo, or taking steps to remove a person from a public-facing position after an offensive comment is to recognize the science behind network structures.

There's "abundant and [...] empirical evidence of increased returns to brokerage" as Burt put it in 2004.[25] Organizations with management structures that build and encourage brokerage learn faster, synthesize and use the new information they learn better, are more creative, and have more and better ideas. To my mind, brokerage is practically indistinguishable from equity and inclusion. Equity and inclusion is the practice that welcomes, facilitates, and constantly hones an organization's ability to capture the value from diverse backgrounds, perspectives, and lived experiences. Those organizations that do it are realizing the power and value of brokerage. Those that aren't are just behind their competition.

Brokerage can happen within organizations as well. Hewlett-Packard credits much of its early innovation prowess to management practices that intentionally facilitated it. Engineers were moved between projects rather than project heads hiring and firing team members which cross-pollinated ideas and, according to one engineer, resulted in "a paradise of creativity."[26] Burt studied brokerage within a large electronics company in "Structural Holes and Good Ideas" and found that managers who brokered connections across structural holes in the company were viewed as having a higher quantity of ideas. They also saw higher compensation, more positive performance evaluations, and more promotions.

The drumbeat of this entire book pulses with the knowledge that creativity is the practice of finding meaning by synthesizing material from different domains. Structural nodes in our network help us see across ideas and break through our biases to make these syntheses. Artists know that the myth of the loner-creator exists only as outliers. My music studies at a music college taught me that if you stay in the practice room you'll sound like a practice room. A dense network with strong ties is essentially limiting itself to the practice room.

Granovetter also found a three-degree path of influence, foreshadowing Christakis & Fowler's work. Job seekers received job information from so-called short information paths, up to but usually not exceeding three nodes. "Just as reading about a job in the newspaper affords one no recommendation in applying for it," a fifth-hand recommendation provides no value beyond awareness.[27] From a structural perspective, networks can be long, but influence occurs in them only among the short paths.

Granovetter goes on to make another important point about the value of weak ties. Individually, the value is clear. When we maintain some degree of connection with our weaker ties, we can capture the value of mobility into other clusters. Not burning the bridge with the cubicle mate who never paid you back that ten bucks can help you get a new job. But there's also macro value to consider. When I move to a new network cluster—when I take its connection and thus a bridge to a new network cluster to my new job—I'm building a bridge, a link that establishes a connection from one network to another by way of weak ties. This is social cohesion: it creates community and adds value to both networking clusters (assuming they're led by social-capital savvy leaders capable of taking advantage of them). It's like building the infrastructure of the idea import-export business. If your organization is at all involved in the community-building business, like say a chamber of commerce or a professional organization, embracing DEI is a necessity, full stop. Prioritize it, or you're exposing a high level of ignorance about your core function.

Burt explores this information exchange in another paper titled "Structural Holes and Good Ideas."[28] People with connections outside their immediate network cluster fill in the gaps, or structural holes, in networks. And they're really valuable from a predictive analysis perspective.

People whose networks bridge the structural holes between groups have an advantage in detecting and developing rewarding opportunities. Information arbitrage is their advantage. They are able to see early, see more broadly, and translate information across groups. Like over-the-horizon radar in an airplane, or an MRI in a medical procedure, brokerage across the structural holes between groups provides a vision of options otherwise unseen.[29]

But remember an earlier principle from Burt: networks do not act. They are contexts for action. Information flowing from node to node is the value, not the source of the idea or even the idea itself. Networks actually generate brokerage value through four different levels, each one more valuable than the next. The first is simple awareness. A colleague of mine brought LEAN software development project management processes into a marketing department, generating awareness of a new way of approaching marketing project management.

The ability to help marketers understand a new concept for

managing their workflows was a breakthrough, and created value. Transferring best practices is the second level, which means my friend's LEAN process from his software project management background had to be (and was) actually integrated into the marketing setting, not just conceptualized.

The third level is the ability to draw lines-of-sight from one seemingly disparate discipline or world to another. Aakash Mittal is brilliant at this, generating all kinds of value for businesses by animating his world of music in such a way that business people are able to make connections to the practice of creativity in theirs. Mittal and people like him are the peacemakers, the connectors, of our world. When we become consumed with our own perspectives, our natural inclination is to build walls and protect our world views and beliefs. Special are the Mittals who break those down for us.

The fourth level is synthesis, when we combine practices and beliefs from two connected networks and integrate them. Artists like Mittal live in this place, constantly seeking, synthesizing, and making new information and ideas a part of their core practice. Mittal's work with business is very much a two-way exercise.[30]

Interceding in social networks to encourage action is difficult and sophisticated work. Social scientists are getting better and better at mapping and understanding the vast differences of networks and how they operate (motivated as they are for mitigating the spread of things like COVID-19), and as leaders of social groups the least we can do is keep an eye on the discipline.

So what do we *do*? How do we intercede in and build online social networks that return value? Again, I'm a strong believer that tactics should be situation-driven, which makes such suggestions problematic to say the least. The network you're interested in working with is structurally very different from another. Still, we know that on the whole, curating a social network that balances and realizes the value from strong and weak ties requires abundant nodes of both, recognizing and making them visible, then rewarding the behavior you wish to see from them. With that as a roadmap, and the framework we just explored (Rule One: We Like to Control Our Networks; Rule Two: Our Network Shapes Us; Rule Three: Networks Have a Mind of Their

Own; Rule Four: We're Connected by Six Degrees, but Influenced by Three; and Rule Five: Weak Ties Matter), here are a few suggestions for action.

1. **Stay consistent, transparent and honest.** These obligatories make yet another an appearance here. The rules of network structures demand consistency, transparency, and honesty for several reasons additional to those we've already covered. First, we need to control our networks because we know they shape us, which in turn amplifies the need to build immediate trust. Encouraging someone to take a leap of faith and join an online social group that is created for them requires trust, and bait-and-switches kill social capital. Second, the more trust there is between nodes, the more likely information will flow and the network will mature in the four different levels of value. And as we've discovered, trust is built over time with consistent action, not words. So if your boss or client is unwilling to build a social community without promotion or dedicate the channels fully to service, consider funneling resources to other efforts. If you already have a channel that's promotion-heavy, consider starting new ones with a customer-first, social capital-building focus. I recognize the heavy lift that this represents, but brands serious about their social capital efforts do it all the time.

2. **Be flexible.** We use our social networks with varying degrees of engagement throughout our lives, constantly changing them and dropping in and out of them. Also, social groups have minds of their own. They will experience murmurations and change. Listen to the community and be willing to shift with it. Is your original goal for the group still top of mind? Are they reacting to different topics? Use the Zappos model for this by asking your customer care team to help inform the overall direction of your social interactions. Remember, you're in a position of responsibility to a diverse set of stakeholders. And mature networks—the

goal of social capital-savvy leaders—will have emergent properties.

3. **Get to know the nodes in your networks at an individual level.** As we've discussed, nodes are not homogenous. Track influencers, watch for patterns, ask questions, rank the levels of engagement. Social scientists have terms and mapping techniques you can borrow from, or you can simply add a few fields in your CRM. Either way, begin to innovate your discipline into the area of structural awareness.

4. **Intercede in your network at an individual level.** Use your CRM to find customers and clients, follow them and their organizations, and support their online efforts by commenting, retweeting, or otherwise giving kudos to things that matter in their lives. Give them some capital in order to build it for yourself. Reach out to influencers and ask them for input and (maybe someday) support. Get to know people. Ask their names and titles. Ask them to participate in feedback sessions, to present at conferences, or write guest blog posts. Ask them if you could write non-promotional guest blog posts for them.

5. **Work on transitivity.** Because we're influenced by three degrees, watch for connections between network nodes and introduce them to each other. Tighten your clusters, increase the transitivity. Remember: greater transitivity means more trust and efficient transfer of knowledge and ideas.

6. **Build a culture of inclusion and equity.** So-called weak ties are incredibly powerful and add tremendous value to networks. But ties with diverse backgrounds and from diverse networks won't add that value without a welcoming landing place. So engage with newcomers intentionally and frequently. Kill trolls immediately. Have zero tolerance for intolerance. Support and amplify the voices and causes of the marginalized. Ask where and how you or your brand can bring value to networks outside of the one you're managing. When it comes to building an inclusionary environment, my personal manifesto comes from James

Baldwin: "We can disagree and still love each other unless your disagreement is rooted in my oppression and denial of my humanity and right to exist."

Christakis & Fowler believe in a notion that we, as social beings, are so driven to connect that we are, in a way, already connected through a structure, sophisticated and incomprehensible though it may be. "Seeing ourselves as part of a superorganism," as they put it. This perspective, in my opinion, necessitates a deeper understanding of how the superorganism operates. It's a human response to this awareness. A response that, to Christakis & Fowler, "allows us to understand our actions, choices, and experiences in a new light [...] It is as if we can feel the pulse of the social world around us and respond to its persistent rhythms."[31]

This is a reality that a drummer like me can live with.

Another thing I can live with? In keeping with Pierre Bayard, I can live with assuaging the guilt of non-reading. That's one of the reasons I included a summary, up next.

Chapter 9
SUMMARY: THE SKIPPERS, THE SKIMMERS, THE READERS, AND ME

Quick shout-out to the skimmers of books: Welcome. I see you. I'm glad you found this section, the section where you hope I've saved you the time of reading the entire thing so you can talk about it confidently. The shared purpose of this chapter is to synthesize things nicely for those who have read it, but also to satisfy your, the skimmer's, needs. I honor the skimmers among us.

Since you probably skipped Chapter 6, I want to provide some quick context by way of a book suggestion before we get to the part you're here for. I recommend *How to Talk About Books You Haven't Read* as a top-five book everyone should read or engage in with some degree of active non-reading, somewhere on a continuum between skimming or gaining an awareness of, that its author Pierre Bayard if not actually advocates at least legitimizes.

Bayard is a wonderful writer. Somehow achieving wit with insight, sarcasm with scholarship. And he gives us space and permission to have a much more honest conversation about what, exactly, we're supposed to do with and how we're supposed to talk about all these books we're supposed to read. A conversation free from shame, without mendacity, where we're free to break those intellectual rules where "we tend to lie [about reading a book] in proportion to the significance of the book under consideration." No, this is a stigma-free zone. Here we do away with the "lies we tell to others [and] first and foremost [...] ourselves" to avoid the "trouble acknowledging [...] that we haven't read the books that are deemed essential."[1]

This is a particularly pressing issue for business professionals trying to prioritize their time with the sea of business books before them. Other than my editors, I doubt very seriously anyone will bill for the time they take to read (or skim) this book.

If this is striking you as subversive, as somehow exposing a forbidden rule you were shamed into accepting in school, consider that taking the time to read something is actually itself an act of non-reading. After all, while you're reading this book, you're actively not reading another.

All of this is to say, basically, that if you're a skimmer, and this chapter is one or one of a few places you're stopping, welcome. If you want to flesh out any of these concepts with data, sources, real-world examples, interviews, and stories about jazz musicians, San Francisco activists, business school deans, and Dead Heads, rest assured they're all waiting for you if and when you're ready.

For those of you who prefer the complete picture, I hope this synthesis brings things together in a tidy place for you.

Leading in a Social World is decidedly not tactical because leading in a social world is highly contextual. Humans are messy, and our relationships are exponentially more so. We form and build our groups around specific needs and wants that look as different as our personality and interests, and we change them constantly to suit our evolving needs and wants.

When it comes to connecting with and having some degree of influence within social groups in digital circles, there's a better way forward than the tactics-focused social media marketing approach on which so many marketing professionals, leaders, organizations and brands currently rely. Creating social capital, a leadership discipline, is that way.

For leaders willing to hone the necessary skills, social capital returns value well beyond what can be derived from online social groups, especially as organizations currently measure (or try to measure) it. Organizations rich in social capital can see better efficiency of action, reduced transaction costs, more efficient knowledge creation and sharing, deeper absorptive capacity, and enhanced group sharing for coherent action. It has been shown to help talent flow—recruiting, smart hiring, transitions, reduced turnover and churn costs, and even create environments with more equitable executive compensation—and helps individual career success. It has been shown to fuel innovation, intra- and entrepreneurship pursuits, more effective collaboration, and cooperative behavior. More intellectual capital is generated in environments with flowing social capital, as well as stronger human capital development.

That may seem like a dream list, the kind of thing promised by con men with silver-bullet solutions. Until you find out how hard building social capital actually is to do.

Especially online. The first order of business for organizations interested in seeing the kind of serious returns social capital can bring them from their online social groups is to prise social media away from the hands of their marketing departments and agencies. This starts with accepting the problem.

SHEDDING BIASES

Headspaces

The first thing business people and especially marketers need to tackle is shedding biases about how social groups in digital spaces operate, and how ineffective the tactics they're currently using really are. These biases were born in an age when social media blossomed into a promise of connecting with consumers in social and personal ways marketers had never imagined possible. Marketing, though, is rejected in social groups because our social wiring isn't compatible with it. And marketing-oriented brains are literally in a different headspace as they watch social activity as those non-marketing brains participating in social groups are. The science behind this is fascinating, and something that can serve business and especially marketing professionals well.

Data Toxicity

Businesses and especially marketing professionals don't have an honest relationship with their data, and when it comes to social media marketing, it's used more to confirm biases than actually drive informed decisions. By evaluating over 50 studies, interviewing several professionals involved in case studies, and through almost two decades of client-side and consulting and agency work, these are our takeaways:

- The data received to make digital marketing decisions is coming from marketing departments who self-report an inability either to collect it or understand it very well. Garbage in, garbage out.
- When it comes to measuring actual business results, social media marketers either don't know or don't care to know how to do this. Instead, they fall back on indicators that are leading at best, and vanity at worse.
- Much of the data used to support social media marketing is highly biased and has an agenda driven by billion-dollar interests. Countless reports and studies are generated by social media marketing companies and their content marketing and PR machines, or even worse, provided by the tools themselves.
- When it comes to marketing effectiveness, our research was confirmed by other anti-social media marketing authors and thought leaders: it isn't a preferred channel for consumers to learn about brands; it isn't a preferred channel to find more information about purchase decisions; it isn't reliable in

effectively building brand trust; it isn't reliable in effectively building brand awareness; it's a poor lead-generation tool; the fans and followers that make up its audience do not equate to brand affinity; it doesn't drive purchase intent; and social media isn't a cost-effective reach tool.

There are three relatively narrow contexts where sustained social media marketing works with any degree of consistency:

1. Brands with inherent and unusually powerful scroll-stopping content or what I like to call Remarkability (think GoPro, ESPN, and celebrities).
2. Brands with cause or purpose built in, like nonprofits, issue or political campaigns, or the very rare corporate brands that contrive it (Charity: Water, Obama for America).
3. Brands that follow tried and true marketing principles and have built global, hardcore support over time with unique, solid quality in their products or services (Harley-Davidson, BMW). Such groups also integrate their social activities with well-funded traditional marketing activities making it difficult if not impossible to tell what's responsible for what.

A culture of using pot-of-gold case studies combined with marketers' biases make us believe that we can apply what we see from GoPro, Obama for America, and Harley-Davidson to our restaurant and accounting firm clients. And that's just fantasy.

WHAT IS SOCIAL CAPITAL?

Creative minds draw richer meaning out of the relationships between seemingly disparate data. Understanding social capital, from a leadership and social sciences perspective, provides a much better way for anyone interested in influencing social groups than marketing ever can. Seeing the intersections of branding, leadership, and building online communities is a creative exercise, and ultimately a sustainable way forward for leaders because it focuses on building social capital in social groups instead of chasing tails with ever-changing tactics.

For the purposes of this book, in business and similar organizational settings, social capital is a resource of value for individuals and groups, created by investing and managing the configuration and operation of social networks and their durable social relationships. Exploring the meaning of social capital is much more helpful than simply defining it, though.

Because we're surrounded by social connections and we intrinsically see the value of them all the time, every day, it's easy to underestimate social relationships and the capital exchanged between them. However, it's "hidden in plain sight," and is actually quite sophisticated stuff. The elements of social capital are also fluid: what's required to build social capital can often be its resulting value. Some elements of social capital are both cause and effect, "simultaneously its underlying conditions, indicators of presence, and chief benefits" as Laurence Prusak and Don Cohen, leading social capital scholars, wrote.[2] Trust is a good example of this. Trust is absolutely foundational to building social capital. An organization can't begin to see the benefits of social capital—on the social web or in their organizations—until it establishes some modicum of trust. But trust is also how we measure strong social capital efforts. It's an outcome. Trust can lead to organization and online value in such areas as collaboration speed, knowledge transfer, and speedier, customer-driven customer service results.

'Social' isn't an adjective. It isn't even a frame. It's the constantly shifting and changing relationships of all things human. It's the water we're swimming in. Embracing the ambiguity can actually help understand social capital better if you're willing to let go and just swim in it.

Still, like human, intellectual, and physical capital, organizations can measure and manage social capital. Arms can be put around it, and leaders can learn to build and use it with well-researched techniques, such as applying authenticity and consistency to the values of the group. But it isn't a balance sheet and it doesn't come from oversimplified tactics as the social media marketing industry would have us believe.

Social scientists have found that there are rules that govern the influence within social groups, and how their structures can be built to return different kinds of value. And we know what kills social capital in social groups: bait-and-switches and, as troubling as it may be for marketers to hear, selling.

Critically, social capital occurs in a group when it achieves *associability*, a process of trust-building that can take some time. Sociability refers merely to a group coming together for a mutual interest. But networks do not create value. Their actions do. When associability is achieved in groups, value is generated by the group acting together for a collective purpose while putting individual desires and goals in an ancillary position. Most social media marketers stop their efforts at sociability, perhaps because that's where their understanding stops, too. Or perhaps because the draw of immediate returns is too strong and their patience has run out.

Social capital is generated in groups when trust is high, reciprocity is fully mutual, and everyone is acting consistently in accordance to the norms and expectations of the group. This is a big reason why marketing departments usually fail to realize it, and why organizations are better off moving it into a different function.

SOCIAL CAPITAL IN CUSTOMER CARE

Customer care is a democratized arrangement between brands and their customers, and it's based on the notion of equal reciprocity. Brands are forced into this relationship in order to serve the needs of the customer. This is why organizations are realizing significant returns by using social media in their customer care teams.

Marketers are still unwilling (or unable) to hear what that data is telling them, though, and cling to the social media levers to the detriment of their brands and organizations. For those that can break through the bias—like Zappos, Xbox, and British Telecom—the returns are handsome.

For those who are ready to make the switch, here are the rules, synthesized from my experience with clients, years of social capital research, and digging into effective online customer care environments like Zappos, Xbox, and CareOne:

1. Figure out what the customer wants, and let them lead.
2. Appreciate online communities as people with various life experiences and levels of expertise all coming together to build value.
3. Think democratized and horizontal.
4. Extend this to 'newbies' and actively stick up for them.
5. If you don't understand customer care, or don't care to understand it, learn up or hand off social media to a different team.
6. Make adding value to the community the goal and view commercial returns as outcomes.
7. Reframe commercial return expectations as bottom-of-the-funnel value, not top or middle.
8. Create your Net Easy score.
9. Declare your intentions, gain alignment from your organization, and hold them to it.
10. Get ready for the long haul.
11. Evaluate response rates and be honest about your ability to meet demand.
12. Put yourself in the capital creation and exchange position.
13. Be human.
14. Finally, be ready to make mistakes, own them, and improve.

THE SECRET LIFE OF SOCIAL CAPITAL

As I mentioned, building social capital is a learnable skill for any leader willing to put in the work. And while (surprisingly) there aren't many sources in the leadership milieu with a direct and intentional focus on building and exchanging social capital, most of the standard leadership material weaves dimensions of the practice in and out of their other themes. Social capital is almost always there, hidden in plain sight.

And with some fine-tuning, you can see clear lines-of-sight and intersections between these leadership best practices and those of brand management. Chapter 6 weaves in and out of these concepts freely.

I contend that leadership itself is a social exercise. A 2009 study published in *Leadership and Organization Development Journal* titled "Social Capital and Leadership Development" by Shelly McCallum and David O'Connell synthesizes five leadership studies that focused on human and social capital. In it they define leadership as "a relational process between leader and followers [...] [L]eaders must focus on their credibility and legitimacy with followers, then the development of a relationship via identification of followers' needs and motivations."[3]

They also lay out three areas that leaders interested in building social capital use to frame up their work:

1. They view leadership as a position with responsibility to a diverse set of stakeholders.
2. They take a partnership approach with constituents, asking good questions of community members, and empowering them to work as partners.
3. They work as coaches in their community, sharing with constituents to build collective energy for creation and sharing.

Social communities require facilitation, at times moderation, and brands have a certain degree of power. Leaders of social groups recognize the need to act in that role as one of responsibility to the group, no more valuable than the others participating in it.

One important tactic for this type of leadership is asking good questions. Questions empower constituents, provide agency (the most powerful and sustainable force of influence available to a leader), and build democratized relationships. Good questions focus on a constituent's needs, not the leader's, which is probably why marketers aren't very good listeners: we're too focused on the conversion, not the relationship.

With this foundation, together with a solid understanding of social capital and its mechanics, it's possible to spot social capital-focused lessons in a number of leadership books and thought leadership material. Here are four that have troves for the social-capital curious:

1. Robert Greenleaf's *The Servant as Leader* (1970): The founding treatise on servant leadership and the notion of people-building.
2. James Kouzes and Barry Posner's *The Leadership Challenge* (1982): A stand-by leadership book that encourages the liberating of visions and walking the talk.
3. Stephen M. R. Covey's *The Speed of Trust* (2006): A book that deals with trust, something inextricably linked to social capital, aka the confidence to connect.
4. Dr. Brené Brown's *Dare to Lead* (2018): The most meaningful leadership book I've ever read, helping us find the courage to drop the armor.

Examples and techniques for leaders to build social capital abound in these works, as are the intersections with brand management, influence, and online community building. A few of the more important syntheses are:

- **Embrace the complexity. Acknowledge the sophistication.**
- **You're interacting with people, not segments; and unlike segments people are made of emotions.**
- **Get your Self/brand together first.**
- **Credibility follows Self, and it matters.**
- **Be ready for and OK with uncertainty.**
- **Get ready for the long haul.**
- **Ask questions: coach and learn.**
- **People-build, don't people-use.**

NETWORK STRUCTURES: THE NEW FRONTIER FOR SOCIAL MEDIA

In a paper titled "Social Capital, Intellectual Capital, and the Organizational Advantage" published in *The Academy of Management Review*, authors Janine Nahapiet and Sumantra Ghoshal identify three 'clusters' that leaders interested in developing social capital concern themselves with: Cognitive (shared representations, interpretations, and systems of meaning), Relational (the relationships and trust built between people in networks), and Structural (the impersonal configuration and linkages of nodes in networks).[4] I've come to call them 'bonds' and they can help professionals interested in building social capital in digital spaces focus their tactical efforts.

Marketers already know how to work cognitive bonds. We're trained to use the power of stories, symbols, and language to influence others and we do it all the time and in our sleep. The leadership techniques explored above offer a guide to strengthening relational bonds in social groups. Structural bonds, on the other hand, are entirely new to the marketing discipline, a new frontier for leaders to master in order to consistently build social capital in digital spaces.

Social networks are sophisticated, have minds of their own, and each node in the network brings with it a different level of influence and value. Influencer marketing is an indication that marketers understand this, but it's in its infancy as a practice.

Christakis & Fowler's book *Connected* gives us five rules that social networks follow. Using them, plus an insight from social scientists Robert Burt and Mark Granovetter, we have a framework that can help leaders interested in building social capital better understand the structural bonds of their networks. This is something we don't spend a lot of time with as marketers, but in my opinion it's the next evolution in a leader's ability to effectively lead social groups, including those online. The five rules are as follows:

1. **Rule One: We Like to Control Our Networks**
2. **Rule Two: Our Networks Shape Us**
3. **Rule Three: Networks Have a Mind of Their Own**

4. **Rule Four: We're Connected by Six Degrees, but Influenced by Three**
5. **Rule Five: Weak Ties Matter**

With these rules as a backdrop, here are some suggestions for action:

1. **Stay consistent, transparent and honest.**
2. **Be flexible.**
3. **Get to know the nodes in your networks at an individual level.**
4. **Intercede in your network at an individual level.**
5. **Work on transitivity.**
6. **Build a culture of inclusion and equity.**

Leading by developing social capital is a deeply significant connection to the human condition. I believe it's a life-affirming pursuit, a path that recognizes and honors the humanity in all of us. I hope you'll join me in exploring this further in the Epilogue, starting with a Thanksgiving turkey.

Epilogue
SOCIAL IS THE OPPORTUNITY–AND
CHALLENGE–OF OUR TIMES

We're prisoners of our moments. Like Nassim Taleb's Thanksgiving turkey, we tend to live in the now, believing that recent events (love and care from the butcher) are predictors of the future.[1] As humans we're as wired this way just as we're wired to be social. We best remember the things we learned most recently, and while there are exceptions and it's contextual, we tend to believe that recent history is a distillation of longer time periods than is actually the case. Psychology has thoroughly defined and tested this wiring as recency biases, recency effects, and forgetting curves.

In marketing we see these biases raise their heads in many ways, not least in our tendency to forget that what we're working with is in its infancy. IBM famously reported in 2017 that 90 percent of the data businesses we're working with were created in just the previous two years. In fact, as Taleb also teaches us, history is only helpful when there's been enough time to distill it and filter out the randomness. Otherwise it can mislead us. When it comes to digital marketing, and especially social media, we haven't distilled much of anything yet.

To illustrate this, let's create a timeline of the history of business in the United States, laid out on the sidewalks of New York City. Because we need a starting place, and because many of us are in the business of content, we'll start with Adam Smith publishing *The Wealth of Nations* 245 years ago and end with Netflix releasing *The Social Dilemma* in 2020. Each year on our timeline will be the length of the average person's walking step, and so it will stretch two city blocks. (We considered starting with the invention of the printing press, but that would have required an additional two-and-a-half blocks and we couldn't get the permit.) Let's fire up our FitBits and go for a walk.

We take five steps from Smith's treatise and stop to marvel at the invention of the steam engine. It isn't until we're halfway down the block, 55 steps, that the first corporation is formed. We reach the end of the block at 138 steps and the opening of the Panama Canal. At the start of the second block, Ford's assembly line and the Federal Reserve make an appearance. A quarter of the way down, at around 160 steps now, the first TV broadcast. Nine steps later, the invention of the transistor. It will be 34 steps later, a little more than halfway down the second block and a full 205 steps since we started, when we arrive at Microsoft's creation of IBM's operating system. We'll walk half as much again—16 steps—to arrive at the launch of a barely-known startup called Six Degrees, a platform based on a newly-coined *Web of Contacts* model that allows friends and acquaintances to invite each other to connect through a web-based technology.

We stop here for a moment, more than 220 steps taken, and look toward the end of the block, to the end of our timeline, when *The Social Dilemma* is released. We're barely over 20 steps away from it, and in that space we still have to experience what to social media marketing professionals represents huge shifts in the way they've done business. We walk on. Six Degrees goes out of business in four steps. Friendster and MySpace launch (five, six steps from the launch of Six Degrees), Facebook goes live (seven steps), YouTube launches (eight), Twitter goes live (nine), Facebook launches its ad platform (ten), Facebook unveils its Like button (12), Pinterest launches (13), Snapchat launches (14), Facebook goes public (15), TikTok launches (19), the Cambridge Analytica scandal hits (21), TikTok becomes the most downloaded social media app in the world (22), and finally *The Social Dilemma* is released (23 steps from the launch of Six Degrees).

Now we turn around, and look back. To cover the whole of social media history, we took ten steps *fewer* than we did to cover the distance between Microsoft developing what would become Windows and the invention of the first social media platform. We took double the number of steps to get from the first television broadcast to the invention of Windows than we did to cover social media's history, and *seven times* as many steps to progress from Adam Smith's book to TV. Social media history represents about nine percent of our Business in the US Timeline and less than one half of a percent of the timeline we wanted to build (the one that included the printing press).

Social media still has some maturing to do. The warp-speed spin of technology can dizzy us into believing we're advancing faster than we actually are. Sure, Facebook going public just nine short years ago (as of 2021) and exploding into a monopolistic behemoth with manipulation powers that some say can sway elections and motivate insurrections seems like a huge disruption. But our understanding of it and similar technologies as social forces—how their algorithms interface with our social wiring—is essentially just poking its beak out of the egg. We're still in the midst of gathering data about online social constructs and their place in our world and businesses. We haven't even got to the place of deciding what to do with the data.

One thing is certain, and it can ground us (thanks to scientists like Dr. Lieberman): we're social creatures. We can't help it. It's in our wiring and we'll keep crafting and molding everything around us, including technology, to satisfy our primal need to connect. For leaders, whatever the Facebooks or Twitters look like next year or in twenty years is far less important than our ability to build and use social capital, no matter the platform, environment, or context.

Think about it. How many steps on our New York City timeline do you think we are from the next big shift in the social media landscape? And how much of your and your company's resources are you willing to bet on it? Many of us barely finished our Google searches on what exactly Clubhouse meant to our marketing department and Podcasting investments by the time we had to open a new tab to hunt down a workable definition of *NFT*. Even that sentence will become obsolete before this book is published.

More importantly, how many steps until a new regulation, a new

Reddit movement, or brands and consumers themselves start storming various online spaces demanding change? The fidelity of technology's future is always unstable, but social media's is downright rickety. Social media's foundation has been shaken by the common understanding that misinformation and manipulation seem to operate at the core of the large platforms (which is why we put the documentary *The Social Dilemma* on our timeline). It's a moral inflection point, and one that is dissonant to our understanding of our social wiring. Our very humanity. The stakeholders propping it up are pointing fingers of blame in all directions, a situation that usually results in a collapse of trust.

The worrisome news for business professionals and especially marketers is that all the data point to the fact that brands, not the platforms and certainly not consumers, are in danger of finding themselves under the bus of this pending calamity. According to the *2018 Edelman Trust Barometer Special Report: Brands and Social Media*, 70 percent of digital consumers say brands themselves need to put pressure on social media sites to do more about the proliferation of false information, and 71 percent put the expectation on brands to pressure social media platforms to protect their personal data. Nearly half of customers say it's a brand's own fault if its advertising appears next to hate speech, violent or sexually inappropriate content, and that any point of view appearing near a brand's advertising and marketing are an indication of that brand's values.[2]

Who is leading these brands? What choices will they make? Us marketers will certainly be at the center, which presents yet another reason for marketers to bravely step up and accept our role as leaders, declare our values, and learn the discipline of leadership along with our technical marketing chops so we can lead the kind of change we wish to see. This will likely entail recognizing the need for balance between community and conversion, and the courage to advocate for enacting such balance in spaces where we most feel the pressure to drive revenue at all costs. Community building means honesty, consistency and honoring the humanity of those in the group. In this way marketers will have a significant hand in the direction of social media platforms, make no mistake.

After all, what's behind the brands? You and I, fellow marketers. People. Making decisions.

As I've said before, I'm no futurist. It seems fairly obvious to me, though, that the more we understand the mechanics of the social connection algorithms, the more likely we are to reject them in favor of our biological need to connect with one another. I don't consider myself an optimist, I've just become convinced that we'll have to follow some such path. We're wired to. The web is and will always be social. I don't know how many more steps down the timeline it will take, but some such changes will happen. There are small flares of hope to be found, like Pinterest's cold shoulder to Facebook and Google-esque practices, iPhone users' power to turn off app tracking, the ease of installation and use of other anti-tracking apps, and the slow simmering of alternatives like Mastodon and Friendica. Who knows? Maybe a step or two down the timeline and the perfect storm of a willing legislative body and a few Redditors with nothing better to do will give the social media platform giants something to think about.

It's also my hope that a more sophisticated understanding among all of us related to social groups, how they operate, and the creation and exchange of social capital, will drive change. My personal (limited) understanding of human beings and our innate desire to connect casts a sobering light on the platforms that manipulate us. Doing business by way of a one-way algorithm that takes advantage of humanity's social wiring becomes a moral choice, not just one of marketing effectiveness.

For moral reasons or otherwise, the social media landscape will change. That much is certain. It follows that leaders are much better served mastering sustainable skills, like building and using social capital, than wasting time and resources adjusting to shifting sands. Plus, investing in a culture rich in social capital will pay off in a multitude of other ways. Setting aside the benefits we discussed like knowledge transfer, trust, innovation, and talent flow in organizations, a culture rich in social capital drives value in customer care and marketing by acting as a multiplier to any investment made in the technical capital of the type favored by those organizations. A *Journal of Business Research* article titled "Social Media Technology Usage and Customer

Relationship Performance: A Capabilities-Based Examination of Social CRM" empirically demonstrates that CRM technologies are more deeply embedded and have a greater impact when used by organizations that already have customer-oriented cultures. Culture eats strategy for breakfast, as Peter Drucker famously said. Or in Clay Shirky's words way back in 2009 which sparked all of this in me in the first place: it isn't the technical capital that matters, it's the social capital. Nothing builds culture—a social construct—like social capital.

An internal culture rich in social capital can't help but spill over into the marketplace. Zappos exemplifies this. An internal culture that values servant leadership and democratized hierarchy is reflected in the way Zappos interacts with the outside world, and it's the most profound lesson I learned from my time with their team members. Social capital actually fuels seeking more of it, ignites wanting to share it, and clarifies how to break down the impenetrable walls between brands and their external stakeholders. Social media provided one mechanical opportunity to do this, but we need to turn to leadership, not marketing, to understand how both offer and extract value from these social groups. It's tempting to confuse this pursuit with something easier like the transactional relationship in a crowdsourcing construct, even when haloed by inflated terms. Transactional relationships are fleeting, usually punctual, and when the funding stops, the value between the connections dies. Remember: connections and networks don't add value. The associability within them does.

Building such value is a human pursuit, rooted in our hard-coding, and requires the integration of another human system hard-wired in our neurology: creativity. Leading with a social capital mindset takes more than lists with clever alteration, clickable listicles, or TED talks. It isn't easily trained, either. But it affirms connections and creativity, two vital dimensions of our humanity. McCallum & O'Donnell said that leadership through building and using social capital "is more of an organic than mechanistic undertaking, where systems adapt to changing environments."[3] Social capital-savvy leaders listen, empower, absorb diversity by welcoming it with inclusion, and change their approach based on the needs of the community they're a part of. The creative muscles required for this are many, finding richer meaning in multiple data sets and improvisation above all. I happen to believe that creativity is actually what provides purpose in our lives and that exercising these muscles and, more importantly, facilitating it in others is a life-affirming pursuit. Along the way, sparking creativity and kindling social connections adds virtuousness to our community and world. Practicing social capital-focused leadership is a kind of social *keiretsu*.

As convinced as I've become with the notion that weak-tie networks find homes for good ideas across all networks, and thus create value across larger communities, I'll reiterate that leading with a strong-tie network orientation denies a place for an idea to find a home elsewhere and thrive. In this way, decisions regarding DEI efforts in organizations impact everyone, not just the CEO who's choosing to prioritizing it (or not) in their organization. Choosing to not wear a mask in the midst of a pandemic doesn't just risk one's own health.

Leadership is also a creative and moral pursuit to James O'Toole, one of the more influential thought leaders in my early professional life. In his book *Leading Change: Overcoming the Ideology of Comfort and the Tyranny of Custom*, he lays out the case for a then-emerging style of leadership called *values-based leadership*. Rooted in understanding and aligning the values of the group, leaders create ownership and agency in their groups and can anchor themselves with values so as to flex with changing situations. To Dr. O'Toole, it's the only approach to leadership that is both moral *and* effective. And once a leader finds (and acknowledges) something that is both moral and effective, what choice is there but to put it to use? "There is no longer a need to lead by command, manipulation, or paternalism," Dr. O'Toole wrote back in 1995, two steps before the launch of Six Degrees on our New York City timeline. "If one wishes to learn this particular art, the first piece that must be put into place is personal acknowledgment that no other form of leadership can be both moral and effective. Once a leader makes that difficult commitment, all the other pieces will eventually fall into place."[4]

It's this reasoning that draws me so strongly to Dr. Brené Brown's work as well. If there's a path to accomplishing the things we wish to accomplish with and through others while recognizing and helping elevate the dignity and humanity of those involved, is there really any other choice? Dr. Brown is helping leaders help their communities "walk into our story and own it [so that we] get to write the ending."[5] Is there any other calling that honors our humanity and dignity more than that?

Both Dr. O'Toole and Dr. Brown echo and align with current Diversity, Equity, and Inclusion practices, ones I'm convinced transcend the DEI efforts they're usually pigeonholed into. DEI is not that complicated, in my experience, if people like me, in positions of privilege and relative power, are willing to drop the armor, listen, and use our privilege to act. And the roots of DEI, in my view, align with the ways to lead we've explored in this book. Recognizing everyone's dignity and humanity and choosing a course of action that is both effective and moral.

Christian Aniciete is a marketing pro in Portland who serves on a DEI committee within an all-volunteer group through the American Marketing Association I've been lucky to be a part of. One day on a Zoom meeting the committee was (as I recall) overcomplicating a concept, and getting wrapped around the axle. Christian chimed in with a concise thought, as he so often does. "For me, it just comes down to 'What kind of organization do you want to be a part of? Does it reflect the larger community? Is it welcoming?' Figure it out and go make that community." Christian cut to the chase of not just DEI, but the social nature of a leader's work. If there's an effective and moral way to build the kind of community we *all* wish to be a part of, what choice do you as a leader really have?

With apologies to Dr. O'Toole, building and using social capital may be today's only moral and effective way to lead. It affirms our hard-wiring to make social connections, and its construction requires creativity to identify and align values for a collective purpose. It requires us to give agency to those involved in the effort, and elevates humanity by putting some social connections, creativity, and a little art into the world. Deciding to lead in a social world requires that a leader affirm that the world is social, not disconnected, even when we're physically distanced. And it demands that we figure out influence and motivation in a human way, not with manipulation or artificial technologies. Likewise for marketers, an alternative world of AIs that manipulate our human wiring and traffic in misinformation is an unviable status quo not only from a moral perspective but probably from an effectiveness one as well. That status quo may very well kill what sustains us. Leading in a social world with acumen tuned into building social capital is the only effective and moral way to build communities online. What choice do we really have?

With Christian's thoughts in mind, leading in a social world means deciding what kind of community you want to be a part of and building it. And what kind of leader you want to be and becoming it.

Acknowledgments

Just a quick, unsolicited tip for first-time authors: The very second you think you might want to write a book, start writing down the people who help you. I didn't do this, so I'm no doubt going to forget some people to whom I owe a debt of gratitude. There were so many helpful and generous souls along this path, and by way of apology to those I've missed here, I'll simply promise to pass on your generosity by offering to others what you all gave to me.

To Paula Lee, The Asset, thank you for your help with some research and all things minutiae, but mostly for just keeping everything rolling all the time for Three Over Four. You give me the bandwidth and optimism to do these things.

Glen Turpin, you sat down with me over ten years ago and provided feedback on a social media presentation I was putting together. Your input, and really your always-present technology expertise, are the rich soil for this book. Thank you.

Erik Proulx, you gave me plenty of your time, yes. But it's your living example that motivated much of my entrepreneurial life and the thinking behind many of the ideas in this thing. Thank you.

Thank you to early sounding-board authors, who provided their experience on writing, publishing, and general feedback on a few early drafts: Erika Napoletano, Adrian Miller, Carl Larson, Scott LaFasto, and Tama Kieves. Thanks also to Saira Rao for the support and introductions to Jessica Fellman, Jess Regal, and Yfat Gendell at Foundry. Yfat, our conversation was the final impetus for me to publish this myself. Thank you for that final push.

Thank you to Julia Roth for the terrific research. The volumes of bad marketing data you waded through? I wouldn't wish that on anyone. Thanks to Augie Ray for setting more than a few tones, particularly around data and speaking and thinking clearly. To Stewart Law of Evolve Research and David Kennedy of Corona Insights for keeping my research honest. And to Mac Clouse for at least trying to plow through my wacky finance musings.

Big thanks to Amy Favreau for the cheerleading and the belief. To Mihali Stavlas and Holly Zachman and all the PCC family for similar support and back-having.

Much gratitude to the people who answered cold requests for interviews from an unknown aspiring book writer. Your time is valuable, and you gave it generously. Shout out especially to McKenzie Eakin (formerly Xbox), Nichole Kelly (formerly CareOne), Aisha Quas (SproutSocial), Madison Leupp (Adobe) and Dan Wilkens (haarper). HUGE shout out to the amazing folks at Zappos for their time and insights: Rob Siefker, Kelsey Walsh, and Amy Gilmer. HUGER shoutout to Laura Davis at Zappos for the ridiculous amount of time and patience you gave me for this project. Totally above and beyond. Zappos is lucky to have you.

Thanks to the always-connective John Wilker for the publishing guidance. Gratitude to David Port for the developmental edit, and to the beta readers—Robin Tooms, Jill Geisler, and Bill Silver. Your time is valuable, and your insights influenced a much, much stronger output.

And to the patient, insightful, and fastidious Bruce Taylor: thank you for keeping this thing 'me' (or should that be in italics?) while challenging my blind spots. That dram soon.

Deep gratitude to Buie Seawell, a mentor and leadership role model who's always believed in me and taken my call no matter how random the need or how little I've given back. And an adjacent final thankyou to Dr. James O'Toole, among the first thought leaders on the topic of leadership of whom I became aware. While not called out much by name, his leadership ideas are the foundation of this book. I was deeply honored to have his time and input.

I'll give Aristotle the last thought, Buie and Jim: May my gratitude never grow old.

Notes

How to Read This Book

1. "Glenn Loury, Distinguished Fellow 2016." *American Economic Association,* www. aeaweb.org/about-aea/honors-awards/distinguished-fellows/glenn-loury.
2. Loury, Glenn. "Re: The term "social capital."" Received by Aaron Templer, 21 February 2021.
3. Loury, Glenn. (1976). "A Dynamic Theory of Racial Income Differences." In Wallace, Phillis & Annette LaMond. *Women, Minorities, and Employment Discrimination.* Lexington, Mass., Lexington Books. p. 153. (Need full page spread of article)
4. Ibid.
5. Prusak, Laurence, & Don Cohen. "How to Invest in Social Capital." *Harvard Business Review,* 2001, pp. 86–93.

Chapter 1

1. globalwebindex.com. *Social: GlobalWebIndex's Flagship Report on the Latest Trends in Social Media.* Flagship Report 2020, e-book ed., https://resources.enterprisetalk.com/ebook/GWI-2020-Social-Report.pdf, GlobalWebIndex, 2020.
2. Boyle, Michael J. "Unemployment Rate, Effect, and Trends." *The Balance,* 21 Nov. 2020, www.thebalance.com/unemployment-rate-3305744.
3. Coined by Harvard professor Clayton M. Christensen through research and in his book *The Innovator's Dilemma,* published in 1997 and taken and run with by Silicon Valley legion. By the time it leaked into marketing, who really knew?
4. Oettinger, Callie. "Erik Proulx." *Steven Pressfield,* 20 Aug. 2010, stevenpressfield.com/2010/08/erik-proulx.
5. Proulx, Erik. Personal interview. 10 August 2010.
6. http://edwardboches.com/this-film-brought-to-you-by-twitter (URL defunct).
7. Shirky, Clay. "Institutions vs. Collaboration." *TED Talks,* uploaded by TEDGlobal 2005, 10 July 2008, www.ted.com/talks/clay_shirky_institutions_vs_collaboration.
8. "Level 5 Leadership: The Triumph of Humility and Fierce Resolve." *Harvard Business Review,* 28 Sept. 2017, https://hbr.org/2001/01/level-5-leadership-the-triumph-of-humility-and-fierce-resolve-2.
9. Nahapiet, Janine, & Sumantra Ghoshal. "Social Capital, Intellectual Capital, and the Organizational Advantage." *The Academy of Management Review,* vol. 23, no. 2, 1998, pp. 242–66. JSTOR, www.jstor.org/stable/259373. Accessed 9 June 2021.
10. Ibid.
11. Shirky, Clay. "Institutions vs. Collaboration." *TED Talks,* uploaded by TEDGlobal 2005, 10 July 2008, www.ted.com/talks/clay_shirky_institutions_vs_collaboration.
12. Ireland, R., & M. Hitt. "Achieving and Maintaining Strategic Competitiveness in the 21st Century: The Role of Strategic Leadership." *Academy of Management Executive,* 2005, Vol. 19, No. 4, pp. 63–77.; Prusak, Laurence, & Don Cohen. "How to Invest in

Social Capital." *Harvard Business Review*, 2001, pp. 86–93.; Nahapiet, Janine, & Sumantra Ghoshal. "Social Capital, Intellectual Capital, and the Organizational Advantage." *The Academy of Management Review*, 1998, vol. 23, no. 2, pp. 242–6.

13. Faucher, Kane X. *Social Capital Online: Alienation and Accumulation*. Vol. 7, University of Westminster Press, 2018. JSTOR, www.jstor.org/stable/j.ctv5vddrd. Accessed 9 June 2021.

14. Lieberman, Matthew D. *Social: Why Our Brains Are Wired to Connect*. New York: Crown Books, 2013; pp. 16–23.

15. Putnam, Robert. *Bowling Alone*. Simon & Schuster, 2001. Print.

16. Granovetter, Mark S. "The Strength of Weak Ties." *The American Journal of Sociology*, Vol. 78, No. 6, 1973. pp. 1360–80.

17. Ronald S. Burt. "Structural Holes and Good Ideas." *American Journal of Sociology* 110, no. 2 (September 2004): DOI: https://doi.org/10.1086/421787

18. *The Social Dilemma*. Directed by Jeff Orlowski. Exposure Labs, 2020. *Netflix*, https://www.netflix.com/title/81254224.

19. Brown, Brené. *Dare to Lead*. New York: Vermilion, 2018, Kindle Location 71.

20. Perez, Sarah. "Videoconferencing Apps Saw a Record 62M Downloads during One Week in March." *Tech Crunch*, Verizon Media, 30 Mar. 2020, techcrunch.com/2020/03/30/video-conferencing-apps-saw-a-record-62m-downloads-during-one-week-in-march.

21. Yuan, Eric S. "A Message to Our Users." Zoom Blog, Zoom Video Communications, Inc., 1 Apr. 2020, blog.zoom.us/a-message-to-our-users.

22. @roto_tudor (unpleasant breakfast burrito). "These are iPad stations being prepared for virtual ICU end of life visits by a palliative care doc I know. Jesus." *Twitter*, 3 Dec. 2020, 8:24 a.m., https://twitter.com/roto_tudor/status/1334534101265682434?s=20.

23. Perez, Sarah. "Houseparty Reports 50M Sign-Ups in Past Month amid COVID-19 Lockdowns." Tech Crunch, Verizon Media, 15 Apr. 2020, techcrunch.com/2020/04/15/houseparty-reports-50m-sign-ups-in-past-month-amid-covid-19-lockdowns.

24. Read, Max. "How Much of the Internet Is Fake? Turns Out, a Lot of It, Actually." *Intelligencer*, Vox Media LLC, 26 Dec. 2018, nymag.com/intelligencer/2018/12/how-much-of-the-internet-is-fake.html.

25. Grimaldi, James V. "FCC's Net-Neutrality Proposal Marred by Millions of Fake Comments." *The Wall Street Journal*, 6 May 2021, www.wsj.com/articles/fccs-net-neutrality-proposal-marred-by-millions-of-fake-comments-11620309351.

26. Fou, Augustine. "Artist Sells Invisible Sculpture—Adtech Sells the Same Thing." *Forbes.com*, Forbes, Inc. https://www.forbes.com/sites/augustine-fou/2021/06/04/artist-sells-invisible-sculpture-adtech-sells-the-same-thing/?sh=785cc28467a0

27. O'Toole, James. "Notes Toward a Definition of Values-Based Leadership." *The Journal of Values-Based Leadership*, vol. 1, article 10, Issue 1, 2008.

Chapter 2

1. Shirky, Clay. "How Social Media Can Make History." *TED Talks*, uploaded by TED@State, 16 June 2009, www.ted.com/talks/clay_shirky_how_social_media_can_make_history.

2. Ibid.
3. Brodie, Roderick J., et al. "Consumer Engagement in a Virtual Brand Community: An Exploratory Analysis." *Journal of Business Research*, vol. 66, no. 1, 2013. *Crossref*, doi:10.1016/j.jbusres.2011.07.029.
4. Lieberman, Matthew D. Social: Why Our Brains Are Wired to Connect, 2013, Ch.1 n. 14. New York: Crown Books, 2013; pp. 42–3. Print.
5. A quick digression here to point out that it looks like we've been mindlessly attributing Maslow's work incorrectly for many years. The concept of his *Hierarchy of Needs* actually may have been appropriated from the Blackfoot Nation. While this is hardly the topic of this book and I'm not at all an expert in the matter, I'm compelled to mention this as we search for ways to properly attribute and honor where we develop our belief systems, especially when something may have been appropriated from a culture that has had so much stolen from it. It's a serious issue about which the least I can do from my position of privilege is provide a footnote. Please Google the issue, and bring up what you learn in your presentations, your classrooms, and in your conversations when referring to Maslow's *Hierarchy of Needs*.
6. Ibid., p. 67.
7. Hibbard, Casey. "How Microsoft Xbox Uses Twitter to Reduce Support Costs." *Social Media Examiner*, 27 July 2010, www.socialmediaexaminer.com/how-microsoft-xbox-uses-twitter-to-reduce-support-costs.
8. Eakin, McKenzie. Personal interview. 11 December 2020.
9. Siefker, Rob. Personal interview. 5 February 2021.
10. Kelly, Nichole. Personal interview. 3 December 2020.
11. Lieberman, Matthew D. *Social: Why Our Brains Are Wired to Connect*. New York: Crown Books, 2013; p. 272. Print.
12. Good Growth. "Social Media Effectiveness Report." *Good Growth*, no. 5, 2018, pp. 1–8, goodgrowth.co.uk/wp-content/uploads/2019/10/Good-Growth-Social-Media-Report-Oct2018.pdf.

Chapter 3

1. Ray, Augie. "What If Everything You Know About Social Media Marketing Is Wrong?" *Experience: The Blog*, 3 Apr. 2014, www.experiencetheblog.com/2014/04/what-if-everything-you-know-about.html.
2. Hootsuite Inc. "Digital in 2018." *Hootsuite*, 2018, www.hootsuite.com/pages/digital-in-2018.
3. The CMO Survey. "The CMO Survey—February 2020." *The CMO Survey*, World Market Watch LLC, Feb. 2020, cmosurvey.org/results/february-2020.
4. Sprout Social. "Turned Off: How Brands Are Annoying Customers on Social." *The Q3 2016 Sprout Social Index*, 2016, p. 11, media.sproutsocial.com/pdf/The-Q3-2016-Sprout%20Social-Index-Sprout-Social.pdf.
5. HubSpot. "Not Another State of Marketing Report." 2020, cdn2.hubspot.net/hubfs/53/tools/state-of-marketing/PDFs/Not%20Another%20State%20of%20Marketing%20Report%20-%20Web%20Version.pdf.
6. Peters, Brian. "We Analyzed 43 Million Facebook Posts From the Top 20,000 Brands." *Buffer | Blog*, 7 Aug. 2018, buffer.com/resources/facebook-marketing-strategy.

7. Social Media Examiner. "The Social Media Marketing Industry Report—2017." 2017, https://www.socialmediaexaminer.com/social-media-marketing-industry-report-2021/

8. Hultgren, Kaylee. "INFOGRAPHIC: Five Insights From the 2020 Chief Marketer B2B Marketing Outlook." *Chief Marketer*, Access Intelligence LLC, 3 Jan. 2020, www.chiefmarketer.com/infographic-five-insights-from-the-2020-chief-marketer-b2b-marketing-outlook.

9. Hootsuite & Altimeter. "Beyond ROI: Unlocking the Business Value of Social Media." 2017, https://hootsuite.com/pages/altimeter-report-2017.

10. Williamson, Debra Aho. "Organic Social Marketing: Why Some Brands Still Make It a Priority." *EMarketer*, 20 Nov. 2017, totalaccess.emarketer.com/view/Report/Organic-Social-Marketing-Why-Some-Brands-Still-Make-Priority/2002150? ECID=TA1000.

11. Bango. "Board to Death." *Bango*, bango.com/board-to-death. Accessed 2021.

12. Buffer & Social Chain. "State of Social 2019." *Buffer*, 2019, buffer.com/state-of-social-2019.

13. Sprout Social. "Index." *Sprout Social*, 2019, media.sproutsocial.com/uploads/Sprout-Social-Index-2019.pdf.

14. Bango. "Board to Death." *Bango*, bango.com/board-to-death. Accessed 2021.

15. Good Growth. "Social Media Effectiveness Report." *Good Growth*, no. 5, 2018, pp. 1–8.; goodgrowth.co.uk/wp-content/uploads/2019/10/Good-Growth-Social-Media-Report-Oct2018.pdf.

16. Taleb, Nassim N. *Antifragile: Things That Gain From Disorder.* New York: Random House, 2012. Kindle location 143.

17. Sprout Social. "#BrandsGetReal: What Consumers Want from Brands in a Divided Society." *Sprout Social*, 2018, sproutsocial.com/insights/data/social-media-connection.

18. Ray, Augie. "The Problem with Social Media Case Studies." *Experience: The Blog*, 1 Apr. 2014, www.experiencetheblog.com/2014/04/the-problem-with-social-media-case.html?m=1.

19. Curalate. "Curalate Consumer Survey: Social Content Is the New Storefront." *Curalate*, 2017, cdn.relayto.com/media/files/Ee7ZjWeXSgyL6YGAiCZV_Curalate_-Consumer-Survey_Nov17_V4%20(1).pdf.

20. John, Leslie K., et al. "Does 'Liking' Lead to Loving? The Impact of Joining a Brand's Social Network on Marketing Outcomes." *Journal of Marketing Research*, vol. 54, no. 1, Feb. 2017, pp. 144–55, doi:10.1509/jmr.14.0237.

21. De Vries, Lisette, et al. "Effects of Traditional Advertising and Social Messages on Brand-Building Metrics and Customer Acquisition." *Journal of Marketing*, vol. 81, no. 5, Sept. 2017, pp. 1–15, doi:10.1509/jm.15.0178.

22. John, Leslie K., et al. "What's the Value of a Like?" *Harvard Business Review*, Mar. 2017, hbr.org/2017/03/whats-the-value-of-a-like.

23. Cialdini, Robert B, & Robert B. Cialdini. *Influence: The Psychology Of Persuasion.* London: HarperCollins, 1993, Brown, Kindle Location 43–87.

24. John, Leslie K., et al. "What's the Value of a Like?" *Harvard Business Review*, Mar. 2017, hbr.org/2017/03/whats-the-value-of-a-like.

25. Zhang, Kunpeng, & Wendy W. Moe. "Bias on Your Brand Page? Measuring and Identifying Bias in Your Social Media Community." *University of Maryland*, 2017, marketing.wharton.upenn.edu/wp-content/uploads/2016/12/Moe-Wendy-PAPER-ver2-Marketing-Camp.pdf.

26. Ibid.

27. Kaushik, Avinash. "Stop All Social Media Activity (Organic) | Solve For A Profitable Reality." *Occam's Razor by Avinash Kaushik*, 7 June 2017, www.kaushik.net/avinash/stop-organic-social-media-marketing-solve-for-profit.

28. SharpSpring. "The State of Social Lead Generation." *SharpSpring*, sharpspring.com/resources/social-lead-gen-ebook. Accessed 2021.

29. Chief Marketer. "2019 B2B Marketing Outlook Survey." *Chief Marketer*, 2019, www.chiefmarketer.com/special-reports/2019-b2b-marketing-outlook-survey.

30. Meeker, Mary. "Internet Trends 2018." *Kleiner Perkins*, 2018, www.kleinerperkins.com/perspectives/internet-trends-report-2018.

31. WARC. "Warc's 'Seriously Social 2016'—Trends in Effective Global Social Strategy." *ACN Newswire*, 29 Nov. 2016, www.acnnewswire.com/press-release/english/33740.

32. Koltun, Natalie. "Mobile Campaign of the Year: Starbucks Unicorn Frappuccino." *Marketing Dive*, 4 Dec. 2017, www.marketingdive.com/news/mobile-campaign-of-the-year-starbucks-unicorn-frappuccino/510799. Poynter, Ray, et al. "Measuring Not Counting." *IPASocialWorks*, 2014, newmr.org/wp-content/uploads/sites/2/2014/10/Guide-to-Evaluating-Social.pdf.

33. HubSpot. "Not Another State of Marketing Report." *Fresh off the Press*, 2020, cdn2.hubspot.net/hubfs/53/tools/state-of-marketing/PDFs/Not%20Another%20State%20of%20Marketing%20Report%20-%20Web%20Version.pdf. Moorman, Christine, et al. "Highlights & Insights Report." *The CMO Survey*, 2019, cmosurvey.org/wp-content/uploads/2019/08/The_CMO_Survey-Highlights-and_Insights_Report-Aug-2019-1.pdf.

34. Sherman. "Top 10+ Social Media Marketing Agencies & The Definitive Guide to Selecting One for Your Business." *LYFE Marketing*, 2 Oct. 2019, www.lyfemarketing.com/blog/social-media-marketing-agencies.

35. Gabbert, Elisa. "State of the Digital Marketing Agency in 2018." *WordStream*, 3 July 2020, www.wordstream.com/blog/ws/2018/04/12/state-of-the-agency-report.

36. Statista. "Most In-Demand Agency Services in the U.S. 2016." *Statista*, 24 Aug. 2017, www.statista.com/statistics/627953/agency-services-demand-usa.

37. "30 Day SMMA." *Choose Pristine*, Choose Pristine Inc., www.choosepristine.com/order-28582136. Accessed 2021.

38. Shmoney. "Why Freelancing SUCKS for Digital Nomads | Is Freelancing Worth It?" *YouTube*, uploaded by Shmoney, 10 Dec. 2018, www.youtube.com/watch?v=CHeUiHkoiuY.

Chapter 4

1. Eagleman, David, & Anthony Brandt. *The Runaway Species: How Human Creativity Remakes the World*. New York: Catapult, 2017, Kindle location 170.

2. Cohen, Don, & Laurence Prusak. *In Good Company: How Social Capital Makes Organizations Work*. Boston: Harvard Business School Press, 2001, p. 9.

3. Ibid.

4. Ibid., p. 7.

5. Lin, Nan. *Social Capital: A Theory of Social Structure and Action (Structural Analysis in the Social Sciences)*. 1st edition, Cambridge University Press, 2001, Kindle Locations 433–7.

6. Latour, Bruno. *Reassembling the Social: An Introduction to Actor-Network-Theory*. Oxford: Oxford University Press, 2005, pp. 1–21.

7. Ibid., p. 7.

8. Granovetter, Mark S. "The Strength of Weak Ties." *American Journal of Sociology*, vol. 78, no. 6, 1973, pp. 1360–80. JSTOR, www.jstor.org/stable/2776392.

9. Adler, Paul S., & Seok-Woo Kwon. "Social Capital: Prospects for a New Concept." *Academy of Management Review*, vol. 27, no. 1, 2002, pp. 17–40. *Crossref*, doi:10.5465/amr.2002.5922314.

10. Cohen, Don, & Laurence Prusak. *In Good Company: How Social Capital Makes Organizations Work*. Boston: Harvard Business School Press, 2001, p. 7.

11. Ibid.

12. Ibid.

13. Nahapiet, Janine, & Sumantra Ghoshal. "Social Capital, Intellectual Capital, and the Organizational Advantage." *The Academy of Management Review*, vol. 23, no. 2, 1998. *Crossref*, doi:10.2307/259373.

14. Hoffman, Donna L. & Marek Fodor. "Can You Measure the ROI of Your Social Media Marketing?" *Sloan Management Review*, Vol. 52, No. 1, Fall 2010 (October, 24 2010). Available at SSRN: https://ssrn.com/abstract=1697257

15. "How Nestlé Dealt with a Social Media Campaign against It." *Financial Times*, 3 Dec. 2012, www.ft.com/content/90dbff8a-3aea-11e2-b3f0-00144feabdc0.

16. Lazerson, Mark. "A New Phoenix?: Modern Putting-Out in the Modena Knitwear Industry." *Administrative Science Quarterly*, vol. 40, no. 1, 1995, p. 34. *Crossref*, doi:10.2307/2393699.

17. Zwick, Detlev, & Alan Bradshaw. "Biopolitical Marketing and Social Media Brand Communities." *Theory, Culture & Society*, vol. 33, no. 5, Sept. 2016, pp. 91–115, doi:10.1177/0263276415625333.

18. Mathwick, C. et al. "Social Capital Production in a Virtual P3 Community." *Journal of Consumer Research* 34 (2008): 832–49.

19. Assenza, P., A. B. Eisner, & J. C. Kuperman. "Ann Taylor: Survival in Specialty Retail", *The CASE Journal*, Vol. 5, No. 2, 2009, pp. 44–68.

20. Bourne, Leah. "Social Media Is Fashion's Newest Muse." *Forbes.com*, Forbes Media LLC., 7 Sept. 2010, www.forbes.com/2010/09/07/fashion-social-networking-customer-feedback-forbes-woman-style-designers.html?sh=6b98a69032a1.

21. Putnam, Robert D., Robert Leonardi, & Raffaella Nanetti. *Making Democracy Work: Civic Traditions in Modern Italy*. Princeton, N.J.: Princeton University Press, 1993. Print.

22. Leana, Carrie R., & Harry J. Van Buren. "Organizational Social Capital and Employment Practices." *Academy of Management Review*, vol. 24, no. 3, 1999, pp. 538–55. *Crossref*, doi:10.5465/amr.1999.2202136.

23. Portes, A. "Social Capital: Its Origins and Applications in Modern Sociology." *Review of Sociology* 24 (1998), pp. 1–24.

24. Portes, Alejandro, & Julia Sensenbrenner. "Embeddedness and Immigration: Notes on the Social Determinants of Economic Action." *American Journal of Sociology*, vol. 98, no. 6, 1993, pp. 1320–50. JSTOR, www.jstor.org/stable/2781823.

25. Christakis, Nicholas A., & James H. Fowler. *Connected: The Surprising Power of Our Social Networks and How They Shape Our Lives*. New York: Little, Brown & Co., 2009, pp. 7–9.

26. Leana, Carrie R., & Harry J. Van Buren. "Organizational Social Capital and Employment Practices." *Academy of Management Review*, vol. 24, no. 3, 1999, pp. 538–55. *Crossref*, doi:10.5465/amr.1999.2202136.

27. Ibid.

Chapter 5

1. Reuters. "Zappos Gets Savvy with Social Media." *Reuters*, 19 Oct. 2009, www.reuters.com/article/idUS280016341920091019.

2. Denning, Steve. "Making Sense of Zappos and Holacracy." *Forbes*, 15 Nov. 2014, www.forbes.com/sites/stevedenning/2014/01/15/making-sense-of-zappos-and-holacracy/?sh=19da20bb3207.

3. Davis, Laura. "Re: Social Media Interview?" Received by Aaron Templer, 9 December 2020.

4. Gilmer, Amy. Personal interview. 8 January 2021.

5. Ross, Jeanne W., et al. "Why Nordstrom's Digital Strategy Works (and Yours Probably Doesn't)." *Harvard Business Review*, 14 Jan. 2015, hbr.org/2015/01/why-nordstroms-digital-strategy-works-and-yours-probably-doesnt.

6. Ibid.

7. "The State of Digital Care in 2018." *Conversocial*, vol. 2, 2018, p. 7, www.conversocial.com/hubfs/2018-State-of-Digital-Customer-Service.pdf.

8. Spector, Robert, & Patrick D. McCarthy, *The Nordstrom Way to Customer Service Excellence: The Handbook for Becoming the "Nordstrom" of Your Industry.* Hoboken, N.J.: Wiley, 2012.

9. "The State of Digital Care in 2018." *Conversocial*, vol. 2, 2018, p. 7, www.conversocial.com/hubfs/2018-State-of-Digital-Customer-Service.pdf.

10. Dixon, Matthew, et al. "Stop Trying to Delight Your Customers." *Harvard Business Review*, 2010, hbr.org/2010/07/stop-trying-to-delight-your-customers.

11. Huang, Wayne. "Consumers Spend after Positive Customer Service Interaction on Twitter." *Twitter*, Twitter, Inc., 7 Dec. 2015, blog.twitter.com/en_us/topics/insights/2015/Consumers-spend-after-positive-customer-service-interaction-on-Twitter.html.

12. Huang, Wayne, et al. "How Customer Service Can Turn Angry Customers into Loyal Ones." *Harvard Business Review*, 16 Jan. 2018, hbr.org/2018/01/how-customer-service-can-turn-angry-customers-into-loyal-ones.

13. "The State of Digital Care in 2018." *Conversocial*, vol. 2, 2018, p. 7, www.conversocial.com/hubfs/2018-State-of-Digital-Customer-Service.pdf.

14. Microsoft Dynamics 365. *State of Global Customer Service Report.* PDF edn., Microsoft Corporation, 2019.

15. Baer, Jay. "5 Social Media Customer Service Stats You Must Know." https://medium.com/convince-and-convert/5-social-media-customer-service-stats-you-must-know-19040b50fe4.

16. Mangles, Carolanne. "The Rise of Social Media Customer Care." *Smart Insights*, 18 Dec. 2017, www.smartinsights.com/customer-relationship-management/customer-service-and-support/rise-social-media-customer-care.

17. Walsh, Kathy. Personal interview. 5 February 2021.

18. IPA, et al. "BT Customer Services: Social Media Helped BT Improve Service and Cut Costs." *Institution of Practitioners in Advertising*, 2014.

19. Khoros. "How Microsoft Shifted from Support to True Engagement with Khoros Communities." *Khoros*, ... 5.; March. 2020, https://assets.khoros.com/content/case-studies/Microsoft-PDF-Case-Study.pdf.

20. Social Media Today & SAP. *The Social Customer Service Index: Results, Analysis, and Perspectives.* 2015

21. Ibid.

22. Ibid.

23. Leupp, Madison. Personal interview. 11 May 2021.

24. Ireland, R., & M. Hitt. "Achieving and Maintaining Strategic Competitiveness in the 21st Century: The Role of Strategic Leadership." *Academy of Management Perspectives* 13 (1999), pp. 43–57.

25. Mathwick, C. et al. "Social Capital Production in a Virtual P3 Community." *Journal of Consumer Research* 34 (2008), pp. 832–49.

26. Ibid.

27. Ibid.

28. Toller, Carol. "How Nordstrom Built the World's Best Customer Service Machine." *Canadian Business*, 5 Mar. 2015, www.canadianbusiness.com/innovation/secrets-of-nordstrom-customer-service.

Chapter 6

1. Bayard, Pierre. *How to Talk About Books You Haven't Read*. New York, Bloomsbury USA, 2007, e-book location 13.

2. Ibid., e-book location 17.

3. Greenleaf, Robert. *The Servant as Leader*. The Robert Greenleaf Center, 1991, Kindle. Kouzes, James M., & Barry Z. Posner. *The Leadership Challenge*. San Francisco: John Wiley & Sons, Inc, 2007. Print. Covey, Stephen M. R. *The Speed of Trust*. New York: Simon & Schuster, 2008. E-book. Brown, Brené. *Dare to Lead*. New York: Vermilion, 2018, Kindle.

4. Social Media Examiner. "Case Study: Social Media Customers Are More Valuable Customers." *Social Media Examiner*, 8 February 2011, https://socialmediaexplorer.com/social-media-marketing/social-media-customer-value/

5. McCallum, Shelly, & David O'Connell. "Social Capital and Leadership Development: Building stronger leadership through enhanced relational skills." *Leadership & Organization Development Journal*, vol. 30, no. 2, March 2009.

6. A quick hat tip to Bob Sutton's excellent LinkedIn post *Hierarchy is Good. Hierarchy is Essential. And Less Isn't Always Better* for the fountainhead on our holacracy research.

7. Reuters. "Zappos Gets Savvy with Social Media." *Reuters*, 19 Oct. 2009, www.reuters.com/article/idUS280016341920091019

8. Bryant, Adam. "Paint by Numbers or Connect the Dots." *The New York Times*, 22 Sept. 2012, www.nytimes.com/2012/09/23/business/mark-templeton-of-citrix-on-the-big-career-choice.html?_r=0.

9. Stanford eCorner, & Bob Sutton. "Hierarchy Is Good. Hierarchy Is Essential. And Less Isn't Always Better." *Stanford eCorner*, 7 Apr. 2016, ecorner.stanford.edu/articles/hierarchy-is-good-hierarchy-is-essential-and-less-isnt-always-better.

10. Bourne, Leah. "Social Media Is Fashion's Newest Muse." *Forbes.com*, Forbes Media LLC., 7 Sept. 2010, www.forbes.com/2010/09/07/fashion-social-networking-customer-feedback-forbes-woman-style-designers.html?sh=6b98a69032a1.

11. Carmicheal, Kayla. "10 Cause-Related Marketing Campaign Examples that Inspire Us." *HubSpot*, 9 July 2020, blog.hubspot.com/agency/5-tips-to-boost-your-next-cause-marketing-campaigns-reach.

12. Cohen, Don, & Laurence Prusak. *In Good Company: How Social Capital Makes Organizations Work*. Boston: Harvard Business School Press, 2001, p. 7.

13. Hibbard, Casey. "How LIVESTRONG Raised Millions to Fight Cancer Using Social Media." *Social Media Marketing*, Social Media Examiner, 13 Apr. 2010, www.socialmediaexaminer.com/how-livestrong-raised-millions-to-fight-cancer-using-social-media.

14. San Francisco Chronicle. "Frances Peavey." *SFGATE Powered by Legacy*, Legacy.com, 8 Oct. 2010, www.legacy.com/obituaries/sfgate/obituary.aspx?n=frances-peavey&pid=145847098.

15. Peavey, Fran. "Strategic Questioning Manual." *Transformer Leadership*, 2018, transformerleadership.com/wp-content/uploads/2018/03/Strategic-Questioning-Manual-11b4d4l.pdf, p.10.

16. Jung, C. G., & W. S. Dell. *Modern Man in Search of a Soul*. Translated by W. S. Dell & Cary F. Baynes, New York: Harcourt Publishers Group, 1955, Kindle location 49.

Chapter 7

1. Greenleaf, Robert. *The Servant as Leader*. The Robert Greenleaf Center, 1991, Kindle Edition.

2. Bass, Robert E., et al. "Scientific Autobiography and Other Papers." *Philosophy and Phenomenological Research*, vol. 12, no. 2, 1951. *Crossref*, doi:10.2307/2103486.

3. Sinek, Simon. "Why Good Leaders Make You Feel Safe." *TED Talks*, uploaded by TED2014, 19 May 2014, www.ted.com/talks/simon_sinek_why_good_leaders_-make_you_feel_safe?language=ig.

4. Jung, C. G., & W. S. Dell. *Modern Man in Search of a Soul*. Translated by W. S. Dell & Cary F. Baynes, Harcourt Publishers Group, 1955, Kindle location 49.

5. Kouzes, James M., & Barry Z. Posner. *The Leadership Challenge*. San Francisco: John Wiley & Sons, Inc, 2007. Print.

6. Covey, Stephen M. R. *The Speed of Trust*. New York: Simon & Schuster, 2008. E-book.

7. Mathwick, C. et al. "Social Capital Production in a Virtual P3 Community." *Journal of Consumer Research* 34 (2008): 832–49.

8. Ibid.

9. Covey, Stephen M. R. *The Speed of Trust*. New York: Simon & Schuster, 2008, E-book location 372.

10. Nahapiet, Janine, & Sumantra Ghoshal. "Social Capital, Intellectual Capital, and the Organizational Advantage." *The Academy of Management Review*, vol. 23, no. 2, 1998. *Crossref*, doi:10.2307/259373.

11. Mathwick, C. et al. "Social Capital Production in a Virtual P3 Community." *Journal of Consumer Research* 34 (2008): 832–49.

12. Oh, Hongseok, et al. "A Multilevel Model of Group Social Capital." *Academy of Management Review*, vol. 31, no. 3, 2006, pp. 569–82. *Crossref*, doi:10.5465/amr.2006.21318918.

13. McCallum, Shelly, & David O'Connell. "Social Capital and Leadership Development: Building stronger leadership through enhanced relational skills." *Leadership & Organization Development Journal*, vol. 30, no. 2, March 2009, pp. 152–66. *Crossref*, doi:10.1108/01437730910935756.

14. Kogut, Bruce, & Udo Zander. "What Do Firms Do? Coordination, Identity, and Learning." *Organization Science*, vol. 7, no. 5, 1996, pp. 502–18. *Crossref*, doi:10.1287/orsc.7.5.502.

15. Nahapiet, Janine, & Sumantra Ghoshal. "Social Capital, Intellectual Capital, and the Organizational Advantage." *The Academy of Management Review*, vol. 23, no. 2, 1998,

p. 242-246. *Crossref,* doi:10.2307/259373.

16. Covey, Stephen M. R. *The Speed of Trust.* New York: Simon & Schuster, 2008, E-book location 422.
17. Brown, Brené. *Dare to Lead.* New York: Vermilion, 2018, Kindle location 19.
18. Ibid., Kindle location 96.
19. Ibid., Kindle location 20.
20. Ibid., Kindle location 38.
21. Pink, Daniel H. *To Sell Is Human: The Surprising Truth About Moving Others.* New York: Riverhead Books, 2012
22. Brown, Brené. *Dare to Lead.* New York: Vermilion, 2018, Kindle location 75

Chapter 8

1. Nahapiet, Janine, & Sumantra Ghoshal. "Social Capital, Intellectual Capital, and the Organizational Advantage." *The Academy of Management Review,* vol. 23, no. 2, 1998, p. 242-246. *Crossref,* doi:10.2307/259373.
2. Lin, Nan. *Social Capital: A Theory of Social Structure and Action.* Cambridge: Cambridge University Press, 2012.
3. Balkundi, Prasad, & Martin Kilduff. "The Ties That Lead: A Social Network Approach to Leadership." *The Leadership Quarterly,* vol. 17, no. 4, 2006, pp. 419–39. *Crossref,* doi:10.1016/j.leaqua.2006.01.001.
4. Christakis, Nicholas A., & James H. Fowler. *Connected: The Surprising Power of Our Social Networks and How They Shape Our Lives.* New York: Little, Brown & Co., 2009. Burt, Ronald S. "Structural Holes and Good Ideas." *American Journal of Sociology,* vol. 110, no. 2, 2004. *Crossref,* doi:10.1086/421787. Granovetter, Mark S. "The Strength of Weak Ties." *American Journal of Sociology,* vol. 78, no. 6, 1973, pp. 1360–1380. JSTOR, www.jstor.org/stable/2776392. Accessed 9 June 2021.
5. Christakis, Nicholas A., & James H. Fowler. *Connected: The Surprising Power of Our Social Networks and How They Shape Our Lives.* New York: Little, Brown & Co., 2009, p. 156.
6. Association of National Advertisers. "Survey Report: How ANA Members Are Using Influencer Marketing." 2018.
7. Nickalls, Sammy. "Infographic: Nearly Half of Americans Make Purchases Based on Influencer Recommendations." *Adweek,* 6 May 2019, www.adweek.com/brand-marketing/infographic-nearly-half-of-americans-make-purchases-based-on-influ-encer-recommendations.
8. Petrarca, Emilia. "Body Con Job." *The Cut,* 11 May 2018, www.thecut.-com/2018/05/lil-miquela-digital-avatar-instagram-influencer.html.
9. Allgaier, Joachim. "Science and Environmental Communication on YouTube: Strategically Distorted Communications in Online Videos on Climate Change and Climate Engineering." *Frontiers in Communication,* vol. 4, 2019. *Crossref,* doi:10.3389/fcomm.2019.00036.
10. Suciu, Peter. "Can We Trust Social Media Influencers?" *Forbes,* 20 Dec. 2019, www.-forbes.com/sites/petersuciu/2019/12/20/can-we-trust-social-media-influencers/?sh=663f2f1a63e8.
11. Morning Consult. "The Influencer Report: Engaging Gen Z and Millennials." *Morning Consult,* 2019, morningconsult.com/form/influencer-report-engaging-gen-z-and-millinnials-download-thank-you.

12. Lin, Nan. *Social Capital: A Theory of Social Structure and Action (Structural Analysis in the Social Sciences)*. 1st edition, Cambridge University Press, 2001, Kindle location 48.

13. Christakis, Nicholas A., & James H. Fowler. *Connected: The Surprising Power of Our Social Networks and How They Shape Our Lives*. New York: Little, Brown & Co., 2009, p. 28.

14. Nahapiet, Janine, & Sumantra Ghoshal. "Social Capital, Intellectual Capital, and the Organizational Advantage." *The Academy of Management Review*, vol. 23, no. 2, 1998. *Crossref*, doi:10.2307/259373.

15. Uzzi, Brian. "Social Structure and Competition in Interfirm Networks: The Paradox of Embeddedness." *Administrative Science Quarterly*, vol. 42, no. 1, 1997, pp. 35–67. *Crossref*, doi:10.2307/2393808.

16. Lin, Nan. *Social Capital: A Theory of Social Structure and Action (Structural Analysis in the Social Sciences)*. 1st edition, Cambridge: Cambridge University Press, 2001, Kindle locations 423–4.

17. Granovetter, Mark S. "The Strength of Weak Ties." *American Journal of Sociology*, vol. 78, no. 6, 1973, pp. 1360–1380. JSTOR, www.jstor.org/stable/2776392. Accessed 9 June 2021.

18. Uzzi, Brian, & Jarrett Spiro. "Collaboration and Creativity: The Small World Problem." *American Journal of Sociology*, vol. 111, no. 2, 2005. *Crossref*, doi:10.1086/432782.

19. Burt, Ronald S. "Structural Holes and Good Ideas." *American Journal of Sociology*, vol. 110, no. 2, 2004. *Crossref*, doi:10.1086/421787.

20. Gladwell, Malcolm. *The Tipping Point*. Back Bay Books, 2002.

21. Granovetter, Mark S. "The Strength of Weak Ties." *The American Journal of Sociology*, Vol. 78, No. 6, 1973. pp. 1360–80. JSTOR, www.jstor.org/stable/2776392.

22. Hunt, Vivian, et al. "Delivering through Diversity." *McKinsey & Company*, 2018, www.mckinsey.com/business-functions/organization/our-insights/delivering-through-diversity#.

23. "Rewriting the Rules for the Digital Age: 2017 Deloitte Global Human Capital Trends." *Deloitte University Press*, 2017, www2.deloitte.com/content/dam/Deloitte/global/Documents/About-Deloitte/central-europe/ce-global-human-capital-trends.pdf.

24. Mind Gym. "Diversity, Equity & Inclusion." *Mind Gym*, 2020, themindgym.com/solutions/diversity-inclusion.

25. Burt, Ronald S. "Structural Holes and Good Ideas." *American Journal of Sociology*, vol. 110, no. 2, 2004, pp. 349–99. *Crossref*, doi:10.1086/421787.

26. Fleming, L. "Finding the Organizational Sources of Technological Breakthroughs: The Story of Hewlett-Packard's Thermal Ink-Jet." *Industrial and Corporate Change* 11 (2002), pp. 1059–84.

27. Granovetter, Mark S. "The Strength of Weak Ties." *The American Journal of Sociology*, Vol. 78, No. 6, 1973. pp. 1360–80. JSTOR, www.jstor.org/stable/2776392.

28. Burt, Ronald S. "Structural Holes and Good Ideas." *American Journal of Sociology*, vol. 110, no. 2, 2004, pp. 349–99. *Crossref*, doi:10.1086/421787.

29. Ibid.

30. Ibid.

31. Christakis, Nicholas A., & James H. Fowler. *Connected: The Surprising Power of Our Social Networks and How They Shape Our Lives*. New York: Little, Brown & Co., 2009, p. 30.

Chapter 9

1. Bayard, Pierre. *How to Talk About Books You Haven't Read.* London: Bloomsbury Publishing PLC, 2009., e-book location 12.
2. Cohen, Don, & Laurence Prusak. *In Good Company: How Social Capital Makes Organizations Work.* Boston: Harvard Business School Press, 2001, p. 7.
3. McCallum, Shelly, & David O'Connell. "Social Capital and Leadership Development: Building stronger leadership through enhanced relational skills." *Leadership & Organization Development Journal,* vol. 30, no. 2, March 2009.
4. Nahapiet, Janine, & Sumantra Ghoshal. "Social Capital, Intellectual Capital, and the Organizational Advantage." *The Academy of Management Review,* vol. 23, no. 2, 1998, pp. 242–6. *Crossref,* doi:10.2307/259373.

Epilogue

1. Taleb, Nassim N. *Antifragile: Things That Gain From Disorder.* Random House, 2012. Kindle location 108.
2. Edelman. "Special Report: Brands and Social Media." 2018 *Edelman Trust Barometer,* 2018, www.edelman.com/sites/g/files/aatuss191/files/2018-10/2018_Edelman_Trust_Barometer_Brands_Social.pdf.
3. McCallum, Shelly, & David O'Connell. "Social Capital and Leadership Development: Building stronger leadership through enhanced relational skills." *Leadership & Organization Development Journal,* vol. 30, no. 2, March 2009. *Crossref,* doi:10.1108/01437730910935756.
4. Sherman, W. Scott. "Book Review: Leading Change: Overcoming the Ideology of Comfort and the Tyranny of Custom James O'Toole San Francisco: Jossey-Bass, 1995." *Journal of Leadership Studies,* vol. 3, no. 1, Jan. 1996, doi:10.1177/107179199600300118.
5. Brown, Brené. *Dare to Lead.* New York: Vermilion, 2018, Kindle location 249.

About the Author

R. Aaron Templer is a polymathic, 25-year marketing leader. He is a marketing firm owner (threeoverfour.com), occasional speaker and professor, and hobby percussionist. His firm, speaking engagements, teachings, and writings are at the intersection of strategy, creativity, brand, influence, and leadership. Some call him the Gora Dhol Wallah. *Leading in a Social World* is Aaron's first book.

http://aarontempler.com

Made in the USA
Columbia, SC
22 November 2021